Spellbound by Beauty

Alfred Hitchcock and His Leading Ladies

Donald Spoto

HUTCHINSON
LONDON

Published by Hutchinson 2008

2 4 6 8 10 9 7 5 3 1

Copyright © Donald Spoto 2008

Donald Spoto has asserted his right under the Copyright, Designs
and Patents Act 1988 to be identified as the author of this work

First published in Great Britain in 2008 by Hutchinson

Random House, 20 Vauxhall Bridge Road,
London SW1V 2SA

www.rbooks.co.uk

Addresses for companies within The Random House Group Limited can be found at:
www.randomhouse.co.uk/offices.htm

The Random House Group Limited Reg. No. 954009

A CIP catalogue record for this book
is available from the British Library

ISBN 9780091797232

The Random House Group Limited supports The Forest Stewardship Council (FSC),
the leading international forest certification organisation. All our titles that are printed on
Greenpeace approved FSC certified paper carry the FSC logo. Our paper procurement
policy can be found at: www.rbooks.co.uk/environment

Typeset in Bembo by Palimpsest Book Production Ltd,
Grangemouth, Stirlingshire

Printed and bound in Great Britain by
Clays Ltd, St Ives plc

Spellbound by Beauty

for Mona and Karl Malden
with grateful love and devotion

. . . why are we so haggard at the heart,
so care-coiled, care-killed . . . so cumbered,
when the thing we freely forfeit is kept with fonder a care,
fonder a care kept than we could have kept it . . .

Gerard Manley Hopkins,
'The Leaden Echo and the Golden Echo' (1882)

Contents

Acknowledgements

My first debt is to Alfred Hitchcock, with whom I spent many hours between 1975 and 1980. He granted me a number of taped interviews in which I found him astonishingly frank on a variety of important issues. He also invited me to lunch more than once, and during those times, the talk flowed very freely indeed.

Conversations with those who appeared in his films were of critical significance in the original preparations for both *The Art of Alfred Hitchcock* and *The Dark Side of Genius*. During the years of my research for those books (1974 through 1982), several people asked me to suppress some material for a period of time, because of his recent death; in some cases, they asked that details not be set down during their own lifetimes. That explains both the lacunae in my earlier work and the main reason for *Spellbound by Beauty* – which, of course, contains very much new material.

I wish to acknowledge, therefore, especially the following actresses, who spoke to me on the record: Diane Baker, Anne Baxter, Ingrid Bergman, Karen Black, Doris Day, Joan Fontaine, Dolly Haas, Barbara Harris, Tippi Hedren, Grace Kelly (Princess Grace of Monaco), Janet Leigh, Margaret Lockwood, Vivien Merchant, Mildred Natwick, Claire Griswold Pollack, Elsie Randolph, Eva Marie Saint, Sylvia Sidney, Jessica Tandy, Ann Todd, Kathleen Tremayne, Alida Valli, Josephine Wilson (Lady Miles) and Teresa Wright.

A number of actors also cooperated generously: Brian Aherne, Martin Balsam, Hume Cronyn, Bruce Dern, William Devane, Jon Finch, John Forsythe, Barry Foster, Sir John Gielgud, Farley Granger,

Lord (Bernard) Miles, Reggie Nalder, Paul Newman, Gregory Peck, Anthony Perkins, James Stewart and Rod Taylor.

Hitchcock's writers knew him in ways others never could, for they sat with him for months and came to know how his prodigious mind worked. I was fortunate to have the confidence of Jay Presson Allen, Charles Bennett, David Freeman, John Michael Hayes, Evan Hunter, Arthur Laurents, Ernest Lehman, Brian Moore, Anthony Shaffer, Joseph Stefano and Samuel Taylor. Among Hitchcock's close creative team, I also knew and interviewed Henry Bumstead, Herbert Coleman, Edith Head, Peggy Robertson, Leonard South and Albert Whitlock.

The original idea for this book derived from conversations with two of my closest friends, Gerald Pinciss and Lewis Falb. They have enthusiastically endorsed my writing for many years.

Once again, my brother-in-law, John Møller, dispatched the difficult creative task of transferring photographs onto disks. John is not only a talented designer but also a superb technician, and I am grateful for his generous allotment of time on behalf of this book.

Claus Kjær and his colleagues at the Danish Film Institute, Copenhagen, have welcomed me most warmly to this prestigious archive and library, and they have graciously invited me to be a frequent guest lecturer at the Cinematek. I am grateful to be associated with them and their audiences.

My London literary agent, Elizabeth Sheinkman, at Curtis Brown Ltd, is the attentive advocate and guide of my British interests, and I am grateful for her caring and her friendship. In her office, Felicity Blunt has supervised a myriad details with unfailing cheerfulness.

Once again, I am very fortunate to be published at the Hutchinson imprint of Random House UK by Paul Sidey, whose friendship for three decades I count as a signal blessing. His creative contributions and his generous camaraderie benefit my life as they do my career. His assistant, Tess Callaway, had dispatched the daily round of chores with graceful efficiency, and Ilsa Yardley was the keen-eyed copy editor.

Ole Flemming Larsen, with whom I share my life, gives me more than I can ever deserve.

★   ★   ★

Acknowledgments

With enormous gratitude and devotion, I dedicate this book to my dear friends Mona and Karl Malden. Their presence in my life means more than I can say.

D.S.

Sjælland, Denmark

Christmas 2007

Foreword

The book you are holding is my third volume on the life and work of the great director. The first, *The Art of Alfred Hitchcock*, is an analysis and critical appreciation of each of his films; it was first published in English in 1976, during the director's lifetime and after I had interviewed him on several occasions. I was very gratified indeed when he celebrated and promoted the book, which is still in print, and in many languages. *The Dark Side of Genius: The Life of Alfred Hitchcock* appeared in 1983, three years after his death; it, too, is still available and has appeared in several dozen foreign-language editions.

Why, then, another book, with specific reference to the director and his actresses?

First, because it is remarkable how infrequently, over a period of more than fifty years, Hitchcock said anything – much less something favourable – about his players. His most repeated remark about them became a famous personal motto: 'Actors are cattle' – or, more puckishly, 'I never said actors are cattle – I said that actors should be treated like cattle.' Actors and audiences laughed together at this, but behind the sardonic statement was the undeniable fact that, while he knew that he needed good and attractive talent to draw audiences and so to guarantee the commercial success of his movies, he seems to have had no great opinion of actors, and he often openly resented their stardom, privileges and salaries. 'Actors! I hate the sight of them!' he cried in one unusually bitter fit of pique.

Hitchcock rarely had anything to say about his male stars – estimable performers like John Gielgud, Michael Redgrave, Laurence Olivier, Cary Grant, James Stewart, Sean Connery and Paul Newman, who were well established in their careers when they came to work for him. Many of his leading ladies, on the other hand, achieved international stardom precisely because of their Hitchcock roles – Madeleine Carroll, Joan Fontaine, Grace Kelly, Janet Leigh and Tippi Hedren are good examples. That he maintained an insistent silence about the quality of their performances is a curiosity that cannot be ignored.

'Some of us actors have ideas,' Ingrid Bergman said at a tribute to him, in his presence, a year before his death – 'and then Hitch can become a little truculent.' Princess Grace of Monaco wrote, in her Foreword to my first book, that 'sometimes he merely wears [actors] down until he gets what he wants.' They spoke these words in the context of affectionate and laudatory remarks, and they were not nearly as taciturn about their appreciation as he was. Nor is there anything unusual or malevolent about directors making demands or seeming defiant with their actors, as Ingrid and Grace attested. Moviemaking, after all, is a collaborative craft, movie sets (even those of the punctilious Hitchcock) are usually chaotic places, laced with the strong aroma of ego and dependent on the countless variables of human temperament and technical accidents. Hitchcock had a lot to put up with from eccentric, sometimes boorish studio moguls, from mediocre workmen and moody colleagues. But his reticence, his refusal to praise or thank those who gave him their best, must be explored.

In François Truffaut's book-length series of interviews with Hitchcock – which covers the production of every one of Hitchcock's films – I have counted more than 140 references to actresses. Hitchcock's remarks about them were mostly neutral but frequently hostile. Indeed, he did not have a good word to say even about the women he apparently liked: Ingrid Bergman and Grace Kelly. The best he could manage about the others was the mildly affirmative opinion that Sylvia Sidney (in *Sabotage*) 'had nice understatement' and that Shirley MacLaine (in *The Trouble With Harry*) 'was very good'. Otherwise, one finds only Hitchcock's indifferent references to his actresses; more to the point, he never once so much as uttered the names of those who contributed enormously to the success of some of his finest works – Madeleine

Carroll (in *The 39 Steps* and *Secret Agent*), Nova Pilbeam (in *Young and Innocent*) and Margaret Lockwood (in *The Lady Vanishes*), for just a few examples.

In the summer of 1975, during the first of our many long interviews, I asked Hitchcock about the achievements of his actresses – just how *did* he work with them to evoke such magnificent performances? 'I think it has to do with the way in which one photographs them,' he replied, and that was that – not a word in favour of the women.

'As far as Hitchcock was concerned,' recalled Joseph Stefano, who wrote the screenplay for *Psycho*, 'if he decided to use you, that was compliment enough.' John Michael Hayes, who wrote *Rear Window*, *To Catch a Thief*, *The Trouble With Harry* and *The Man Who Knew Too Much*, elaborated: 'Hitch was an enigma – personally as well as professionally. He never once congratulated me or thanked me for anything I did. In his mind, if you did well, he thought it was just expected of you.' One had to learn of Hitchcock's satisfaction through others, as Hayes continued. 'Hitch's wife Alma came up to me once and said, "Don't breathe a word of this to anyone, but Hitch is *immensely* pleased with you."' Doris Day interpreted Hitchcock's stony silence as his disapproval of her performance during the shooting of *The Man Who Knew Too Much* in 1955. It took her offer to withdraw from the film to evoke Hitchcock's lukewarm response that if he did *not* like what she was doing, he would have said something. Some might consider such ungenerosity more than merely enigmatic.

These were matters I subsequently discussed in some detail with a number of his leading ladies – among them, Margaret Lockwood, Sylvia Sidney, Joan Fontaine, Teresa Wright, Ingrid Bergman, Alida Valli, Anne Baxter, Grace Kelly, Janet Leigh and Tippi Hedren. His male stars seemed, for the most part, to have little to say on the matter, although Michael Redgrave, Hume Cronyn, Joseph Cotten, Gregory Peck, Farley Granger, Reggie Nalder, Rod Taylor, Paul Newman, Jon Finch and Barry Foster were singularly perceptive in their observations.

In *Spellbound by Beauty*, I detail the fine points of the significant contributions leading ladies made to Hitchcock's films – contributions often made under difficult and even painful circumstances. To a person, none of them ever defended, praised or justified herself – that would not have done much good in any case, for he was the powerhouse, they the mere exponents, expendable and often doomed to the merciless scythe of transient popularity.

In addition, there have been many rumours about his treatment of women – not only in the films themselves, but also behind the scenes, during production. Stories have circulated about Hitchcock's sadistic behaviour and his occasional public humiliation of actresses. The fact is that these accounts turn out to be alarmingly true in a remarkable number of cases. There is no doubt that he was enormously helpful in the advancement of some careers. But he was, equally often, unhelpful to himself when he was unkind to people – especially to women, for whom he had a strange amalgam of adoration and contempt, and whom he felt he could control in a way he dared not attempt with men. Hitchcock had many professional admirers among his actresses, but no true and lasting friends. Ingrid Bergman and Grace Kelly kept in contact with him over the years, but he was slow to reciprocate. The fact is that he had not the gift of friendship; there are few comparable sadnesses in any life.

Hitchcock was evidently attracted to women (to blondes especially), but he never spoke well of them, and most of them did not have the remotest idea of his reactions toward their work. To him, they were foolish, capriciously sensual and at the mercy of wildly improbable sexual urges. This attitude of stony indifference characterised his relationships with his male players, too, but he had few emotional requirements to make of men in his work, and for the most part, he neither challenged them nor showed much interest in them. No, it was the women who preoccupied him – 'Torture the women!' he said, repeating the advice of the nineteenth-century playwright Victorien Sardou about plot construction.

Hitchcock took that counsel to heart. In his first English movie, *The Lodger*, he put his star (known simply as June) in manacles, which caused her no little upset and discomfort. Madeleine Carroll was dragged around the sets of *The 39 Steps* for long periods over several days, handcuffed to her co-star Robert Donat until she showed painful bruises. Such incidents occurred at regular intervals during his career, but nothing compared with the physical torture inflicted on Tippi Hedren during the filming of *The Birds*, or the sexual harassment she endured during the production of *Marnie*.

★   ★   ★

But a potential objection must be faced at the outset.

Why does a biographer describe Hitchcock's strange psychology and even stranger conduct, however fastidiously and accurately one can document them? What does this sort of thing add to our knowledge or appreciation of a great film artist and perennial entertainer?

Alfred Hitchcock died in 1980, and in the intervening years, his legion of admirers have too often mythologised him out of all resemblance to reality. Indeed, he has become in the eyes of many a genius *tout court*, without much humanity to make him recognisable. More unrealistically, he is regarded by many as a warm and cuddly gentleman, adorably amusing, like an eccentric grandfather who tells bedtime stories – a man unworthy of what is sometimes called meretricious treatment at the hands of some writers. I have not escaped the occasional opprobrium of some Hitchcock partisans who will not hear a syllable against him and are shocked that such anecdotes are included in a biography.

But there can be a dangerous hypocrisy – and a fearful scholarly deficiency – at the root of such objections when they come from people who ought to know better about the links between art and life, and who ought to have a deeper appreciation of human longing and pain. In this regard, I was immensely gratified when Hitchcock's close collaborator, the playwright and screenwriter Samuel Taylor (who gave him the final script for *Vertigo*), proclaimed that *The Dark Side of Genius* was a sympathetic biography *not* of an angel or a demon, but of 'a human being in all his complexity'.

Writing or speaking anything other than the highest praise and promoting the most affectionate encomia for so august an icon as Alfred Hitchcock has become, in the eyes of many, equivalent to cultural sacrilege. But the craft of biography requires that the shadow side of subjects be set forth and comprehended – otherwise, their humanity is diminished, their pain minimised, and those they hurt are ignored. Any serious appreciation of Hitchcock's art and life must take into account the enormity of his psychological, physical and social suffering, as well as that which he (perhaps unintentionally) caused others. From his suffering came the obsessively recurring themes and the constant sense of dread with which he continues to astonish, entertain and enlighten.

History provides a very long list of the names of great artists whose characters were not always sterling and whose lives were variations on misery. No one disputes either the genius of Richard Wagner or his enduring significance in the history of great music. But Wagner was also dishonest, untruthful, unfaithful, temperamental, rude and virulently anti-Semitic. He sacrificed everything for his art, even putting up and losing his mother's pension to pay his gambling debts. He was, to put it mildly, a person to be avoided except from a distance, in his work for the opera and concert halls. Similarly, Pablo Picasso was a deeply misogynistic man whose art was great but whose personality was profoundly flawed.

In the annals of filmmaking, it is well known that D. W. Griffith risked actors' lives for the sake of dramatic scenes; that Carl Dreyer contributed directly to the emotional collapse of his leading lady during the making of *The Passion of Joan of Arc*; that John Huston very nearly killed Gregory Peck during the production of *Moby Dick*; and that Otto Preminger routinely brought actors to tears and even the brink of nervous breakdown by his cruel public humiliation of them.

But Hitchcock was different. His particular, lifelong fantasies informed just about every one of his motion pictures – and alarmingly often, the frustration of his romantic fantasies or his harbouring violent ones sprang into life. His movies were consistently self-revealing in ways that Griffith's, Dreyer's, Huston's and Preminger's were not.

When I began *The Art of Alfred Hitchcock* in 1974, I was committed to the idea that he was history's greatest filmmaker. This I maintained because so many of his films defy the passage of time and the inevitable changes of cinematic style. I also discovered that very many of his movies continue to entertain audiences worldwide even as they deal, remarkably often, with perennially significant issues of human life and destiny. Decades later, I have no reason to alter my high estimation of his genius.

The Dark Side of Genius, which appeared in 1983, was the first of my sixteen biographies (up to 2008). From it, I felt obliged to withhold some information, as several of my sources asked me to omit certain comments either for some years or until after their own deaths. I honoured those requests, but now an important element of Hitchcock's life story must supplement what has preceded.

Apart from his memorable achievements, his biography remains a cautionary tale of what can go wrong in any life. It is the story of a man so unhappy, so full of self-loathing, so lonely and friendless, that his satisfactions came as much from asserting power as from spinning fantasies and acquiring wealth. The fact is that some of his conduct can only be called sexual harassment, and I do not believe that there is ever any justification for that: no artistic goal justifies cruelty or exploitation. It is important to know this about Hitchcock, especially at a time when raising an artist to the pantheon leads to an injudicious minimising or even ignoring of episodes that cast light on the strange links that can bind confident genius to a domineering cruelty. He could not have got away with some of his conduct today; and no one should ever be permitted to act as he often did.

This book is not a revisionist biography, but in a sense, it is the life story of a sad motif – in the broadest sense, the motif of a consuming selfishness. Sometimes he could not foresee the suffering his actions would cause; sometimes, he seemed to anticipate that suffering quite clearly. He never forgot Sardou's injunction to 'torture the women'.

All motifs or themes in our lives have bases and backgrounds, beginnings, developments, climaxes and conclusions. Therefore, I have considered it essential to treat the subject chronologically and to provide important contextual material on the matter of some films, for Hitchcock's relationships did not occur in a professional vacuum.

Spellbound by Beauty: Alfred Hitchcock and His Leading Ladies aims to explore the life of a brilliant, strange, tortured and essentially unhappy man, who left us a legacy of great art, perhaps in spite of himself. It also attempts to offer new insights into Hitchcock the filmmaker – in particular, how he understood the element of collaboration. Finally, this book is a tribute to a number of extraordinarily talented women, without whose courage, grace and patience we would almost certainly not have these enduring, moving, deeply rewarding motion pictures.

I

Love in Handcuffs
(1920–1926)

For five years beginning in 1920, when he was twenty-one, Alfred Hitchcock worked in London for Famous Players-Lasky, the British production branch of Hollywood's Paramount Pictures. Most of the senior technical staff were Americans, imported to work on the two small stages, once a power station in the borough of Islington.

Hitchcock's first job, illustrating the title cards of silent movies, gave him access to various jobs on an ad hoc basis: designer for this picture, or art director, co-writer or production manager for that one. Unlike the job specialisation in the American movie industry, labourers hired by English studios were encouraged to perform multiple tasks, working wherever their talents could be exploited – hence the multi-talented young Hitch became a jack-of-all-work on at least eighteen British silent movies. 'All my early training was by Americans,' he said years later, 'and it was far superior to the British.'

In 1924, he was still putting in long hours and learning new, up-to-date production methods. That year, producer Michael Balcon took over the studio when Paramount withdrew; Balcon's goal was to sponsor entertainment for an international (especially an American) audience. Accordingly, Balcon brought over Hollywood's Betty Compson to star in a picture called *Woman to Woman*, on which Hitchcock worked, as he said, as 'general factotum. I wrote the script. I designed the sets, and I managed the production. It was the first film that I had really got my hands onto.'

I

It was also the first of five films on which he worked for the studio's leading director, Graham Cutts, with whom he had an increasingly hostile relationship. The trouble was caused, it seems, by Cutts's increasingly indiscreet sexual liaisons (which even interrupted production) and by Hitchcock's evident ambition to supplant him and to secure additional credits, the better to impress Balcon. 'I was quite dogmatic,' he said of this time. 'I would build a set and say to the director, "Here's where it's shot from!"'

Cutts resented Hitchcock's assertive style and said so, but Balcon was impressed with the younger man's talent and ambition – especially after Cutts returned to London in early 1925, after filming *The Blackguard* in Berlin. While in Germany, Hitchcock had expeditiously resolved many logistical problems caused by Cutts's ineffective balancing act of work, wife and women on the side. Soon after, Balcon asked Hitchcock to direct a motion picture.

'I had no intention of becoming a film director,' Hitchcock always said of this time in his career. 'I was very happy doing the scripts and the art direction. I hadn't thought of myself as a director' – which was obviously not the case. Working on productions six days weekly for almost five years, he was clearly eager for promotion: he was writing scripts, designing sets, working with editors, and was, to his chagrin, paid miserably in comparison with established directors. Eager to perform any task on a picture by dispatching quickly and effectively every challenging aspect of production, Hitchcock (according to Balcon) 'wanted to be a director, but it was not easy to get a young man launched in so important a job' because financiers and distributors were wary of promoting an assistant.

And so Balcon turned to his foreign partners: 'I had to arrange to have [Hitchcock direct his first two pictures] in Germany because of the resistance to his becoming a director' in London. With the screenwriter Eliot Stannard; the assistant director Alma Reville; and the cinematographer Gaetano di Ventimiglia, Hitchcock headed for exterior location shooting in northern Italy and then for studio work in Munich, where they were joined by a crew of international technicians and co-producers. Hitch absorbed enough rudimentary German to communicate his wishes.

His assignment was *The Pleasure Garden*, based on an unexceptional but once popular novel about two London showgirls, their shifting fidelities to the difficult men in their lives, and their dangerous sojourn in the tropics – all of it wrapped up in a dénouement of madness and murder. The principal characters were portrayed by American stars acting in Germany and Italy as if the settings were London and the Far East. Hitchcock had the task of making all this appear realistic and emotionally credible, and for the most part, he succeeded admirably.

Balcon imported a pair of Hollywood's top glamour girls, Virginia Valli and Carmelita Geraghty. Virginia had already appeared in forty-seven pictures under the direction of John Ford, King Vidor and others. She wanted to hear what Hitchcock planned and how she would look in the finished film.

'I was in a cold sweat,' Hitchcock admitted later. 'I wanted to disguise the fact that this was my first directorial effort. I dreaded to think what she, an established Hollywood star, would say if she discovered that she had been brought all the way over to Europe to be directed by a beginner. I was terrified at giving her instructions. I've no idea how many times I asked my future wife [Alma Reville] if I was doing the right thing. She, sweet soul, gave me courage by swearing I was doing marvellously.'

So began an historic collaboration. Alma had a keen eye, she knew how stories should be structured and rendered visually, she had worked as an editor, and she was not hesitant to tell Hitchcock just what she thought. Tiny and titian-haired, she gave a first impression of shy gentility, but the real Alma Reville was an acutely intelligent, self-assured woman of steely resolve, quite different from the insecure Hitchcock, who was ever self-conscious about his appearance, his tastes and modest Cockney background. When a tough decision had to be made in business or private life, Alma acted fearlessly.

Hitchcock was uncomfortable around his two pretty American stars, but he knew how much he needed them. He also resented their enormous salaries, and his budget forestalled their expectations of Hollywood-style luxury they had enjoyed there. 'Valli was big stuff and knew it,' according to Hitchcock. 'She expected a brass band. She expected the red carpet. But she didn't get them. Valli was peeved, but she turned out to be sweet enough.'

Filming began in June 1925 in northern Italy, before moving to the studio interiors in Munich, which were suffocatingly hot that summer, for the ceilings were glass and air-conditioning was unknown.

Everything seemed to go wrong: there were numerous delays from uncooperative extra players, and then a trained dog simply wandered off, and his replacement insistently licked off the make-up designed to replicate his predecessor. After that, a woman hired to play a native girl arrived on the day for her swimming scene, but she promptly announced that her monthly period prevented her going into the water.

This bit of news, Hitchcock claimed, was an educational experience for him. He insisted that he had never heard of the menstrual cycle because it had not been included in his schoolboy education – nor, one might add, was production design or scriptwriting. But like his assertion that he had no thought of becoming a director, this statement of ignorance simply cannot be taken at face value. He was twenty-six, had an older sister and brother, and had worked at a movie studio during the freewheeling 1920s – not generally a place and time of polite discourse. Sexually inexperienced though he claims to have been, he was not a backward, pre-adolescent country boy from an earlier century. Ordinary curiosity surely must have supplemented his formal education.

But word circulated that Hitch was an unsophisticated innocent, which (as he may have intended) evoked the benignly maternal, protective reactions of Valli and Geraghty and much improved the tone of the production and their pliancy in his hands. Thus, he won them over not by exhibiting his sophistication, but by feigning ignorance. He employed, in other words, whatever it took to achieve the desired effect – including his demand that Virginia Valli wear a blonde wig for her role.

When Balcon arrived in Munich to have a look at Hitchcock's first cut of the picture, he agreed with the director that rearrangements were called for, but, for his marketing purposes, he also said he liked the American look of the picture. *The Pleasure Garden* revealed, too, Hitchcock's skilful use of hallucinatory cinematic techniques (dissolves and double printing, for example) – and, for commercial appeal, the emphasis on fast-paced action alternating with scenes of violence and boudoir sex.

The final form of *The Pleasure Garden* contains several elements that would intrigue Hitchcock throughout his career: the theatrical setting, the motif of voyeurism, sudden emotional breakdown, and the psychological torture and physical pain inflicted on women by deceitful and violent men. The last element is not peculiar to his entertainments, of course: the damsel in distress is virtually an ancient archetype, long a staple of literature, poetry, theatre, opera and movies. Hitchcock showed the world, in stark close-up, that misogyny is part of a pandemic social pathology. He was neither moralist nor preacher, but his work consistently reveals that the fine arts of human exploitation and cruelty are symptoms of a deep fissure in the human spirit.

The Pleasure Garden opens with a close shot of women's legs, hastening down a spiral staircase toward the stage of the eponymous theatre, where they dance with wild abandon typical of the Jazz Age; the movement is so animated that this silent film suddenly becomes a kind of vivid flip-book. Hitchcock then shows the men in the theatre audience, formally dressed but leering as they gaze at the dancers through their opera glasses. These will become mainstream themes and images for Hitchcock – characters in the world of theatre, drawn into bizarre real-life dramas; voyeurism; the camera observing an observer; the rapid transitions from the watcher to the watched; the dizzying staircase – and the mischievous humour. 'What every chorus girl knows,' announces a title card – and the movie then shows a woman washing her stockings in a basin. Hitchcock's bedroom scenes occur later in the movie, and there is nothing coy, bashful or boyish about them.

Life within and outside this pleasure garden, from London's Piccadilly to the tropics, is a perilous paradise – thus the ominous snake entwined round a tree, and on the title card designs Hitch devised, adding another layer of meaning to the film's title. The chase and nick-of-time rescue at the finale reveal his familiarity with film-makers like D. W. Griffith, and he was certainly inspired by Charles Chaplin and Buster Keaton as much as by Germans like F. W. Murnau and Fritz Lang, whom he had met in Berlin. One conceit particularly marked the Hitchcock style from this year forward: characters often gaze directly at the camera, thus making the audience a corresponding player, a participant in the drama.

Hitchcock boldly added his initials (and sometimes his full signature) to the intertitle designs. In this regard, he was taking a page from Chaplin and Griffith, who were among the first to understand that the marketing of their own names was as critical as the selling of the properties or presenting an attractive leading lady. 'Actors come and go,' Hitchcock told his colleagues at London's Film Society that year, 'but the name of the director should stay clearly in the mind of the audiences.' That spirit would lead to his cameo appearances: he was the artist signing his canvas, reminding viewers that this was an Alfred J. Hitchcock production.

When Balcon screened the film in London for the press, they were enthusiastic – 'a powerful and interesting story [that] promises well for Hitchcock's future efforts', proclaimed the trade journal *Bioscope* on 25 March 1926. But the financiers working with Balcon would not distribute the picture, claiming that its content and style would alienate British audiences accustomed to more straightforward and less visually inventive movies. Hence Balcon decided to shelve *The Pleasure Garden* for a while – but he had not lost faith in Hitchcock, to whom he gave another crack at directing. (Later, American journalists were scathing, calling the picture 'sappy' and 'a Wiener schnitzel', and banishing it straightaway.)

As for Virginia Valli and Carmelita Geraghty, they apparently never spoke on the record about Hitchcock, even after his international fame was secure. That was perhaps due to the dramatic changes in their lives, which led them to reject all later requests for interviews about their days as movie stars. Carmelita worked in an additional fifty-three pictures during the next decade, but then, at thirty-four, she retired and became a successful professional artist whose paintings were sold at galleries across America; she died in 1966.

Virginia turned her back on Hollywood after appearing in eighteen more movies. Real-life romance then replaced the imaginary sort, when she met the dashing actor Charles Farrell, whom she married in 1931, when she was thirty-three. For the next thirty-seven years, until her death in 1968, she lived more happily than any heroine she portrayed. For her as for Carmelita, glamour-girl vanity was no longer important. Hitchcock referred to his first leading ladies only to cite the costs of their excess personal baggage and their refusal to eat food served on European trains.

Balcon told Hitchcock to remain in Germany, where the producer had lined up another movie with another American beauty, but this time the director was unflappable, even in the face of her frank and sassy sex appeal. After a spin with the Ziegfeld Follies, Brooklyn-born Anita Donna Dooley was brought to Hollywood by John Barrymore, with whom she co-starred in *Dr Jekyll and Mr Hyde* in 1920. Theodosia Goodman had been renamed Theda Bara, and so a publicist changed Anita's name to Nita Naldi. With that, Nita was promoted as the daughter of a famous Italian diplomat and a descendant of Dante's Beatrice. In fact, her family background was far humbler, for she had left school to work as a model before joining Ziegfeld's chorus line. The highlight of her career had been acting opposite Rudolph Valentino in *Blood and Sand* and in De Mille's original *The Ten Commandments*. Incredible though it seems decades later, audiences in the silent movie era often confused the role with the actress, and Nita's notoriety as a vamp on-screen made her unwelcome in many restaurants, on public beaches and at polite social gatherings.

When she arrived in Munich, Nita at once put Hitchcock at ease with her tough humour and lack of guile. Travelling with an older gentleman she winkingly referred to as 'Daddy', she whisked Hitchcock and his assistant off for a visit to a famous brothel that was on her list of tourist attractions. Invited to participate in the customary recreations, Hitch and Alma demurred, while the activities of Nita and Daddy have not been documented. It may have been at this time, or in Berlin the previous year, that Hitchcock also rejected the advances at some pleasure palace of two young German girls who then shrugged indifferently and got into bed together. Hitchcock remained to observe at close range the lesbian encounter. 'It was a very *gemütlich* [cosy] family soirée,' he said.

But there was work to do with his cast that autumn of 1925. *The Mountain Eagle*, based on a story by Balcon's story editor, concerned (of all things) scandal among Kentucky hillbillies, which was not exactly familiar territory for Hitchcock or his writer, the prolific Eliot Stannard. Very quickly, the finished film, partly shot in the snowy Tyrol, vanished into oblivion, and only some still photographs survive – no loss, said Hitchcock, calling it 'a very bad movie'. But the trade review in London's *Kinematograph Weekly* for 7 October 1926 disagreed, praising the direction as 'thoroughly imaginative . . . [despite the] slow tempo and a story too full of unconvincing twists.'

Nita Naldi came to the production with all sorts of suggestions as to how she might make the role of a doughty schoolmarm more alluring. 'She arrived on the set with fingernails like a mandarin's,' Hitchcock recalled, 'and with four-inch heels and a black dog to match her black, swathed dress. She was dark, Latin, Junoesque and slinky, with slanting eyes, and her maid followed her – it was like the royalty Germany hadn't seen for years! I was thinking of a simple Kentucky Miss in a gingham gown and a cotton apron. I had to turn her into a strong woman of the Midwestern mountains who handled a gun instead of a lipstick.'

So began a little conflict. First the director and his star quarrelled about her fingernails, which she gradually trimmed. The high heels also came down, and the make-up was altered, shade by shade. After a loud altercation, Nita finally agreed to change her hair, curl by curl – always a Hitchcock fixation.

In silent films, dialogue was created only for close shots; in grand emotional scenes (as Hitchcock said), 'we allowed people to say just whatever came into their heads. One day, Nita was playing a scene in which she had been run out of town by a Kentucky farmer. She had to turn on them and tell them just what she thought of them. I called out to her, "Give them all you've got!"

'And she did! She gave it to them in English, Italian, American, Bowery, Park Avenue and maybe double Dutch. She called them anything and everything she could lay her tongue to. She told them where they got off, where they came from, where they were going. She used words we had never heard before. When I called "Cut!" she was shuddering and shaking with emotion, and the whole studio – none of whom had understood a word she said – burst into spontaneous applause.'

That was Nita Naldi's last scheduled task in *The Mountain Eagle*. She took no time to change her clothes, but instead she called at once for her dog and her 'Daddy', hurried to a waiting taxi and raced off to the train for France, 'still in her gingham dress, with make-up on her face'.

She made two more films in quick succession, one in Paris and one in Berlin. Her energy was prodigious, but her strong New York accent was unacceptable with the arrival of talking pictures. In the 1930s, she appeared on Broadway in a forgettable trio of plays with very short runs, and when she died alone in a Manhattan hotel room in 1961, she had been a widow for sixteen years, living on a meagre stipend from the Actors Fund. 'Nita turned out to be a grand person,' Hitchcock said later. 'For all her entourage, there was really nothing high-hat about her. She talked to everybody in her heavy New York drawl, and the Germans fell hard for this American royalty.'

★   ★   ★

Like *The Pleasure Garden*, *The Mountain Eagle* left exhibitors luke-warm, and it was put on the shelf next to its predecessor until after the eventual critical and popular success of Hitchcock's third picture, *The Lodger: A Story of the London Fog*. This was Balcon's idea, and Hitchcock and Stannard were at once enthusiastic: it was based on a superb and successful 1913 thriller by Marie Belloc Lowndes that was inspired by the ghastly crimes of Jack the Ripper in 1888. The real-life slayer was never identified, but a series of copycat murders ensued, and a general paranoia afflicted London life for years.

Eliot Stannard was the main writer on no less than eight Hitchcock silent pictures, and his contributions must be stressed. But as the British scholar Charles Barr observed, Hitch 'fostered the impression that he used screenwriters like secretaries, as skilled agents for writing up his own ideas.' Sidney Gilliat, who co-wrote *The Lady Vanishes* in 1937, recalled that Hitch routinely told the press that he alone was respon-sible for 99 per cent of his script material. That is especially ironic in the case of *The Lady Vanishes*, which was virtually complete when Hitch came to the project.

However, it must be added that this young director also took enor-mous care in shaping whatever written material he received, and his increasing success, his cameo appearances, his interviews with the press (and later his television programmes) made him a celebrity and bestowed a power he exploited even as he affected a cool, detached and remote diffidence. In addition, he had a rare technical genius and had ideas for every element in visual storytelling, from pre-production to final release. Unfortunately, he never mentioned Eliot Stannard's signal contributions, and throughout his lifetime, Alfred Hitchcock seemed to believe that sharing credit diminished the praise due solely to himself.

In the novel *The Lodger*, the title character, who calls himself Mr Sleuth, appears to be a refined gentleman who comes to rent rooms in the home of a London family, Mr and Mrs Bunting. 'It hadn't taken the landlady very long to find out that her lodger had a queer kind of fear and dislike of women. When she was doing the staircase and landings, she would often hear [him] reading aloud to himself passages in the Bible that were very uncomplimentary to her sex. But that didn't put her out. Besides, where one's lodger is concerned, a dislike of women is better than – well, than the other thing.'

As it turns out, the lodger is indeed no merely eccentric gentleman: he is the self-styled 'Avenger', a mad serial killer responsible for the death of a dozen poor girls. The Buntings are both frightened and fascinated as the Avenger's crimes multiply.

Mrs Bunting's seventeen-year-old stepdaughter, Daisy (her husband's child by a previous marriage), does not live with them, and is very much a secondary character in the novel. She comes to visit and is courted by Joe Chandler, a detective on the Avenger case, whom she eventually marries. Daisy does not meet the lodger until very near the end, and then only briefly. Despite Mrs Bunting's conviction that her lodger is a serial murderer, she says nothing to Joe, nor does she go to the police, despite the accumulating evidence.

In the final pages of the novel, the lodger escapes and never returns to the Bunting house. The landlady 'had sheltered him – kept his awful secret . . . that [he] was victim of no temporary aberration, but that he was, and had been for years, a madman, a homicidal maniac . . . [He] never came back, and at last, after many days and many nights had gone by, Mrs Bunting left off listening for the click of the lock which she at once hoped and feared would herald her lodger's return.'

At the core of this profoundly disturbing book is Mrs Bunting's fascination for a smoothly stylish lunatic. Marie Belloc Lowndes brilliantly explored the clash of repulsion and attraction that is often linked to the desire to experience the darkest aspects of danger and dread – but from a distance, in both art and entertainment. Very often in her novel, she describes the frank excitement of the newspaper reports, and of the public's relish for the daily instalments of a real-life horror thriller.

Hitchcock insisted that the central characters of the movie must be the lodger and Daisy, not the lodger and the landlady, and so the part of the girl was much enlarged, and the central conflict became the detective's jealousy of the lodger's attentions to Daisy. Mr and Mrs Bunting, therefore, became faintly comic characters, Cockney simpletons whom the movie treats with some condescension.

Balcon decided that *The Lodger* would be perfect for the reigning matinée idol of the day, Welsh actor-author-composer Ivor Novello, star of Balcon's major hit that year, *The Rat*. Novello also composed successful West End musicals, and his tunes were heard everywhere ('Keep the Home Fires Burning' had been the sentimental standard all during the World War). According to Hitchcock, Novello's enormous popularity would not permit him to undertake the role of a murderous madman – hence, the script could not conclude (like the novel) with a clear establishment of the lodger's guilt: 'They wouldn't let Novello even be considered as a villain,' Hitchcock insisted. 'We had to change the [book] to show that without a doubt he was innocent.'

But this statement, too, must not be accepted at face value. The novel had been freely adapted by H. A. Vachell for the London stage in 1915 as *Who Is He?*, which Hitchcock saw before he read the novel. In this serio-comic theatrical adaptation, the lodger turns out to be an innocent young aristocrat who takes refuge in lodgings after being jilted by his lover. The darker psychological complexity of Stannard's and Hitchcock's film treatment would have been much attenuated by a straightforward tale in which a suspect turns out to be the villain after all.

Novello was a rather unctuous over-actor, ferociously protective of his glamorous profile to the point of applying thick lipstick and eyeliner in the style of antique theatrics. He was also clever and witty, enjoying the advocacy of Noël Coward, who nevertheless preferred Ivor from a distance: 'Before a camera, his face takes on a set look, his eyes become deceptively soulful, and frequently something dreadful happens to his mouth.' Novello was quite flamboyantly gay. The poet Siegfried Sassoon was among his lovers, although Novello eventually settled down to many years of domestic bliss and professional success with the actor Robert Andrews, who appeared in a number of Novello's musicals.

Unlike many of his contemporaries, Hitchcock was always comfortable working with male and female homosexuals. 'Some people might be surprised by this,' said the musical star Elsie Randolph, who appeared in two Hitchcock movies over the span of forty years. 'He was always at ease with homosexual or bisexual people. Hitch often told actors – for what mix of reasons I won't guess – that they really had to be part masculine and part feminine in order to get inside any character.' Throughout his life, Hitchcock burnished his public image as a bourgeois middle-class Edwardian gentleman, but he nursed no prejudices against gay men and women.

Ivor was an amusing colleague during the making of *The Lodger*, and Hitchcock was not hesitant to pull a practical joke, taking great care as he set up a shot with a flowerpot strategically placed on a shelf behind his leading man, so that the actor appeared to be wearing a woman's outlandish hat. 'It was just too tempting,' Hitchcock told the actor-writer Rodney Ackland. 'I couldn't resist it. Anyway, with that profile, why should Ivor mind having a flower pot on his head?'

For an actress to portray Daisy Bunting, Novello suggested a former colleague, twenty-five-year-old June Howard-Tripp, a popular musical comedy star since childhood. Known professionally and credited in *The Lodger* simply as June, she had appeared in a few previous films, was quickly hired to play Daisy, and readily complied with Hitchcock's requirement that she wear a bright blonde wig over her brown hair.

So began the type of woman Hitch preferred – Nordic, he called them. Blondes were easier and more dramatic to photograph in monochrome, and he considered their 'coolness' and elegance appropriate contrasts to the kind of passion he wanted to reveal beneath the surface. In the years to come, he obliged many actresses to dye their hair a luminous, even glossily burnished blonde. During his black-and-white period, he took special care with the hairstyles of Anny Ondra, Joan Barry, Madeleine Carroll, Joan Fontaine and Ingrid Bergman, while Grace Kelly, Kim Novak, Eva Marie Saint and Tippi Hedren received even more obsessive concern in his colour films.

'Hitch had very strong feelings about women in his films,' recalled Joseph Cotten, who appeared in two of the director's features. 'To him the most feminine and most vulnerable women were usually blondes. He loved blondes and couldn't understand women not bleaching their hair for the privilege of working with him.' Usually, they complied.

In addition to his personal predilection for fair-haired ladies, Hitchcock shared the popular notion that brunettes have a serious nature, while blondes are frivolous – an idea perhaps based on the assumption that comparatively few women are naturally blonde, and because hair-dying was considered a characteristic of idle, shallow women. In ancient Rome, prostitutes were required to dye their hair yellow-gold with saffron, and literary history is full of blonde women of doubtful intelligence and virtue. In George Eliot's Victorian novel *Middlemarch*, for example, the noble and self-sacrificing Dorothea is dark-haired, in contrast to the shallow, selfish, pale and blonde Rosamond. 'Gentlemen prefer blondes' perhaps because 'blondes have more fun,' as the sayings go, and rude mid-twentieth-century jokes about 'dumb blondes' abounded.

Hollywood's images of Jean Harlow, Marilyn Monroe, Jayne Mansfield and others reinforced the unwholesome and erroneous conjunction of blondness with ignorant hypersexuality – a prejudice often imitated by the cinema worldwide (as in the cases of England's Diana Dors and Sweden's Anita Ekberg, for example).

June recalled that Hitchcock 'spoke in a curious mixture of Cockney and North Country accents, with a laboured stress on elusive aitches [h's]. His humour was salty or subtle, according to his mercurial moods, and his brilliance was patent. Hitchcock was being hailed as the Great White Hope of the lagging British motion picture industry, [and] he was so imbued with the value of unusual camera angles and lighting effects with which to create and sustain dramatic suspense, that often a [very brief] scene would take an entire morning to shoot.' For one sequence, Hitchcock insisted that she repeatedly carry an iron tray of breakfast dishes up a three-storey flight until he was satisfied with both 'the expression of fear on my face and the atmosphere established by light and shadows. I must have made the trek twenty times, the tray seeming to grow heavier with every passing minute.'

Another scene requiring multiple takes was far more unpleasant for the actress. Daisy's detective boyfriend (played by Malcolm Keen), comes to visit the Buntings, with the news that he is on the case of the killer. 'I'm keen on golden hair myself, same as the lodger is,' according to his words on an intertitle. 'When I've put handcuffs on the Avenger and a noose around his neck, I'll put a ring on Daisy's finger.' With that, he makes real the picture on the lodger's wall of a woman in bondage, as he playfully snaps handcuffs on Daisy – a gesture that does not amuse the girl but causes sheer panic, which was precisely what June felt when Keen snapped on the cuffs. She had not been prepared for this, and later she reasoned that Hitch wanted to record her shock. During many takes, she was required to run from one room on the set to another, crying out for her manacles to be removed.

Thus another Hitchcockian motif was introduced for future recurrence. 'Psychologically, of course,' Hitchcock said years later, 'the idea of the handcuffs has deeper implications. Being tied to something – it's somewhere in the area of fetishism, isn't it? There's also a sexual connotation. When I visited the Vice Museum in Paris, I noticed there was considerable evidence of sexual aberrations through restraint.' As for Novello, he, too, had an ordeal toward the end of the picture – handcuffed and suspended from an iron fence before being rescued from a vengeful mob.

Beginning with *The Lodger*, it is most often the blondes in Hitchcock's movies who are put through an ordeal, thrown into danger, humiliated and assaulted. As no less a venerable organisation than the British Film Institute stated in a glowing tribute to Hitchcock, he seemed to have 'a murderous fascination with blondes'. That language may be a bit extreme, but even a cautious film historian like Philip Kemp agrees: 'Like Hitchcock himself, the serial killer in *The Lodger* seems to have it in for blondes . . . [and] Hitchcock's mischievous, semi-sadistic treatment of blondes hit its stride in Hollywood, perhaps provoked by the flawless glamour of its screen goddesses', for whom Hitch felt both attraction and resentment. Kemp, too, cites Hitchcock's preference for Victorien Sardou's advice to playwrights: 'Torture the women!' Added Hitch puckishly, 'The trouble today [in the 1930s] is that we don't torture women enough' – a statement he could not have made decades later without risking serious reprisals. Concluded Kemp: 'Hitchcock, at least, did his best to make up for the omission.'

2

Of Sound and Sense
(1926–1934)

The *Lodger* was June's last English movie. In 1929, she married John Alan Burns, the fourth Baron Inverclyde, and retired to take up the quiet life of a titled socialite and hostess. But this did not endure for the new Lady Inverclyde, and the marriage collapsed. She obtained a divorce, married an American businessman and relocated to New York. Her only two subsequent film appearances, both brief and ignored, were in Hollywood productions many years later. June died in 1985, remembered by movie historians for her anxious portrayal of a woman attracted to a fey lodger whom she neither comprehends nor resists.

'*The Lodger* was really my first picture,' Hitchcock said. 'It was the first time I really exercised my style' – or at least one kind of it, for he would modify that style markedly in the years to come. In this case, his technique or design was somewhat influenced by Robert Wiene's recent German film, *The Cabinet of Dr Caligari*, a morbid horror tale about somnambulism, lunacy and murder, played against deliberately artificial and angular studio sets reflecting disordered minds. This extreme example of expressionism Hitchcock downplayed, making the sets more realistic, stressing deep shadows and disorienting camera angles – and so giving *The Lodger* an acute sense of uneasy imbalance from first frame to last.

The picture opens with a close-up of a blonde-haired woman,

screaming in terror and gazing out at us before she is discovered dead; the scene is briefly interrupted by the blinking lights of a theatre marquee – 'To-Night, Golden Curls'. There follows a virtual documentary of the press reports about the murders – the busy teletype machine, the delivery of newspapers, and the dispatchers in the news office (where Hitchcock made his first cameo appearance). We then see chorus girls backstage, as in *The Pleasure Garden*, but here they are obviously terrified. With a kind of wistful rapture, one of them hears the latest news of a killing on the wireless, while another touches her blonde hair protectively – 'Am I next?' For Hitchcock, victims are as fascinated by the horror as the villains and the audience.

The narrative then moves to Daisy, glamorously outfitted and apparently wealthy – but the camera pulls back, and we see that she is a store mannequin, modelling the latest fashions. At home, she lives in genteel poverty with her parents and her constant visitor, the ambitious detective, Joe. In fact, his jealousy of the lodger's attentions to Daisy will soon convince him that the man is the killer. Meanwhile, the nameless lodger glides around the house, asking that all the Victorian paintings of blondes be removed ('they get on my nerves'); he paces his rooms, too, to the anxiety of the household. Soon he is Daisy's greatest admirer, watching intently as she models fashions, buying her expensive frocks and constantly staring at her. In a real sense, Novello is Hitchcock's alter ego in *The Lodger* – ever aware of the leading lady, indulging her, selecting outfits for her, observing her. In this regard, there is a straight line from *The Lodger* to *Vertigo*.

In due course, the police close in on the Bunting neighborhood as the locale of the Avenger's recent crimes, and we see Joe's mental process as he conjures the lodger's guilt – brief connective images, all passing over a footprint in the mud. The final vindication of the lodger, when the actual killer is apprehended off-screen, is not entirely convincing – nor did Hitchcock intend that it should be. The ambiguity of the situation and the character is deliberate.

Perhaps capitalising on Novello's performance as a distracted neurasthenic, the film has a delicate poise between paranoia and security. The final macabre frisson is that Daisy's engagement to the lodger is visually associated with murder: as they embrace, the show title again flashes on a distant marquee – 'To-Night, Golden Curls'. Murder is thus associated with the 'love night' of Daisy and the lodger and with their future. The link between bondage and pleasure, between hand-cuffs and sexual teasing, has come full circle, and for the first time, Hitchcock established an association between sex and murder, ecstasy and death. This is a key element in the disturbing psychology of his greatest works.

As the last image fades, on Daisy's tentative smile in the arms of her lodger-lover, the convention of innocence is much in doubt. After all, if the lodger is not the Avenger, he is certainly a man who has set out to kill – to track down and murder his sister's murderer. He is nothing but a vigilante on the prowl, and so it is impossible to endorse his union with Daisy.

The Lodger required further work after principal photography. It had atmosphere but seemed, to the distributors, to be *artistic*, which was the ultimate commercial condemnation. In addition, very little was tidy about the picture, and Hitchcock wisely and benignly agreed to rethink, trim and reshuffle several sequences. This task was undertaken with the assistance and guidance of Ivor Montagu, a young zoologist who had given free rein to his passion for films and was much respected by (among others) none other than Michael Balcon.

'Hitch was ungrudgingly warm,' recalled Montagu many years later, '[and] eager to hear of anything that, even by chance, might make his work more acceptable. My suggestions were quickly and gener-ously adopted.' Those suggestions included cutting the intertitles from several hundred down to eighty; repeating the heroine's name alone on several intertitles, for 'a menacing effect'; engaging the American designer E. McKnight Kauffer, who created sinister triangle designs; and reshooting some scenes that failed in their intended effects. Montagu brought out the full potential in *The Lodger*, thus salvaging the young director's fledgling career and effectively enabling Hitchcock to become Hitchcock.

'Among the additions I made to *The Lodger*,' Hitchcock told me in July 1975, 'I had a flashback scene on a dance floor – it refers to the murder of the lodger's sister at her social debut. I began with a close-up of two people dancing. Then I dollied back and showed all the guests dancing, and then I went past people sitting at tables against a wall – and then I seemed to go right through a window, all without a single cut. What I actually did was to put everyone and all the furniture on a platform hooked to the camera. Then I dollied back, pulling everything along – and at a certain moment I unhooked the platform. Everything was hooked to the camera! These were the kinds of little tricks I did in those days.'

And these were among the moments that, as he must have foreseen, the critics would notice and celebrate. An important element in building his career was Hitch's belief that movies had to be made with the press in mind – that is, they had to contain his 'Hitchcock touches' that journalists and critics would recognise and publicise, mostly matters of style and technique. He wanted to make himself known as a director by being mentioned in the press *as a director*; this, he correctly reasoned, would be his ticket to creative independence.

When it was finally released, *The Lodger* was an enormous critical and popular success – 'It is possible that this film is the finest British production ever made' was a typical press response – and so Balcon and Novello decided to proceed with another Hitchcock picture. The star had co-authored a play called *Down Hill*, and very quickly it was turned into Hitchcock's *Downhill* – the rather damp story of a wealthy schoolboy (improbably played by thirty-four-year-old Novello) who nobly takes the blame for his best friend's bad conduct and so is expelled from school and disowned by his family. His life degenerates into a spiral of bad fortune, poor choices, poverty and squalor until he is restored to his rightful station – but not until he has endured a series of humiliations from an array of mean-spirited and exploitive women. The story may well reflect Novello's experience as a gay matinée idol, oppressed by unwanted female ardour. That may have been the case, but the film must be assessed on its own merit, which is often considerable.

There was no single leading lady in *Downhill*, but among the lot was a stylish actress named Isabel Jeans, who had already co-starred in a pair of Novello films. Established in the theatre, aristocratic in deportment and projecting a kind of severe femininity, Isabel infused her role of a jaded, immoral actress with calculated carelessness and a mocking cruelty. All the female characters in *Downhill* are reprehensible cheats, liars or insatiable sensualists, but Isabel's Julia is memorable for the worst sort of chilling exploitation. During production, she impressed Hitchcock with her inventive gestures for the silent film, and with her unerring sense of timing.★ Balcon was pleased to grant Hitchcock's request that she star in his next film, also to be based on a play – Noël Coward's *Easy Virtue.*

In a Roman Catholic ceremony at the Brompton Oratory, Knightsbridge, Alfred Hitchcock married Alma Reville on 2 December 1926 – 'because she asked me to', he said many years later, adding provocatively, 'I could have been a poof [i.e., gay] if it were not for Alma.' According to Hitch, the marriage remained unconsummated for more than a year, but at last, there was one experience of sexual intercourse, which resulted in the conception of his only child. (The girl was born on 7 July 1928, which would put her conception at some time in autumn 1927 – a year after the wedding.) As he routinely said, Hitchcock, for all his fantasies, was not a sexually active man.

'Hitch and Alma were really like brother and sister,' said the American playwright and screenwriter Samuel Taylor. 'In business matters, quiet little Alma could be a scrappy little watchdog, for she was much shrewder about people than Hitch, and a lot tougher. Their relationship was one of working partners.' The Hitchcocks' long-time friend Elsie Randolph, among others, agreed: 'Alma was his co-writer, his cook, his *hausfrau* – but theirs was not a grand passion, and to tell the truth, she bossed him.' As one Hitchcock scholar has observed, Hitchcock gave the impression that his marriage was (after their daughter's conception) 'celibate . . . full of sublimations, foremost among which was his work, but [the sublimations included] travel, exclusive restaurants, attending both wrestling matches and symphony concerts at the Albert Hall, and collecting first editions and original works of art. One hears that the diminutive Alma more than stood up to the often grossly overweight Alfred – [she] being described as peppery and given to bossing her husband.' (Later, one of Hitchcock's granddaughters confirmed this.)

★ In *Downhill*, as later, Hitchcock took up a pen and wrote the 'Roddy letter' to be filmed and inserted. So began another type of cameo appearance, but one unnoticed and unremarked in commentaries on Hitchcock. Hitchcock was having fun, but serious fun. There are dozens of examples of his handwriting in his films, and they are always significant.

At work, he gave the women orders – although such were unnecessary during the production of *Easy Virtue*. Isabel Jeans provided a remarkably sympathetic portrait of a socially maligned woman, and her canny professionalism freed the director to explore just how publicity and the camera probe and pry into people's lives. Hitchcock insists on the potentially destructive effects of newspaper and magazine photos and their coyly suggestive captions, and he instructed Isabel Jeans to throw a book at a camera, the cause of all bad publicity.

Very little studio production material has survived for Hitchcock's British films, and interviews with actors – like celebrity autobiographies – were not commonplace in England at the time. These factors make it difficult to document details of Hitchcock's professional relationships in the first years of his career.* But the director himself provided some critical information.

Following *Downhill*, Hitchcock made two more films in 1927 – one based on an original idea, called *The Ring*, and *The Farmer's Wife*, based on a popular stage comedy. In both, he meticulously exploited the porcelain beauty of twenty-nine-year-old Lilian Hall Davis in two very different roles. For the first, she had a kind of edgy caprice as the fickle object of two boxers' attentions; in the second, she portrayed a widowed farmer's devoted housekeeper.

The Ring revealed Hitchcock's canny ability to combine traditional romantic melodrama – in this case, a love triangle – with a keen sense of the comic-grotesque. The chums of sideshow denizens are introduced as Siamese twins fight over a pew in church; a giant comes to a wedding in the company of a midget; a fat lady enters with delicate tentativeness. The movie's fairground setting will feature significantly later in *Stage Fright* and *Strangers on a Train*, but even in 1927 – under the influence of *Dr Caligari* – Hitchcock knew how to use the raucous, hallucinatory nightmare aspects of the carnival.

---

* For Michael Balcon at Gainsborough, Hitchcock directed *The Pleasure Garden*, *The Mountain Eagle*, *The Lodger*, *Downhill* and *Easy Virtue*; for John Maxwell at British International, he directed *The Ring*, *The Farmer's Wife*, *Champagne*, *The Manxman*, *Blackmail*, *Murder!*, *Juno and the Paycock*, *The Skin Game*, *Number Seventeen* and *Rich and Strange*. Also at BIP, Hitchcock produced a film, contributed to an anthology picture and quickly made a one-reel comedy sketch.

For sheer comic inventiveness, his film of *The Farmer's Wife* succeeded in turning a rustic stage comedy into irresistible, hilarious and even astonishingly tender farce. A formal luncheon descends into madcap chaos; a maid breaks down weeping when ice cream melts; children wreak havoc everywhere; and a sturdy matriarch in an unruly wheelchair tries to negotiate her way through a crowd.

But it was the scenes with the leading lady that everyone on the production recalled – particularly when Hitchcock reduced this sensitive actress to abject tears, proclaiming loudly that she was incompetent, that she ought to go to drama school. It's impossible to know why Lilian Hall Davis was the object of such opprobrium, although it may have had to do with her freewheeling private life, which Hitchcock found both fascinating and offensive. 'Lilian was a good actress,' he told me, 'willing and very efficient, but rather fragile. She was married and had a child, but while we were filming *The Ring* and *The Farmer's Wife*, she had an affair with Gordon Harker [who had supporting roles in both pictures]. He was married, too, and involved with yet another young woman. Then Lilian had a nervous breakdown, and soon her career was over.' Alas, so was her life: in 1933, at the age of thirty-five, Lilian Hall Davis committed suicide.

No such intrigue attended Hitchcock's next silent picture, the 1928 comedy *Champagne*. Producers engaged the immensely popular Betty Balfour to play an irrepressible flapper who is taught a lesson by her wealthy father; her adventures take her aboard a luxury liner and to a Parisian garret. The comedy is thin, but the picture has considerable charm and visual invention. Balfour had a strong sense of her value as the star of a motion picture, however, and this created some tension as she worked with Hitchcock, who was also intent on stardom as a director. She had no hesitation in expressing her opinions of scenes as well as suggesting alternative ideas. Hitchcock, who was none too keen on this assigned project from the start, did not appreciate what he considered undesirable meddling from an actress.

There was no interference from Anny Ondra, the Polish-Czech blonde who had been directed by Graham Cutts in a pair of films and whom Hitchcock requested for *The Manxman*, produced during the summer of 1928. Her English was heavily accented, but this was irrelevant to a silent film, and she took direction to the letter. Based on a Victorian potboiler about romance and betrayal among fishermen on the Isle of Man, the movie is perhaps best remembered for its shimmeringly lovely photography and for the deeply felt performances by Ondra, by the Danish actor Carl Brisson (who had played in *The Ring*) and by Malcolm Keen (from *The Mountain Eagle* and *The Lodger*).

Michael Powell, later a celebrated producer and director, was the on-set stills photographer for *The Manxman* and *Blackmail* (Hitchcock's next picture). 'I am sure he wanted Anny as much as I did,' Powell wrote frankly in his memoirs, recalling that Hitchcock (who liked to direct people in life as much as on a movie set) asked Powell for more than photos of Anny alone. He asked Powell 'to get a boy with her in the hay . . . and she's pressing up against him, to feel his cock against her leg.' Powell recalled how often Hitchcock 'loved to talk bawdy.'

Such was the experience of a young assistant the following year, who was asked to relay quite filthy comments to a German-speaking actress playing in the foreign-language version of one of Hitchcock's films. Recently, a Hitchcock biographer has reported that 'it was outrageous – the sort of remark one might expect in the most permissive of today's scripts, but in 1930 it was outrageous.'

Like the roles undertaken by June and Balfour, that of Kate in *The Manxman* was essentially a coy and fickle blonde – 'that kind makes the best victim,' Hitchcock said. The same biographer added, 'His women must kill or die, be humiliated, or endure a frustrating romance with an impotent hero on the run. One way or another, the beautiful women always suffered.' Sometimes these beautiful women suffered as working actresses as much as their characters did in the stories. Anny Ondra was but the latest in a series of those whom Hitchcock knew how to embarrass, to the point that she was driven to tears.

Anny tried to please her director by shrieking gaily when he played his customary rude practical jokes on colleagues and guests – in other words, she tried to be his perfect audience as well as a docile leading lady. Alma, on the other hand, grew impatient: 'He never stopped playing jokes on people,' his wife said, 'and now and then I got a little apprehensive.' The series of pranks contributed to the Hitchcock legend: the dinner party he gave, for which all the food was dyed blue; the rude 'whoopee cushions' in the Hitchcock flat in Cromwell Road; the horse he sent to the backstage dressing room of a bumptious actor; the cocktails he served, occasionally laced with mysterious (even sometimes cathartic) ingredients.

Later, such shenanigans would not go over well in America, but for a time they were tolerated in Britain, where they were not entirely unknown. When Hitchcock was bored during filming certain scenes of *The Manxman*, recalled Rodney Ackland, 'he was more engrossed in thinking up wicked practical jokes to play on the more vulnerable artists.'

There was no time for boredom on Hitchcock's next project, based on Charles Bennett's play *Blackmail*. As historian Charles Barr has demonstrated, the film's production history is unusually complex. 'It was initially set up and shot as a silent film, but the industry's conversion to sound was gathering such momentum that, at an early stage, a decision was taken by the [studio's] management to add some dialogue, in order to make it, like many films of the period, a "part-talkie." Hitchcock, however, had been astute enough to plan ahead in such a way that it was possible, with the help of judicious reshooting and reworking, to produce a version that could be successfully marketed as a "full talkie" with dialogue scenes spread throughout the picture.' Assistant cameraman Ronald Neame (later also a director) has clarified several points about the production of *Blackmail*. 'We made the film silent,' he recalled in 2003,

> and then in came sound. We didn't want to reshoot the whole picture, just some scenes with important dialogue. We were using arc lights, and the sound people said we couldn't [use them for sound scenes] because they made a loud humming noise. But when we used regular incandescent lights, which were quieter, the camera department said that kind of lighting was not strong enough. There were many such problems we had to resolve – but the greatest challenge was that we had Anny Ondra's thick accent, and she was supposed to be a Cockney girl, the daughter of a newsagent!

Producer John Maxwell was willing to dismiss Anny Ondra and reshoot her scenes with another actress, but to his credit, Hitchcock was adamant that she be retained – not only because he liked her and was somewhat bewitched by her, but because she was a fine and subtle actress.

First, Hitchcock arranged a voice test for her, and the sound film of it survives. He stands with her, beneath a hanging microphone.

HITCHCOCK: Now, Miss Ondra, we are going to do a sound test. Isn't that what you wanted? Now come right over here.

ONDRA: I don't know what to say. I'm so nervous!

HITCHCOCK: Have you been a good girl?

ONDRA (*laughing*): Oh, no!

HITCHCOCK: No? Have you slept with men?

ONDRA: No!

HITCHCOCK: *NO???*

ONDRA: Oh, Hitch, you make me embarrassed. (*She giggles uncontrollably.*)

HITCHCOCK: Now come right over here, Miss Ondra, and stand still in your place – or it won't come out right, as the girl said to the soldier.

Anny knew that her accent was indeed inappropriate for a London girl, but no one wanted to dismiss her, and so Hitchcock came up with a way out of the problem. The actress Joan Barry was brought in to stand just off camera, speaking Anny's lines of dialogue into a microphone as Anny silently mouthed them. This was as good a resolution as could be found, but it had two drawbacks. Joan Barry's diction was too refined for a Cockney character; and there was a series of awkward pauses – viewers then and later sensed the off-camera cues.

For all that, *Blackmail* remains a fascinating, complex and disturbing film. The story concerns Alice White (Ondra) and her beau, detective Frank Webber (John Longden). When they quarrel one afternoon at a crowded restaurant, Alice departs on the arm of a handsome artist (Cyril Ritchard). She accepts an invitation to come to his studio, where she agrees to wear a skimpy tutu and to model for him. But he then attempts to make violent love to her, and she seizes a bread knife and stabs him to death. Webber soon suspects the truth. Then a blackmailer enters the story. He had seen Alice entering the artist's flat, and he wants hush money. But Webber implicates the blackmailer in the murder; a chase ensues; and the blackmailer falls through the dome of the British Museum. Alice tries to give herself up – but Webber prevents her. The film ends with Alice's anguish and the couple's shared, secret guilt. In *Blackmail* as in *The Lodger*, Hitchcock thus explored the perfidy of the officials of law and order – specifically, how they permit passion to corrupt duty.

Hitchcock remains justly famous for the scene (added to the sound version) in the girl's home after she has killed the artist. No one is yet aware of her involvement. A nosy neighbour begins to chat about the recent murder nearby. As she rambles on, the camera moves to Ondra's traumatised face, and Hitchcock imaginatively distorts sound. The audience hears only the subjective impression of what the girl hears, as the neighbour's words blur together until only the word *knife* stabs out at her and at the audience from the soundtrack: 'What an awful way to kill a man – with a *knife*! Now a good stiff whack over the 'ead with a brick is one thing – there's something *British* about *that*! But a *knife*? No, *knives* is not right! Now mind you, a *knife* is a difficult thing to handle. Not just any *knife* will do, because with a *knife* . . .'

Then Alice's father asks her to cut some bread, and she distract-edly grasps a bread knife while the neighbour drones on: 'a *knife* . . . and if you come to Chelsea, you mustn't bring a *knife*!' And with that, the bread knife seems to leap from Alice's hands and fly to the floor. "Ere!' says her father. 'You might've *cut* someone with that!'

From the time of *Downhill*, Hitchcock had known the power of celebrity. Required to film the underground escalator sequence of that film at night, he had come directly to the station from the theatre and was formally dressed in white tie, top hat and tails, an outfit he made certain the media noticed and documented. Now, in *Blackmail*, he devised his most extended cameo appearance. As Ondra and Longden ride in the Underground, a small boy next to them leans over to Hitchcock, as a passenger trying to read a book. The brat pokes Hitchcock's hat down over his brow, then squirms away. The director pokes him back and then cowers in fear when the boy baits him yet again.

Anny Ondra's career in the British cinema ended with *Blackmail*. She went home to Germany, divorced her husband and married the prizefighter Max Schmeling, with whom she lived happily for fifty-five years, until her death at eighty-five, in 1987. She regularly sent Christmas cards to the Hitchcocks. 'Hitchy, I'm so happy here,' she often wrote on her greetings.

In 1930, producer John Maxwell at British International Pictures assigned Hitchcock the task of filming another play – Sean O'Casey's *Juno and the Paycock* – but this brought Hitch little satisfaction. Nor were the notices flattering: 'Hitchcock has been so faithful to his text as almost to forget the medium in which he was working – it is less a film than a play projected on the screen.' And so it was.

His contract with British International, however, eased the pain, for by this time he was England's highest-paid director, with an annual income of at least £65,000 (then about $350,000). The Hitchcocks kept their modest flat in Cromwell Road, but they also purchased a country house in Shamley Green, Guildford.

Blackmail was a huge critical success: 'Under Mr. Hitchcock's guidance, the talking film has taken a very definite step forward,' wrote one critic, to which another added that 'Hitchcock's films resemble the more intelligent and conscientious works of detective fiction.' *Murder!*, the next picture, was also well received – for the first time, Hitch was called a 'creative artist who makes films superior in intelligence and style to any from America or Germany.'

With no audition and little conversation, Hitchcock chose twenty-three-year-old Norah Baring for the leading role. 'I asked him later if he always picked out his stars with as little ado as he did me, because all he seemed to do when we first met was to play silly jokes – I thought he was having a good laugh at my expense.'

'Shows how little you know about it,' Hitchcock told her. 'You see, there you were. You had the type of face and the personality I had in mind, but you were all tied up with nerves and so tense that at first I hadn't a ghost of an idea whether you would be any use to me at all. I didn't know if you would photograph or record well enough.'

'Hitchcock used to make gentle fun of me in the studio,' Baring continued. 'But I had to do as he wanted simply because he did not allow me to get so strung-up that I could not express the emotions the part required.'

Elsie Randolph, engaged to play in *Rich and Strange* the following year, was not the object of any gentle fun. Hitchcock knew that she was allergic to smoke, and one day he summoned Elsie for a scene in a studio telephone call box that property men filled with smoldering steam. 'He was a darling,' she said years later, 'but a darling with a sadistic sense of humour.' This was as it had been during production of Galsworthy's *The Skin Game* in late 1930, another filmed play to which Hitchcock was assigned. Playwright Rodney Ackland, a visitor to that production and subsequently a bit player in it, recalled that the director 'was engrossed in thinking up wicked practical jokes to play on the more vulnerable artists or on his main butt, one of the property men.'

Henry Kendall, the leading man of *Rich and Strange*, recalled his camera test. Instead of directing the actor in a scene from the picture, 'the conversation took a very Rabelaisian turn,' according to Kendall, 'and he kept me in fits of laughter so that I could hardly do more than stand in front of the camera and shake.' Joan Barry (the off-camera voice for Anny Ondra in *Blackmail*) was the leading lady for *Rich and Strange*; she never spoke of her experience with the director.

But Jessie Matthews did. In 1933, she was England's most popular musical star, and producer Tom Arnold cast her in his independent production of Hitchcock's *Waltzes from Vienna*, about the Strauss family. Annoyed as much by her pre-eminence as by her salary in that picture, Hitchcock reduced her scenes whenever he could, moved the camera away from her, interrupted filming with an endless litany of needless corrections and set Matthews on the edge of nervous collapse.

'He sent me up mercilessly,' she recalled, 'and I was always anticipating some ghastly practical joke he was about to play on me. He was just an imperious young man who knew nothing about musicals. I felt unnerved when he tried to get me to adopt a mincing operetta style. He was out of his depth, and he showed that he knew it by ordering me around. I thought the film was perfectly dreadful.' Esmond Knight, co-star to Jessie Matthews in the film, felt 'continually on the qui vive for some elaborate leg pull at my expense, which automatically produced a feeling of nervousness.'

By the end of 1933, Alfred Hitchcock was wealthy and famous – but not happy with his professional prospects. Once again, Michael Balcon came to the rescue, with a deal that gave him extraordinary freedom. His fortunes, and those of British cinema, changed dramatically when he directed *The Man Who Knew Too Much* in 1934. Collaborating with Ivor Montagu, playwright Charles Bennett and no fewer than five additional writers, Hitchcock and company prepared a shooting script about a couple on holiday whose child is kidnapped to prevent them from divulging a plan to assassinate a foreign statesman in London.

The picture opens on the bright ski slopes of St Moritz and concludes on the dark, sloping rooftops of London. In both sequences, the couple's daughter is nearly killed – first by a downhill skier, later by terrorists. Within this framework, her mother (Edna Best) is shown to be a crack shot who loses a match when her daughter (Nova Pilbeam) distracts her. 'Let that be a lesson to you,' she tells her opponent. 'Never have children!' She then turns to her husband (Leslie Banks): 'You take this brat – you *would* have this child!' The film concludes when the same challenger turns out to be an assassin – working with the villainous mastermind (Peter Lorre). Mother wins the final 'match' and, by sharpshooting with a police rifle, saves the daughter she once casually dismissed.

In this first of Hitchcock's classic spy-chase thrillers, as in all those to come, the international political issue or secret is merely the pretext for exploring personal emotions. Hitchcock refuses to specify a national cause or to identify the nations involved, and so his movies never became obsolete. This plot pretext is what Hitchcock called a 'MacGuffin' – what the spies are after, what gets the action going but fades into insignificance for the characters and the audience.

The odd term, Hitchcock always insisted, derived from an anecdote about two men travelling from London to Scotland by train. In the luggage rack overhead is a wrapped package.

'What have you there?'

'Oh, that's a MacGuffin.'

'What's a MacGuffin?'

'It's a device for trapping lions in the Scottish Highlands.'

'But there are no lions in the Scottish Highlands!'

'Well, then, that's no MacGuffin!'

The point is that a 'MacGuffin' is neither relevant, important nor finally anyone's business: it simply gets a story going. Hitchcock's classic thrillers take from standard literary melodrama the motif of the secret or the critical documents, the scientific formula or the papers sought by the heroes. But this device – the thing sought – is utterly unimportant, and finally has no significance for the characters.*

---

* Examples of Hitchcock's MacGuffin: the stolen jewels in *Number Seventeen*; the planned assassination in *The Man Who Knew Too Much*; the design for a new aircraft engine in *The 39 Steps*; the espionage plots in *Secret Agent* and *Sabotage*; the tune containing a diplomatic secret in *The Lady Vanishes*; the secret clause of a treaty in *Foreign Correspondent*; the uranium ore in *Notorious;* the international politics at stake in the remake of *The Man Who Knew Too Much*; the microfilmed secrets in *North by Northwest;* and the secret formula in *Torn Curtain*.

In *The Man Who Knew Too Much*, we're never told just what country is represented by the man targeted for assassination, nor what is at stake, nor for whom the kidnappers work. Topical stories quickly become dated, but Hitchcock knew that tales with a focus on recognisable human feelings are perennials. His concern, therefore, is for the beleaguered family – thus the increasing tenderness between husband and wife.

At the time, leading lady Edna Best was married to stage actor Herbert Marshall, who had been the male lead in *Murder!* and would return even more significantly in *Foreign Correspondent*. Hitchcock was unfailingly courteous to her during production. As for fifteen-year-old Nova Pilbeam, who played the daughter with touching artlessness, Hitchcock said that she 'had to be handled diplomatically [because] she lacked experience and her ideas were not always suitable. At the end of the film, when she is reunited with her parents, I made her so terrified by the ordeal that she had been through that she shrank from them.'

Once the film was completed, the Hitchcocks directed a less upsetting real-life version of the movie: they took an extended holiday – first stop, St Moritz, as in the film – and, like the beleaguered but eventually safe family of *The Man Who Knew Too Much*, they brought along their young daughter, Pat.

3

The Mastery of Mystery
(1934–1935)

From 1925 through 1933, his first nine years as a filmmaker, Alfred
Hitchcock directed sixteen motion pictures; three of these (*The
Lodger*, *Blackmail* and *Murder!*) could be classified as thrillers, and only
one was a 'whodunit' mystery. He was one of Britain's busiest, wealthi-
est and most famous directors, eager for the publicity he himself
initiated and encouraged, and for the prestige and compensation he
believed he had already earned.

But critics mostly rated Hitch as a formidable director of unimportant pictures – mere entertainments, which were held in low
esteem by the guardians of high culture. First for Gainsborough and
then for British International, Hitchcock made what were considered
skilful diversions for the masses, some of them more successful than
others. This subtle condescension began to change when he went
over to Balcon's Gaumont-British Studios, Shepherd's Bush, London,
to direct *The Man Who Knew Too Much*, released in England at the end
of 1934 and in America in early 1935.★ The final script of the movie
was the work of a committee: no less than seven writers worked on
it, among them Charles Bennett.

'I am no longer concerned with cut-and-dried formulae for melo-

---

★ Also at Gaumont-British, Hitchcock directed *The 39 Steps*, *Secret Agent* and *Sabotage*,
all at the Shepherd's Bush studios. Balcon's Gainsborough Pictures then produced *Young
and Innocent* (at Shepherd's Bush and at Pinewood) and *The Lady Vanishes* (at Islington).

drama,' Hitch said at the time. 'Formulae were good enough in the old days when every hero had a heart of gold and every villain was a dyed-in-the-wool minister of the devil. A writer of melodrama merely manufactured a group of villains and a clan of heroes, dropped a plumb line between the opposing camps, cemented the action with a train wreck from which the heroine staggered forth somewhat battered, and wrote FINIS while the villain gave his mustachio a final twirl. This was genuinely touching in the age of bustles and knee breeches, but has not the slightest bearing on modern, robust melodrama, which discards highly fictionalised characters and presents instead a large-sized canvas with everyday life-like people on it.'

He made these comments just after the wildly successful premiere of *The Man Who Knew Too Much*, which was 'glorious melodrama', according to the *Kinematograph Weekly*, and other reviews praised the picture's 'great thrills, human interest, good work by a sterling cast, and excellent production qualities'. An even greater triumph was to come, with *The 39 Steps*, very freely based on John Buchan's 1915 novel *The Thirty-Nine Steps*. With this film, even some serious critics began to take notice, and the Hitchcock blonde was firmly represented by one of the most accomplished, popular and strikingly beautiful women of the time – Madeleine Carroll.

'I had wanted to turn John Buchan's novel into a film for over fifteen years,' Hitchcock said. 'I first read the book round about 1919 or 1920, and when I read it again in late 1934, I received a shock: I found that the story as it stood was not in the least suitable' for a movie. To make it so, he turned again to Bennett for collaboration.

Eleven days older than Hitchcock, Charles Bennett had fought in the World War as a teenager, had dabbled in espionage, and had acted in plays and movies before turning to playwriting. He and Hitchcock were good partners at spinning ideas and mixing potent drinks, and they both saw the value in telling stories about ordinary people suddenly caught in extraordinary circumstances. Most of all, they wanted to avoid a tone of turgid gravity and to find the rich, ironic humour in each sequence they created. With *The 39 Steps*, they succeeded admirably, and the result was a film that survives its era and style and remains a rare and supreme entertainment.

Hitchcock and Bennett both admired the Buchan novel, but they agreed that it lacked humour, strong characters and most of all a woman for the romantic angle. There is actually a climb of thirty-nine steps in Buchan's novel, leading to a nest of spies. But as Hitchcock, Bennett, Alma and dialogue-writer Ian Hay worked on the narrative treatment for a movie, everyone agreed that the 'steps' should merely refer to an organisation of spies, working on behalf of who knows what country. And, they asked each other, what was at stake, what was the secret? Oh, they decided airily – merely some secret formula for the design of British fighter planes. But none of that was important: the hero's relationship to a beautiful blonde – that's what mattered. The dominant issue was to be one of trust between a man and a woman, highlighted throughout the story by contrasting sets of couples on whom the action hinges structurally: a hypocritically pious Scotsman and his benighted wife; a kindly inn-keeping couple; and the gentlemanly villain and his aristocratic wife.

'You owe everything to me,' Hitchcock wrote to Bennett some years later – which led to Bennett's reflection, 'Everything? Hardly! By the time of *The Man Who Knew Too Much*, I had staged seven plays and directed five, written more than fifteen films and had succeeded as an actor. Arguably, Hitch owed me! My Shakespearean experience and sense of melodrama built his reputation for suspense; my play *Blackmail* was his first talkie. My story "The Man Who Knew Too Much" launched his international reputation, and my construction of *The 39 Steps* put him out front by inventing motifs he would use in subsequent films.

'But Hitch would not acknowledge it. It always had to be Hitch! He would not acknowledge any writer. This was a very ungenerous character flaw, actually, as Hitch was totally incapable of creating or developing a story. Without me, there wouldn't have been any story. Hitchcock was never a constructionist, never a storyteller. I would take a story and turn it into something good. After that, Hitch and I would turn it into a screenplay, and then, as often as not, we'd call in certain people to write the dialogue for it. So we were a writer-director partnership, but his vanity could not credit his writers. He could give credit to no one but himself.' Bennett, who collaborated on no fewer than six films with Hitchcock, observed that he 'had a monstrous ego that matched his appetite'.

Hitch could certainly allow himself to be praised for his visual inventiveness, and for his brilliance in taking a script and knowing precisely the right images, the proper tone and atmosphere to enliven them. But screenwriters from Bennett in the 1930s to Ben Hecht in the 1940s, Samuel Taylor and Ernest Lehman in the 1950s and Evan Hunter in the 1960s quickly realised that this director's gift was not for writing dialogue but for minimising it and allowing action and reaction, gaze and glance to tell stories. Perhaps because he wanted to write the script entirely on his own but could not, he sometimes resented his writers. 'If he decided to use you, that was compliment enough,' said Joseph Stefano, who wrote the screenplay for *Psycho*. One need not expect gratifying compliments.

As *The 39 Steps* was being developed, Hitchcock required a personal assistant to read and summarise stories and to help with the many daily details in a busy production office. His choice fell on an educated, attractive twenty-eight-year-old blonde named Joan Harrison. Hitchcock apparently believed that he had to assess her sensibilities and reserve, and so, one day early in her employment, he read aloud to her an explicitly crude scene from Joyce. Unmarried and a university graduate in literature, Joan was unfazed and passed whatever test Hitchcock had in mind; under his tutelage, she quickly advanced from secretary to continuity supervisor to script consultant to dialogue writer. From 1939 to 1941, she received co-screenwriting credit on five Hitchcock films (*Jamaica Inn*, *Rebecca*, *Foreign Correspondent*, *Suspicion* and *Saboteur*), and she later returned as a producer of his television shows.

The 39 Steps tells of Richard Hannay (played by Robert Donat), a Canadian on holiday in London, who must establish his innocence of the knife-murder of a mysterious brunette spy (Lucie Mannheim) and also prevent a critical national secret ('vital to your air defence ministry') from passing out of the country and over to the enemy. In this, Hannay is at first hindered and betrayed, and finally helped, by a woman (Madeleine Carroll), to whom he is handcuffed for a major portion of the interior and exterior action.

'He is blazingly ambitious,' Hitchcock said of Donat soon after *The 39 Steps* was released, 'but difficult to satisfy. He is a queer combination of determination and uncertainty. He is determined to do only pictures that satisfy him' (to which one might reply, 'Indeed – and why not?').

As for Madeleine Carroll, Hitchcock was forthright. She had not been his first choice, nor was it a starring or leading role: she is the leading *lady* of it, to be sure, but she does not appear until well into the story, and there are long episodes from which she is absent. Nevertheless, she accepted for several reasons. First, she had known Hitchcock when they were working on separate projects at British International in 1928. He was polite and respectful, and she liked his fresh ideas for storytelling. In addition, her agents negotiated a very lucrative deal with Michael Balcon for her to appear in two Hitchcock pictures that year.

Born 26 February 1906, she was christened Edith Madeleine Carroll, in West Bromwich, five miles north-west of Birmingham. Her Irish father was a language professor at the university there, and her mother was French. Raised in a bilingual household, she was groomed to be a French teacher, took a degree with honours and then continued her studies at the Sorbonne. But Madeleine had acting ambitions, as she always confided to her closest confidante – her adored younger sister, Marguerite.

Her father, however, brooked no opposition to his professional plans for her, and when she announced that she wanted a theatrical career, he dismissed her from the house and refused to support her. At first, she took tutoring jobs while seeking work as an actress. Her film career, which began with silent films in 1928, owed a great deal to her striking glamour. She projected a rare aristocratic allure, a kind of unstuffy elegance and a restraint that attracted men and commanded the respect, if not the downright envy, of women. Directors like Cecil B. DeMille, Lewis Milestone, Anatole Litvak, Victor Saville and John Ford adored working with her, as did actors Gary Cooper, Brian Aherne, Ronald Colman, Henry Fonda and Tyrone Power. Off-screen, her many suitors included Randolph (son of Winston) Churchill.

'She is both beautiful and convincing. Her performances are full of life, sympathy and perception. She is simply radiant.' So ran the typical press comments, and there was no argument about that. From her first appearances on stage and screen, audiences, critics and the general public who saw her photographs and the increasingly popular movies she made in England, France and America, agreed that Madeleine Carroll was one of the most exquisite women in the world.

If that was hyperbolic language, it was also difficult to counter. Journalists ransacked their vocabularies to describe her expressive, dazzling blue eyes and flawless complexion, her calmly sensual gaze and splendidly enigmatic smile. She had a rare photogenic glow, but she also had genuine talent and a lively intelligence. By 1934, when she was twenty-eight, Madeleine Carroll had appeared in a dozen plays in England and no fewer than thirty-seven movies. Hollywood quickly took note, and soon she was working frequently in American studios. Her appearance in two spy melodramas inspired Hitchcock and Balcon to engage her for *The 39 Steps* and *Secret Agent*, a pair of espionage thrillers made back-to-back in 1935; both projects capitalised on her natural charm and unaffected glamour. Within two years, she was one of the highest-paid actors in the world, receiving more than $250,000 per picture.

'There has been a great deal of controversy over my handling of Madeleine Carroll,' Hitchcock told an interviewer after he completed both films with her. Fearful that she was going to act the spoiled celebrity when she arrived for *The 39 Steps*, he insisted that she submit herself to the uncomfortable demands of the script – especially the long sequences in which she would be painfully handcuffed to Donat. Well, she replied, if that was required . . .

On the first day of filming, in late January 1935, Hitchcock introduced his two stars to one another and tried to put them at ease with his usual blue humour. They should address him by his famous nickname, he said – 'Hitch, without the cock.' Donat and Carroll smiled indulgently. The director then set up the first sequence, in which the couple, handcuffed to each other, flee across the Scottish countryside. He snapped the handcuffs onto their wrists (shades of *The Lodger*), led them through a rehearsal over the dummy bridge and over the fences – and then he announced that some technical problem required his attention, and that they could take a tea break. The key to the handcuffs? Oh, dear, he seemed to have mislaid it. 'There they were,' he said later, 'inextricably bound – and they couldn't get away from one another until I "found" it again.' And with that, he vanished, while his crew wasted no time, photographing several insert shots of sheep.

'Madeleine and I shared this enforced companionship while the hunt for the key was sustained,' recalled Robert Donat. John Russell

Taylor, Hitchcock's authorised biographer (writing while the director was living) states that Hitchcock took 'a gleeful delight in devising indignities for Madeleine Carroll to undergo.'

Eventually, Hitchcock found the key (which had been deposited with a studio guard). The two actors were weary, dishevelled, uncomfortable and acutely embarrassed. Donat recalled that they coped as best they could: 'There was nothing else to do, so we talked of our mutual friends, of our ambitions, and of film matters generally. Gradually, our reserve thawed as we exchanged experiences. When Hitch saw that we were getting along famously, he extracted the "missing" key from his waistcoat pocket, released us, and said with a satisfied grin, "Now that you two know each other, we can go ahead."'

That was not the only day of 'enforced companionship' in handcuffs. 'It would be hard to estimate the number of hours we were handcuffed together in the studio,' Donat continued. 'Shackled to me, she was dragged along roads, through ravines and across moors; humiliations were heaped upon her. Naturally, we had to play these scenes with realism: the weals and bruises which the handcuffs made on her delicate wrists were ample proofs of that – but I never heard her utter one word of complaint.'

'What interests me,' Hitchcock said, 'is the drama of being handcuffed. There's a special terror, a sort of "thing" about being tied up. In *The 39 Steps*, of course, it was fundamental.' A recent Hitchcock biographer further quotes him to the effect that handcuffs 'bring out all kinds of thoughts in [the audience's] minds – for example, how do they go to the toilet was one natural, obvious question. And the linking together relates more to sex than anything else.' There is something more than merely playful about this sort of thing.

'There was no better technician in the business,' said Jack Whitehead, second-unit cameraman on the picture, 'but when it came to personal relations, there was certainly a streak of the sadist in him.' Years later, Ivor Montagu addressed the matter delicately: 'It had long been my conviction, sustained by working with Hitchcock, that a good director must have something of the sadist in him. I do not necessarily mean to a pathological degree, but that his looking at things and telling characters to do this, undergo that, is necessarily akin to dominating them, ordering them about.' Hitchcock himself was frank: 'I sometimes wonder whether I am not – as all my friends insist – a sadist.'

As for Madeleine Carroll, 'she entered into the spirit of the whole thing with zest,' Hitchcock said, 'and I was determined not to let up at all. Dignity or self-consciousness is impossible when you're being dragged along the ground, which I made Donat do to her. I try to make a woman human by making her appear in awkward and comic situations and taking away her glamour.' But in the recounting, Hitchcock softened the event. When he was ready for her, for example, he called out, 'Bring on the Birmingham tart!' He was 'dead set on making every assault on her dignity he could – to prepare her for her on-screen indignities.'

Madeleine Carroll made no noisy objection, but privately, she was weary, confused and angry about the demands placed on her. (When her friend Randolph Churchill visited the set one day, he reproached Hitchcock for the rough handling of her. 'I just gave him a look and then went on with the job,' Hitchcock said later.) Over several days, she was dragged along in handcuffs, pushed behind a waterfall, over a stream and through fences until her hair and clothes were ruined and her wrists bruised. 'The roughness of the scenes was meant to strip Carroll of her poise and dignity,' as one critic wrote, echoing Hitchcock's calm self-defence.

Hitch did have an ally in Ivor Montagu: 'We deliberately wrote the script to include her undignified handcuff scene on the bed, and being led out from under the waterfall looking like a drowned rat. But Madeleine was a trouper and turned the tables on us by appreciating this treatment and asking for more.' It must be pointed out, however, that Montagu, as associate producer, was alone in asserting her compliance: as he said, his job was to be 'the defender of the director's needs [and] to act as cushion between company and creator.'

To achieve his goal – to assure that Madeleine Carroll would 'enter into the spirit of the whole thing with zest' – Hitchcock actually went too far. For one scene (as she confided to her friend, the actress Googie Withers), Hitchcock wanted her to express shock. After several takes, Madeleine had still not given him what he seemed to want. 'We'll do it one more time,' he said, and consulted quietly with the cameraman. Hitch then went back to Carroll, who was the only one who could see that he had unbuttoned his trousers as if to expose himself to her. This produced the desired reaction, and the director had his shot.

Odd though it may seem, very few actors expressed their resentment of Hitchcock's methods – his films, after all, were good for their careers. In addition, as Ivor Montagu said, 'He was essentially a shy man, who would have died rather than give anyone a clue to the heart he hid under his sleeve. So he adopted a tactic of brusque exaggeration, slow sarcasm accented by deliberate articulation, so outrageous that no one could take offence because of the pretense that he must have been joking. Women stars, especially, would at first be taken aback. Soon they would accept it as a sort of compliment of intimacy, which of course it was.'

'Nothing pleases me more than to knock the ladylikeness out of them,' he said when filming was completed, 'I don't exactly hate women, but I certainly don't think they are as good as men actors.' But with Donat as with almost every one of his leading men, he plied no practical jokes or rude tactics.

Hitchcock's attitude toward and treatment of Madeleine Carroll, and of others later, must not be minimised; indeed, one must ask the basis for it. Perhaps he was full of resentments: 'He was sexually impotent,' according to a recent biographer, citing Hitchcock's obesity and quoting the writer Jay Presson Allen, who wrote the final screenplay of *Marnie*. Long afterward, he confided to an unknown number of people that he had sexual intercourse only once in his life. 'I did it with a fountain pen' was his most outrageous statement, sometimes even uttered in his wife's presence. Joseph Stefano, who wrote the screenplay for *Psycho*, heard the same confidence as did I.

The 39 Steps was hailed, then as later, as a hugely enjoyable comic thriller – first-class entertainment was the universal critical response – and even before it was released, Hitchcock, Bennett and Hay were busy on their next production for Balcon. Based on short stories by Somerset Maugham, it would be the third consecutive Hitchcock movie about spies, but more serious than its predecessors. *Secret Agent* (not *The Secret Agent*, as it is usually misidentified) is also Hitchcock's most overtly moral fable up to that time: it denounces killing as a political expedient and insists on the ethical bankruptcy of the espionage enterprise.

Thanks to her contract with Balcon, Madeleine Carroll was ready for the early autumn filming. Her first appearance in the picture continued the deglamorisation process now dear to Hitchcock's heart. In *The 39 Steps*, she is first seen wearing unflattering eyeglasses (which fall to the ground when she is kissed and are never seen again); in *Secret Agent*, she is first shown wrapped in a formless, long bath sheet, cold cream splattered on her face and a make-up cap on her head. For all that, she was still luminously, irreparably beautiful.

Hitchcock had hoped to engage Robert Donat again, too, but the actor did not want to be typed as the leading man of thrillers and had gone to work for director René Clair in the comedy *The Ghost Goes West*. John Gielgud inherited the role of novelist Edgar Brodie, renamed as the spy Richard Ashenden. Hitchcock said the character was rather like a modern-day Hamlet, a man forced to make difficult decisions, and so Gielgud accepted, even though this meant an exhausting schedule, for he was acting onstage every night in *Romeo and Juliet*. Alas, his role was reduced during production, and what was left of it was consistently overwhelmed by the crazy antics of Peter Lorre, whom Hitchcock brought back after *The Man Who Knew Too Much*. 'Peter Lorre was a great scene-stealer,' Gielgud recalled. 'He had all sort of tricks, like adding an extra line when it came to the take, or he'd move an inch and I realised I'd been upstaged by a very clever actor.' To make matters worse, Lorre was a morphine addict who constantly upset the production by disappearing to administer his injections.

Madeleine's role was far more significant than that she had in *The 39 Steps*. As Elsa Carrington, she initially sees the business of spying as 'something worthwhile – a thrill, excitement, a big risk, danger!' She's almost aroused by the thought of mayhem and outspoken in her anger when denied the opportunity to assist in the killing of a spy who turns out to be not a spy at all but an innocent Englishman abroad. 'It's murder, and you call it fun,' says Ashenden. But when she learns that they have all engineered the death of the wrong man – and that the real villain is the charming suitor played by the American actor Robert Young – she has a crisis of conscience that is at the heart of the movie.

'Madeleine Carroll was charming and we got on very well,' Gielgud continued. 'She was a big star, but Hitchcock was beastly to her. He was a very coarse man, fond of making dirty jokes all the time.

He often made me feel sick with nervousness.' That was also the reaction of a fifty-seven-year-old American actress named Florence
Kahn, who was appearing in her first and last movie; unaccountably,
she had never even seen a motion picture in her life. Married to the
English satirist Max Beerbohm, she had been born in Tennessee and
had a modestly successful stage career before retiring quite young;
she accepted on the basis of her acquaintance (through her husband)
with Gielgud. 'She was a very odd woman indeed,' Hitchcock told
me (without elaboration) in 1977; Gielgud shared that view.

The only aspect of *Secret Agent* that exercised the director's daily
ingenuity was his treatment of his leading lady. One moment, he
supervised her hairstyle and wardrobe, the next moment she was the
victim of a practical joke. Devoted one moment, almost cruel
the next, he kept her ever on the alert. This was the first sign of
a trait that marked his dealings with several actresses later: attraction and repulsion, the almost idolatrous gaze of his camera and
the concomitant compulsion to tear her character apart. This bifur-
cated attitude marked the psychological climate of his most mature
films, and it was in real life the emotionally schizoid pattern that
caused him and the women considerable pain during the time of
their work together.

That year, Hitchcock was at his heaviest – just over three hundred
pounds – and his lumbering discomfort must have augmented feelings of social ineptitude. His neatness, authority and unblinking
intelligence scarcely ameliorated the sight of a grotesquely misshapen
man, and his sudden lapses into moody silence and his inability to
praise or thank anyone publicly characterised him as an enigmatic
and ungracious boss. But Hitchcock was capable of surprising acts
of kindness – a case of wine would arrive at a crew member's door
on his birthday, or a colleague's mother would receive a lavish floral
tribute on her birthday.

The train crash finale of *Secret Agent* required considerable physical
discomfort of all the players, and Carroll sustained everyone's spirits
during multiple retakes of that sequence. Seen decades later, the entire
picture has a freshness that was much ignored at the time. Perhaps
because it defied the contemporary assumptions about what constitutes
patriotism and heroism, and because it condemned the nefarious nature
of espionage, *Secret Agent* was unfortunately discounted as both un-
fashionable and insignificant.

Nowhere in his book-length interviews with Truffaut did Hitchcock mention the name of Madeleine Carroll. But she was a memorable actress and a remarkable woman, with an inner strength and a depth of values of which her director seemed unaware. Because her life post-Hitchcock was not only dramatic but also heroic, it is worth summarising; as her friends insisted, the contours of her later years best define the real woman behind the celebrated beauty.

From 1936 to 1939, Madeleine continued to work in London and Hollywood, appearing most memorably in *The General Died at Dawn* (with Gary Cooper), *Lloyd's of London* (with Tyrone Power), *The Prisoner of Zenda* (with Ronald Colman) and *Blockade* (with Henry Fonda). At Christmas 1939, her eight-year marriage to the wealthy, attractive and urbane Captain Philip Astley was dissolved. Randolph Churchill, although married, apparently popped up again in early 1940, but his pursuit of her was futile.

That spring, she was scheduled to appear in a Paramount picture called *Virginia*, delayed several times due to script and casting problems. With permission from the studio, she took a month's leave and headed for Europe in early June, intending to visit her parents in England and the fifty war orphans to whom she had turned over her home, a chateau at Saudreville, near Paris. She also hoped to find her 'fiancé,' as the press termed him – the dashing Lieutenant Richard de la Rozière, who had recently gone missing in the early days of the French stand against Germany.

But in none of these aspirations was Madeleine successful, for her journey coincided with Hitler's incursion into France, and severe restrictions were put on any travel by British nationals. On 13 June 1940, she fled from Paris – there were rumours that de la Rozière was near the Spanish border – and the next morning, she arrived at the strategically significant town of Hendaye, the most south-westerly town in France, within walking distance to Spain. At that very hour, the Germans entered Paris.

There was no sign of the lieutenant in Hendaye, and Madeleine proceeded to the home of some cousins in Biarritz, fifteen miles north. There, on 16 June, there was loud commotion, as all British citizens in the region were to report to Bordeaux for evacuation to England, under threat of imprisonment. One such ship had already been bombed, and there were reports that many Britons were being taken for interrogation or worse. 'I knew that if I went to England, I wouldn't have a chance of getting back to America,' she said days later, 'and I had given my word of honour [to Paramount] to take the July 10 Clipper and return to my work.'

Clutching her passport and a small valise, and hoping somehow to find her way back to the United States via Spain, Madeleine drove to Madrid alone, in her family's old, cranky automobile. There, American Embassy officials could discover nothing of her parents in England or of the children outside Paris, but they were able to tell her that de la Rozière was safe on duty in Tunisia with a small platoon of Free French soldiers. When the diplomats undiplomatically enquired if the film star intended to marry the lieutenant when the war ended, she replied, 'Who knows if any of us is going to be alive even in a month or so?' At this point, Richard de la Rozière vanishes from Madeleine Carroll's biography.

At eleven o'clock on the morning of 11 July, she arrived at La Guardia Field, New York, aboard one of the Pan Am Clippers. In service only a year, this was a legendary airship whose sumptuous accommodations included a dining room where five-course meals were served on antique china; elaborate bars and lounges; private sleeping quarters; and a crew of sixteen to serve the seventeen passengers who paid the equivalent of $4,000 for a one-way passage. Until the Clippers were requisitioned later in wartime, they were the most luxurious means of air travel in history.

Among Madeleine's fellow travellers on the thirty-hour flight were Archduke Otto of Hapsburg, pretender to the non-existent Austro-Hungarian throne; Ralph Paine, European managing director of the Time-Life-Fortune magazine corporation; and Andrew Heiskell, a writer and editor then attached to *Time*'s Paris bureau. He thought Madeleine was 'the most glamorous woman I have ever met. She was wearing a blue hat, not very broad-brimmed, and a blue suit with a white blouse. She had soft blonde hair, large blue eyes and classic features. She was thirty-five, ten years older than I, but there was an instantaneous flash of something between us.'

Heiskell recalled that he and Madeleine 'spent the entire flight talking to each other, mostly in French, which she spoke as perfectly as she did English. We ate all our meals together, had our wine and champagne together.' When they landed in New York, the actress and the writer promised to stay in touch, but travellers who meet on

Alma Reville and Alfred Hitchcock, about the time of their marriage

Hitchcock's first leading lady, Virginia Valli,
in *The Pleasure Garden*

June, the first Hitchcock blonde,
in *The Lodger*

Isabel Jeans, in *Easy Virtue*

Lilian Hall Davis, in *The Ring*

Anny Ondra, in *Blackmail*

(Above right) Joan Barry,
in *Rich and Strange*

(Right) Jessie Matthews,
in *Waltzes from Vienna*

Directing
Madeleine
Carroll and
Robert Donat
in *The 39 Steps*

Madeleine Carroll, in *Secret Agent*

Sylvia Sidney,
in *Sabotage*

Nova Pilbeam, in
Young and Innocent

Directing Cary Grant and Joan Fontaine, in *Suspicion*

With Margaret Lockwood,
during the production of
The Lady Vanishes

Teresa Wright,
in *Shadow of a Doubt*

Directing *Shadow of a Doubt*, in Santa Rosa, California

journeys routinely say such things. Heiskell went home to his wife and children, and Madeleine proceeded to her movie assignment and her co-star, a yachtsman who was making his motion picture debut. At six feet five, with a thick crop of unruly golden hair, Sterling Hayden was touted by Paramount publicists as 'The Most Beautiful Man in the Movies' and 'The Beautiful Blond Viking God.' He hated the hype as much as the work, which he accepted only to afford his beloved boats and schooners. Like Heiskell, he was a full ten years younger than Madeleine, but he was unmarried. They were wed in 1942, but their wartime service forestalled any reasonable facsimile of a solid marriage: their time together was infrequent, and they divorced amicably in 1946.

Just as *Virginia* was completed that autumn of 1940, the Germans began massive air raid attacks on London, Southampton, Bristol, Cardiff, Liverpool and Manchester. And then Madeleine, who had been hoping for a holiday, received tragic news on 7 October. Of this she gave a calm account in fluent French on the Canadian Broadcasting Corporation, hoping that her statement would be heard by her family in England:

> I knew a young Englishwoman – like so many others, she was pretty, fond of laughter and a good comrade. When war came, she wanted to do her share. She was made to understand that she was performing a great service by remaining at her post – continuing, by her good humour and her unswerving faith in the victory of our arms, to sustain the morale of her associates.
>
> So she remained at her work in a London store. Then came the big air raids. Ever smiling, ever confident, she went on doing her daily task. She was the first to jest after a bomb exploded close by. It was to her that her companions turned for comfort when they were in trouble. And when people congratulated her on her devotion to work and her pluck in braving the perils of this war that civilians must face just as the armed forces do, she answered, 'Our airmen and sailors are doing much more, and the Germans would be delighted if they frightened us!'
>
> She was not at all heroic, but she gave an example of the attitude to take in this struggle for our survival – a struggle in

which only the courage to hold out and the will to win will
assure us of our victory.

This girl was killed recently by a German bomb. She was my
sister.

Madeleine at once decided to become directly involved in the
war effort. Without detriment to her performances, she hurried
through three contracted movie projects – one of them with Hayden,
who volunteered for service with the Marines before Pearl Harbor
and quickly rose to the rank of lieutenant. From the end of 1940
and throughout 1941, she repeatedly asked the War Department for
volunteer assignments abroad, anywhere and at any peril. 'In my
French home at Saudreville, outside Paris, I am now sheltering two
hundred homeless children,' she said in her petition. 'And when
the war is over, it is to them and them alone that I will devote
myself.'

After working without compensation for the United Seaman's
Service in New York, she was permitted to train in Washington as a
hospital staff aide for the Red Cross. She served in the Sixty-first
Field Hospital in Bari, Italy, where she tended countless wounded
men and, according to her companions, thought little of working
twenty-hour days. Equally hazardous were her several return trips by
ship to America, where she raised money for the Red Cross and
taught schoolgirls to knit clothing for deprived European children
and soldiers. At no time was she permitted to visit her family in
England, nor even to put through a telephone call to them.

Throughout the years of her service, Madeleine refused all personal
publicity and worked under a pseudonym. When soldiers recognised
her and asked (as they often did), if she was really Madeleine Carroll,
she replied, 'Don't be silly. What do you think Madeleine Carroll
would be doing here?'

For her outstanding humanitarian work, France awarded her the
Legion of Honour in 1946; she also received the Medal of Freedom
from the United States government. In 1951, still dedicated to the
plight of war orphans and working full-time as a volunteer for
UNESCO, she received the Brotherhood Award from the National
Conference of Christians and Jews. 'Representatives of the three great
faiths, working side by side on problems of social and civic concern,'
she said, accepting the award, 'can and will free the world of bitterness

44

and resentment. In the struggle for freedom, at home and abroad, our greatest weapon is our love of and faith in God.'

She made her last film in 1948, when she was forty-two, and then she appeared once on Broadway (in Fay Kanin's play *Goodbye, My Fancy*). In 1950, she married Andrew Heiskell, her companion a decade earlier on the Clipper flight, who had become the publisher of *Life* magazine. She retired completely save for a few infrequent television or radio appearances, and she and Heiskell had a daughter, Anna Madeleine. Her marriage was dissolved in 1965, when she was fifty-nine. She never married again and devoted herself to good causes and to her daughter – who, alas, died of drug addiction at the age of thirty-three.

Madeleine Carroll then moved to Paris and finally to Marbella. She invariably refused requests for interviews and worked tirelessly for poverty-stricken children of the world until her death, at eighty-one, in 1987. Asked how she felt about her movie career, she once said, 'Let's say I got out while the going was good!' She had found her fulfilment neither in fame nor wealth but in devoting more than four decades to the needs of the wounded, the sick and the orphans of war.

4

Shaking the Dust
(1936–1938)

'When moving pictures are really artistic,' Hitchcock said as early as 1927, 'they will be created entirely by one man.'

The convenient fiction that this was possible or even desirable – that he was the sole creative force behind his pictures – became the primary element in his self-promotion. But since the release of massive American production files and studio archives in recent years, it has become clear that Hitchcock was essentially a senior collaborator. Just about the only thing he did on his own was to create a powerful public image, and even for that he had to rely on writers and publicists for help. Otherwise, he depended on the talent and assistance of many people.

Hitch routinely claimed to have planned everything in advance – each aspect of a production, from the original ideas to the final screenplay to camera placement to the length of a cut, from art direction and set design to wardrobe, sound effects and editing. To be sure, he had significant experience in these areas from the beginning of his career, but micromanagement was not realistic. Outtakes, he said, could be rolled up and would fit in a pocket; there were no camera angles to be used except those he had pre-chosen, because he always 'cut in the camera'.

But the reality was quite different. There was no doubt that the choice of stories and the manner of their visual telling were, as François Truffaut rightly described it to me, a 'coherent body of work'. But this is a valuation that could be made only after the fact. Indeed, no screenplay during his American period was complete when filming began; major revisions occurred during shooting; scenes were excised from the final versions; and the nature of certain key characters – far from being perfect on the page – emerged during the making of the film. Late in life (after completing what was his last picture), he seemed to acknowledge this when he and I discussed the subject of the recurring themes and motifs in his films. 'We try to tell a good story and develop a hefty plot,' he told me over lunch in November 1976. 'As for the themes – they *emerge* as we go along.'

In his book *Hitchcock at Work*, scholar Bill Krohn devotes seven oversize pages to the so-called myths Hitchcock promulgated, to the effect that the films as we have them took their final form long before shooting began. Krohn notes that 'what critics consider the key moments – the strongest moments, or the most illuminating – were often not on the map but were discovered during the long journey of making the film.' In other words, themes emerged. 'He thought movies,' said one of his production designers, Robert Boyle. 'He didn't have rules about movies. He was never afraid to try anything, and if it didn't work out exactly as he wished it, it didn't bother him that much, as long as he got the sense correct.'

The 'coherent body of work', in other words, was therefore very much a creative accident whose coherence had as much to do with the collaborators Hitchcock assembled as with any intention about what a film could *become*. His preference was to work repeatedly with writers, craftsmen, editors and artists with whom he felt comfortable; after all, they would come to know just what he wanted, and they would give it to him along with the best of their own talents.

Hence, during the sound era, writer Charles Bennett worked on six complete Hitchcock movies, John Michael Hayes and Ben Hecht on four each, and a number of writers (Ernest Lehman and Evan Hunter, for example) on two each. John J. Cox was cinematographer for ten of Hitchcock's British pictures, and Bernard Knowles for five; in America, Robert Burks filled the same position on twelve Hitchcock films. George Tomasini edited nine Hitchcock pictures, and Robert Boyle and Henry Bumstead were art directors and/or production designers on the same number. Louis Levy composed the music for nine English films, either partly or in their entirety, while Bernard Herrmann wrote the scores for eight in America.

And so it went. Whenever Hitchcock's schedule was congruent with that of men and women he admired and trusted, he saw to it that they were engaged as collaborators: he thrived on uncomplicated, polite teamwork. 'He knew what he wanted' was their constant refrain about working with him. But Hitchcock's genius in visualising a movie was not something that occurred primarily in advance, in his mind. The visual sense accumulated, as he spoke with writers about ideas and dialogue, as he made lists of shots and scenes, as he designed with artists and costumers, and as he discussed mood and effects with composers. Sometimes, Alma participated, too: she was credited on nineteen out of fifty-three Hitchcock films, although it is sometimes thought that she was involved, however tangentially, in the production of every one. At the least, her approval or disapproval of subject matter and detail was very important to her husband.

A movie, therefore, was a process, not something finished in advance; a movie was something for which Hitchcock needed many helpers – all of whom he guided, evoking the best they had to give. But as Charles Bennett (among others) insisted, 'He could give credit to no one but himself.' This was the central element in his self-promotion and in the creation of the Hitchcock myth. Few among the public guessed that it bore little relation to reality.

The inclination to engage familiar collaborators also explains Hitchcock's preference for multiple engagements with stars who were bankable and cooperative – major players like John Longden, Malcolm Keen, Michael Wilding, Ingrid Bergman, Cary Grant, Farley Granger, James Stewart, Grace Kelly and Joseph Cotten; and supporting cast members like Leo G. Carroll, John Williams, Percy Marmont, Jessie Royce Landis and Edmund Gwenn. Rarely but significantly, he set about creating stars – hence his favour fell on Vera Miles and on Tippi Hedren.

In 1936, Hitchcock's next picture was to be no exception to this process. Michael Balcon approved his request, endorsed by Montagu and Bennett, that the project to follow *Secret Agent* should be a film based on Joseph Conrad's novel *The Secret Agent* – whose movie title, for obvious reasons, would have to be changed. When filming began in the spring of 1936, after three more writers contributed dialogue, they finally settled on *Sabotage*; still, the script was incomplete and

Hitchcock and his collaborators made significant decisions during production.

'I discovered while I was in Hollywood that Miss Sylvia Sidney was available for one picture in England,' Balcon recalled. 'I should have been a fool if I let slip the opportunity of signing up such a brilliant actress.' Trained as a stage actress, twenty-five-year-old Sylvia (credited as Sylvia Sydney in *Sabotage*) had appeared in twenty films and had just co-starred with Spencer Tracy in Fritz Lang's powerful drama *Fury*. Under contract to Paramount, she was earning just under $10,000 weekly, or about $60,000 per picture. Her Hitchcock co-stars were John Loder, Oscar Homolka and seventeen-year-old Desmond Tester, who looked much younger, as the story required.

Sabotage concerns a terrorist (Homolka) who is married to an innocent American (Sidney). He manages the Bijou movie theatre, which he uses as a front for meetings with foreign spies and for the planning of violence. At the outset, we see that he has sabotaged a London power plant; his next assignment is to deliver a film tin that contains a time bomb set to detonate and cause death and destruction in Piccadilly Circus. He asks his wife's brother (Tester) to deliver the package, but the boy is killed when the bomb explodes in a crowded bus. When she learns the truth, she is traumatised with shock and rage, and as she prepares dinner for her husband, he seems almost deliberately to step toward her outstretched carving knife and falls dead. Full of remorse, she longs to tell the police, but the local detective (Loder), who is in love with her, prevents her from divulging her conscience and takes her away after another terrorist bomb destroys the cinema.

Perhaps the most brilliant and provocative change Hitchcock and his writers made from the Conrad novel was the alteration of the setting – from a corner shop to a cinema. This gave Hitchcock an opportunity to reflect on the nature of film watching itself, since most of the action occurs in front of or behind the movie screen of the Bijou. At the structural centre of the film are two motifs. First, there is the use of Hitchcock's ubiquitous birds: 'The birds will sing on Saturday at 1.45' refers to the time of the planned bombing, and Verloc urges the boy to 'kill two birds with one stone.' In addition, the bomb-maker uses his bird shop as a cover for terrorist activities. The bird imagery then comes full circle in the inspired use of the Disney cartoon 'Who Killed Cock Robin?' in the Bijou cinema, which links to the second motif: things are always happening 'behind the screen,' as the characters say – that is, where the Verlocs live. With its economic pacing, sustained images and darkly important themes, *Sabotage* may be Hitchcock's profoundest (if not his most popular) British film.

'On the set [of the picture], he's a sadist,' wrote C. A. Lejeune, one of the few English critics Hitchcock invited to watch him at work. 'His language is fierce, and his humour rarely drawing-room. He respects nobody's feelings, but everybody respects him.' Her harsh assessment of the director (although she claimed to be an ardent fan and a good friend) was apparently based on visits during which Hitchcock was particularly severe with Sylvia Sidney and Desmond Tester (whom the director publicly addressed as 'Testicle').

Hitchcock had approved of Balcon's imported American star, who was well known for her portraits of suffering women, and whom Hitchcock referred to as 'the masochistic Sidney' ('Paramount pays me by the tear,' she once joked). The false assumption that she was indeed a masochist led him to discount her questions and to reject her ideas, and he did this bluntly.

'Hitch had called her and courted her for the picture,' according to Bennett, 'and then when she arrived, he virtually ignored her. I think she just wasn't his type. I thought she was very good. But Hitch was Hitch with her – tough to love and easy to hate.' And because the director could not be bothered to explain to his star his intention in breaking up long scenes into separate close-up shots, he found her, one day, sobbing in confusion. Perhaps because she wasn't his 'type,' he was all business and attempted no practical jokes nor indecent scenes. He simply ignored her, as Bennett recalled. That did not make things easier for this serious actress.

'Hitchcock was very strange to be with,' Sylvia said many years later. 'He made it clear that he resented my salary, which was higher than his. I learned that he had a thing about money, and that he felt actors were all paid too much. I had to admit, when I saw the rough cut of the picture, that *Sabotage* was brilliant. What did he teach me? To be a puppet, and not to try to be creative. But at the time, I really took exception to that.' Hitchcock's brief comment years later was that 'she had nice understatement.'

★   ★   ★

After the dark gravity of *Sabotage*, he lightened the tone in his next picture, *Young and Innocent*, made during the spring of 1937 and freely based on Josephine Tey's novel *A Shilling for Candles*. Hitchcock and his writers completely altered the novel, making a young couple the film's major characters, and reducing the detective to nonexistence.

The movie plot repeated Hitchcock's device of an innocent man wrongly accused, which had been so popular in *The 39 Steps* (and was later exploited in *Saboteur, Spellbound, To Catch a Thief, The Wrong Man, North by Northwest* and *Frenzy*). In this case, a young actor (played by Derrick de Marney) is presumed guilty of the murder of an actress who had given him money. He eludes the police with the help of the constable's daughter, and together they track down the real killer, a jazz drummer with a nervous twitch to his eyes.

At fourteen, Nova Pilbeam had done well for Hitch in *The Man Who Knew Too Much*; ripened now to seventeen, she had had considerable stage experience and was a much-admired actress. Her role as the constable's daughter demanded a complex of feelings, as the girl changes from moral outrage against the apparent killer to being forced to assist him, to a conviction of his innocence, to helping him clear his name.

Young and Innocent is a movie of singular mildness, benevolence, humour and charm, with the added themes of play-acting and disguise that were so dear to Hitchcock's heart. The screenwriter-hero filches identity-concealing eyeglasses to make his escape; a tramp disguises himself as a dandy to help smoke out the villain, who wears black-face to play in a band. To top it all off, Hitch makes a hilarious cameo appearance as a photographer, holding a tiny camera in front of his huge torso, trying vainly to get a snapshot of the commotion outside a courthouse. Everyone in *Young and Innocent* deals in illusions, and at the centre of the film is the justly famous birthday party, in which children play a game of blind man's buff – a sequence the director called an obvious symbol for the picture's theme of the quality of vision, of seeing and not seeing.

Hitchcock was enormously fond of Nova, of whom he was almost paternally protective. But this did not short-circuit what she called his 'really wicked wit'. Derrick de Marney agreed: Hitchcock had a sharp tongue, much to the distress of his actors. His aim, de Marney reckoned, was to strip them of their poses 'and he finds he can do this best by infuriating them.' But Hitchcock was curiously tender and patient with Nova. 'He was deferential to her, both on and off the set,' de Marney added; otherwise, 'he spared no one' – not de Marney, not Mary Clare (as Nova's aunt), both of whom heard Hitchcock's sarcastic comments on their performances.

One difficult and dangerous sequence stayed in Nova's memory over the years. Taking refuge from the police in an abandoned mineshaft, she and her young man are almost lost when the floor of the cave collapses. In the largest stage at Pinewood Studios, Hitchcock supervised the building of a set fifteen feet off the ground, enabling him to film a car just before its crash. Nova Pilbeam then struggled to reach Derrick de Marney's outstretched fingers (precisely the setup of the final clinging and reaching in *Saboteur* and *North by Northwest*). The critics liked the picture and loved Nova: 'She imparts sincerity to every gesture, and at the same time invests the stormy love interest with adolescent charm. This is a charming portrayal of innocent girlhood.'

Hitchcock's assistant director on *Young and Innocent*, as on his previous four pictures, was young Penrose Tennyson, great-grandson of the Victorian poet. For the mineshaft scene, no doubles were used, as Nova recalled: 'I did that, and it was my husband-to-be – Pen – who held me up as I dangled there. I was terrified! But Hitch had this quirky sense of humour, and he made the scene go on and on, so that I thought my arm would come out of its socket.'

In 1939, Nova Pilbeam and Pen Tennyson were married. Two years later, when he was twenty-eight and she twenty-one, he was flying for the admiralty's Educational Film Unit during World War Two when his small plane crashed. 'Had my husband not been killed, I suspect I might have stayed in the business of filming.' But after a few more movies, she retired. A decade later, she married again, and in 1972, she was widowed a second time. As of 2008, she had not appeared in a film in more than sixty years and was living quietly in north London. 'Her name, her beauty and her talent remain in the annals and the memory,' as one historian has rightly stated.

If Hitchcock's behaviour toward Nova Pilbeam had an element of benign paternalism, what can be said of his relationship with his real-life daughter, Patricia, who marked her ninth birthday in July 1937?

By this time, she was away at boarding school, where she studied and lived for two years. 'It's what people did at that time,' she said in 1999, but she seems not to have been very happy there: 'I would never send my own daughters to boarding school. I've never understood this thing with the English sending their children away. They should be absolutely shot for sending children away at that age. Well, that's the English – that's what they do.'

At the Hitchcocks' country house in Shamley Green, near Guildford, visitors like Elsie Randolph recalled, 'There was a strange formality when Pat was home for the occasional weekend or on holiday. She had to sit alone at her own little table in the kitchen while the adults dined in grand style, and her father insisted that she curtsy and be very proper with the guests. For all that, she seemed a happy, polite child.' Pleasant memories of her childhood, however infrequently expressed, do not seem to have been unalloyed. 'I never go back to England, not unless I have to,' she said years later. She did not provide reasons.

Did she have a positive sense of her life in England? 'I don't think there's any particular thing that stands out at all,' she said in 2005. There was no mention of friends, of visitors to the Hitchcock home, of travels. As she spoke to an interviewer, her life sounded thumpingly dull – nothing stands out at all. And what of her father? Only this: 'He had a great sense of humour, and he said that if you couldn't look at life with a sense of humour, then you were in a lot of trouble. I inherited a sense of humour. We were a very close family.' Did anything else come to mind? 'My father did a lot of reading, and my parents gave me a toy kitchen set as a gift, and I served cake around to them, several friends and family.' Did she ever watch her father's home movie of this, which has been preserved? 'No.'

After the death of her father and mother, Pat Hitchcock took her place among the great flame-keepers in cultural history. Guardian of the Hitchcock legacy and a wealthy heiress, she has celebrated her parents not as if they were creative geniuses or working artists, but as if they were just an average down-home couple with whom she had 'a perfectly normal life. My parents were ordinary people. I know a lot of people insist that my father must have had a dark imagination. Well, he did not. He was a brilliant filmmaker and he knew how to tell a story. That's all.' This is certainly not high praise.

Pat adored her mother, and years later collaborated on a book celebrating Alma's contributions to Hitchcock's films. Her relationship to her father was more tangled and problematic. Then, on his death, she became a very wealthy woman precisely because of movies she did not always wish to defend, much less praise. 'When my own girls were young, I wouldn't let them see *any* of his movies,' she said at a dinner in autumn 1977. 'My own favourite was *Rebecca* – I thought everything went downhill after that' (although she later added that *Notorious* was a good picture, too). When she asked me, at that same dinner, to name my favourite, I replied that I had many, but that I thought *Vertigo* was a great film. 'Oh,' she said after a pause, as if trying to remember. 'Was that the crazy movie with a bell tower? I never understood what was going on in that picture!'

Hitchcock's next project came to him as a virtually completed screen-play by Frank Launder and Sidney Gilliat; ironically, it turned out to be a crowd pleaser, and so it remains seventy years later – generally perceived as classic Hitchcock. *The Lady Vanishes* (based on a novel by Ethel Lina White) was all but ready for production in the autumn of 1937, and casting was rapidly concluded with the engagement of Margaret Lockwood, Michael Redgrave and Dame May Whitty, among the polished cast. Filming took just five weeks, on the cramped, eighty-foot-long stage of Gainsborough's Islington studio.

'I suppose what surprised me most of all about Hitchcock,' recalled Margaret Lockwood, 'was how little he directed us. I had done a number of films for Carol Reed, and he was quite meticulous by contrast. Hitchcock, however, didn't seem to direct us at all. He was a dozing, nodding Buddha with an enigmatic smile on his face' – the look of pleasure perhaps expressing his thoughts about the negotia-tions then in progress for him to accept a deal in America. Redgrave agreed: 'He wasn't really an actor's director. Everyone knew that his reputation was more for preparation and technique than for working with his cast. In fact, his own nonchalance made it rather easy for us.'

Perhaps it was easy for the two leading players, but for Mary Clare (who had been razzed on the set of *Young and Innocent*), the experi-ence was memorably uncomfortable. Swathed in black for her role as a Middle European baroness, she had to accept the assignment under the terms of her contract with Balcon. Hitchcock, ostensibly to welcome her, had heard she did not drink alcohol, so he politely offered her a fruit drink he had prepared. But the concoction was laced with strong spirits, and soon Mary Clare was hopelessly drunk.

The Hitchcocks made several journeys by ship to the United States from 1936 to 1938 – not primarily for holidays, but for meetings with potential producers and Hollywood moguls. 'He felt that he was not really respected in England,' recalled Samuel Taylor, 'and that British critics regarded him as the house clown. When he finally left for Hollywood, he and Alma shook the dust from their shoes – he couldn't wait to get out.'

Taylor was on the mark. A number of British producers and critics expressed the widely held sentiment that Hitchcock was a great director of unimportant pictures. Such elitists believed that he was a mere technician catering to lower-class audiences – which meant that he was the most popular filmmaker in Britain, and perhaps the only one whose name alone meant success at the box office.

There were other reasons for Hitchcock's desire to quit England. British production was in decline; executives were inefficient and not all were as committed to movies as, say, Michael Balcon had been; craftsmen and other personnel drifted from one studio to another; and budgets dropped precipitously.

'The art of filmmaking was often held in contempt by the intellectuals,' Hitchcock retorted years later. 'And that was truer of the British. No well-bred English person would be seen going into a cinema; it simply wasn't done. You see, England is strongly class-conscious, [and] the general attitude in Britain is an insular one.' He always recognised how much he needed good actors, but those who expressed their preference for the art of the theatre over mere work in film were always the objects of his special ridicule.

For *The Lady Vanishes*, the New York Film Critics Circle cited Hitch as the best director of 1938, and this award certainly helped in his Hollywood negotiations. After complicated, protracted exchanges, a deal was concluded with David O. Selznick, for whom Hitchcock was to begin work the following year.

But there was one more promise to fulfil in London: he had agreed (without, alas, first reading the property) to direct Charles Laughton in a film of *Jamaica Inn*, based on a Daphne du Maurier novel. The beleaguered project, about nineteenth-century pirates on the Cornish coast, could not have not have been less Hitchcockian in content and style, nor could it be salvaged, even by a team that included Joan Harrison (whom Hitchcock now promoted to writer status), Sidney Gilliat and the esteemed J. B. Priestley.

Produced in autumn 1938, *Jamaica Inn* turned out to be one of the few unadulterated failures in Hitchcock's career. Laughton's character (the mad Squire Pengallan, mastermind of cutthroat smugglers) appears nowhere in the du Maurier novel: the role was Laughton's own invention. As co-producer, this brilliant, erratic, self-indulgent actor waved a heavy hand over every element of the picture, which (as his biographer Simon Callow accurately wrote) is 'sloppy, stiff, unrhythmic [and] ugly.' Daphne du Maurier succeeded in having her name removed from the opening credits.

The finished film is remarkable only as Maureen O'Hara's first major role. Then eighteen, she gamely and uncomplainingly submitted to numerous soakings with studio rain, violent wind machines, immersions in tanks designed to mimic seawater – and a torturous binding and gagging by Laughton in the final sequences. As he admitted, Hitchcock was fascinated by the duality of Pengallan's Jekyll-and-Hyde mentality. Apart from those sequences, the young actress felt that 'Hitchcock had little interest in the film, and he didn't make much of an impression on me. His physical appearance was very much a part of his eccentricity. He was always very neat and tidy in his appearance, but he moved very awkwardly because of his weight. He rarely socialised and usually spoke in a low Cockney whisper to keep the set quiet.' Emlyn Williams, already established as both playwright and actor, was once asked what he learned from Hitchcock during *Jamaica Inn*. 'I learned that it was a good time to go to Hollywood.'

By the time *Jamaica Inn* was released, Alfred, Alma and Pat Hitchcock – and the now apparently indispensable Joan Harrison – were settled in Hollywood, where Hitchcock began his seven-year contract with Selznick. The glory was beginning, and with it, more than a few predicaments.

5

Passport to Hollywood
(1939–1940)

'*Rebecca* was a very pleasant experience for my father,' said Patricia Hitchcock many years after the movie was made, 'because [the producer] David Selznick was too busy with *Gone With the Wind* to cause any problems.' *Rebecca* may have been Pat's favourite among all Alfred Hitchcock's motion pictures – but this judgement was very different from his. He always insisted that directing it was nothing like 'a very pleasant experience', precisely because Selznick interfered all the time. Indeed, the producer was constantly and obsessively involved. Eager to sign up England's most popular and successful director, Selznick was shocked to discover how independently he was accustomed to work. Hitch, on the other hand, was keen to make movies with the vast technical and financial resources of Hollywood – but he had no notion of how proprietary the American producer was.

As is well known, Selznick dictated lengthy, exhaustive and exhausting memoranda by the score every day, indicating to Hitchcock as well as dozens of employees and colleagues just what sort of film *Rebecca* should be and what sort of things needed attention. This kind of front-office control came as a great shock to Hitchcock, who had enjoyed enormous directorial freedom under British producers Michael Balcon, Edward Black and John Maxwell, and who saw a book as merely a starting point for a visual tale. Selznick, however, believed that fidelity to the texts of popular fiction would satisfy readers and result in good box office.

The Hitchcocks and Joan Harrison arrived in Los Angeles in March 1939. Principal photography on *Gone With the Wind* concluded in June, while Hitchcock and company were still at work on the screen-play of *Rebecca*. The editing of *Gone With the Wind*, the last pick-up shots, the scoring, the advertising and marketing and hundreds of other details before the release of this extravaganza engaged Selznick virtually around the clock, right up to the Atlanta premiere in December. In fact, Selznick asked Hitchcock for his reactions and advice regarding several sequences of *Gone With the Wind*, and Hitchcock replied with an 'analysis that . . . was cinematic and precise', as Selznick acknowledged.

Rebecca occupied Selznick no less than the completion of *Gone With the Wind*. But he had to proceed cautiously. As his advertising and publicity director, Whitney Bolton, observed, 'Hitchcock was not always the most consistently amiable of human creatures. He delighted in needling those around him. He needled stars, staff, and press agents, any and all. He had a way of speaking that commands attention, and if he didn't get it, he tended to fret a little.'

The Hitchcock picture was, remarkably, Selznick's sixty-ninth production in sixteen years. At the age of thirty-seven, his prodigious energies had many sources and supports: his wife, Irene, the daughter of studio mogul Louis B. Mayer; his meticulous attention to detail; his ability to engage highly talented directors, designers, artists and actors (not to say wealthy investors); his keen intelligence and consider-able charm; and a daily diet of dangerously addictive amphetamines and barbiturates.★ He spent money imprudently, presuming that good luck at gambling would provide what he needed; it never did, and his monthly losses at card games cost him enormously: in the first nine months of 1940, he lost $56,378 at card games.

'It's not a Hitchcock picture,' the director said flatly of *Rebecca*; it was, on the contrary, very much a Selznick picture – a project to which Hitchcock was once attracted, but for which he had lost all interest even before it was assigned to him. The first Selznick-Hitchcock project, wisely abandoned even before there was a draft

---

★ Among Selznick's credits after he began as a producer in 1923: *King Kong, Dinner at Eight, Anna Karenina, The Prisoner of Zenda* and *Intermezzo*. Katharine Hepburn's first film and Ingrid Bergman's American debut were both Selznick productions.

screenplay, was to have been about the sinking of the *Titanic*. But a movie of Daphne du Maurier's best-selling novel was sure to be a hit. Hundreds of thousands of copies had been sold in England and America since its publication in 1938, and dozens of translations were being prepared.

Rebecca is very much a modern Gothic romance, in the tradition of Charlotte Brontë's 1847 novel *Jane Eyre*. Both stories feature shy young women tormented by self-doubt; obsessed, gloomy older men with dreadful secrets; stately, immense and isolated manor houses; the influence of the past and the dead; catastrophic fires; and happy endings that are not entirely so. Perhaps neither *Jane Eyre* nor *Rebecca* is entirely satisfactory for some twenty-first-century readers, but they both retain considerable popular appeal.

'Screen Play by Robert E. Sherwood and Joan Harrison' – so it is noted among the opening credits of *Rebecca*; and below those words, 'Adaptation by Philip MacDonald and Michael Hogan.' After all the script versions are compared and contrasted, Charles Bennett (who was in close contact with Selznick and Hitchcock that year) summarised the facts: 'It's ninety per cent the work of Michael Hogan, with some rewrites by Joan. Very little, at the end, was contributed by the one who is most famous and most prominently credited – Sherwood.' Alma had worked with Michael Hogan on a non-Hitchcock screenplay in 1935. She liked and admired him, and convinced her husband to put him on the project even before they left England; Hitchcock simultaneously promoted Harrison; and MacDonald, a writer of thrillers, worked on the early treatment.

By spring 1939, Joan Harrison was becoming more important – some said indispensable – in the life of Alfred Hitchcock. Alma received proper credit and compensation on four of his later films, and her professional and personal encouragement and persuasion were constant and considerable throughout his life. But her direct, daily presence and detailed involvement on his pictures diminished during the American period. Pat Hitchcock always claimed otherwise, even to the extent of authorising *Alma Hitchcock: The Woman Behind the Man*, one-fourth of which is devoted to Alma's recipes.

Pat's book was lovely evidence of a daughter's affection, but it does not confirm the idea that Alfred Hitchcock would not have been successful without the lifelong collaboration of Alma Reville. Nevertheless, that was precisely the fiction some people have come to believe; it may provide a kind of tender revisionist history in praise of a supposedly neglected heroine, but it does not stand up to scrutiny – and Alma herself would have laughed at such hyperbolic praise. That Alma's mind and voice were respected and often heeded by her husband is beyond dispute; that we would not have his masterworks without her ubiquitous assistance is an absurd idea.

As for Joan, 'she was widely assumed to be Hitch's mistress,' as his authorised biographer, John Russell Taylor, wrote twenty-five years after the director's death. Harrison was never asked about this; Hitch vehemently denied it; and when the subject came up long afterward with producer and actor John Houseman (who worked with Hitch in 1941), Houseman said, 'I would put my hand in the fire to swear that [Harrison] was never his mistress. I ought to know, because for some time she was mine' – and, Taylor asserts, Harrison was also Clark Gable's mistress.

Joan and Alma remained on friendly terms and, from 1939 to 1942, they often conferred on script problems. But everyone near them knew that Hitchcock simply adored the beautiful and lively Harrison, and this Alma endured (not for the last time) in silence. Of his wife, Hitch said simply, 'She puts up with a lot from me.' For Joan, Hitchcock was a valuable mentor-employer; for him, she was the object of a serious fantasy romance and very much a leading lady in his life. In the summer of 1939, Hitchcock turned forty, his doctor noted his weight at 365 pounds, and a morbid situation could have developed at any moment. Most touching and agonising, however, was his yearning for Harrison. That year, he joined history's long list of famous unrequited lovers who drew energy and inspiration for their work precisely from the fact that their passion was indeed unrequited. This was often the single most powerful motif and motive in Alfred Hitchcock's life.

'There are only two women I ever could have married,' Hitchcock told Charles Bennett one evening, 'Alma, whom I did, and Joan, whom I didn't.' It is impossible not to pity the anguish of his suppressed desires, his feelings of isolation and his acute sense of embarrassment in the presence of both his wife and his mistress manquée. Professional and family life proceeded with all requisite politeness, but also with marked awkwardness – especially when Harrison began to enjoy her own scarcely concealed Hollywood romances. In that department, she was apparently a busy little bee, even after Houseman and Gable, until, at fifty-one, she married the writer Eric Ambler.

Rebecca's casting problems, nothing less than an exercise in frustration, have been exhaustively documented elsewhere; the results were fascinating. To portray the handsome and enigmatic hero Maxim de Winter, Selznick signed Laurence Olivier, who had just come to major stardom in the film *Wuthering Heights*. At once, he began an intense campaign for his inamorata, Vivien Leigh, to play the nameless second Mrs de Winter, the title character's successor and the novel's narrator, identified as 'I' in the screenplay. Leigh was just completing *Gone With the Wind*, but there was unanimous judgement that she would have been very wrong in *Rebecca* (as her surviving screen tests indicate). Dozens of actresses were considered for the role all during June, July and August, but Selznick could not make a final decision on the matter until four days prior to principal photography, which began on 8 September.

His favour had come down to a choice among Margaret Sullavan, Anne Baxter and Joan Fontaine. Sullavan, whom many of Selznick's colleagues preferred, finally seemed too quirkily autonomous for the part of a shy, anxious ingénue. Baxter had admirable stage experience and appeared eminently sincere, and she also had the enthusiastic support of many others at the studio. But she was only sixteen, and it was hard for the producer to see her opposite Olivier, who was thirty-two and would be presented as even older. Alma Reville and Joan Harrison supported Anne Baxter, insisting (along with others) that Joan Fontaine was 'too coy and simpering to a degree that is intolerable.' Hitchcock took their point but waited for Selznick's deciding vote. Notwithstanding others' judgements, Fontaine's screen tests for *Rebecca* (which have also survived) revealed a touching simplicity and a muted disquiet. But many thought that those qualities simply reflected her insecurities and lack of experience on the days of the tests.

In addition, David O. Selznick had been (as his authorised biographer wrote) 'much in love with Joan Fontaine from the summer of 1938.' His passion may have been blunted by her marriage, on 20 August 1939, to the actor Brian Aherne − but Selznick's ardour was not forthwith extinguished, and he still believed she was right for the role. When informed that she had won it, Joan interrupted her honeymoon and went immediately to work, the last and most important player to sign on for *Rebecca*.

Born in 1917 to English parents and raised from childhood in California, Joan Fontaine had acted to no great effect in more than a dozen movies, and in 1938 RKO had dropped her from its roster of players. Pretty, slim and photogenic, she was like very many other young Hollywood hopefuls, and nothing like a bankable star. Contrariwise, the career of her sister, Olivia de Havilland, was already impressive and would become more so after the release of *Gone With the Wind*. About to turn twenty-two that autumn, Fontaine was polished and literate, and what she lacked in professional self-confidence, she could handily offset with a certain wry hauteur that later increased with her relatively short-lived stardom. Selznick found her charming; Hitch, who did not, 'knew ways of pressuring her insecurities, and making her his' instead of Selznick's, as David Thomson wrote.

In the two pages Fontaine dedicated to *Rebecca* in her autobiography, she told readers virtually nothing about the film that made her career or the people involved in it – except that she was badly treated by just about everyone in the picture. Of Hitchcock, she wrote, 'We liked each other and I knew he was rooting for me. He had a strange way of going about it, as actors who have worked with him have verified. His technique was "divide and conquer". He wanted total loyalty, but only to him.'

To establish that loyalty and to evoke from Fontaine the anxiety and sense of isolation necessary for the character of the second Mrs de Winter, Hitch told her that Olivier had wanted Vivien in the role; that Olivier disliked her intensely; that Olivier thought she should be replaced. Olivier himself told her that he disapproved of her new husband – whereupon the bride went home and 'gazed upon my Prince Charming with new eyes. Try as I would to forget his remark, Larry [Olivier] had rudely awakened me from my pillow dream.' She was certainly impressionable. In any case, her husband was sanguine during the six years of their marriage. 'Joan is young, pretty, gay and utterly charming – and no actress, thank God,' wrote Brian Aherne in his memoirs.

Hitch's apparent segregation of Fontaine from the rest of the cast was unrelenting. Claiming that she was cold-shouldered on and off the set by Gladys Cooper, Judith Anderson, Nigel Bruce, George Sanders and others, she added, 'The British brigade couldn't be bothered to attend' a little birthday celebration in her honour at the studio on 22 October. Was this collective snub an example of what she termed Hitch's 'divide and conquer' conspiracy, devilishly devised to make Fontaine feel as unwanted and unloved as her character? That is extremely unlikely: no matter how much her co-stars were 'a cliquey lot' (Fontaine's phrase), the entire cast would never have been so rude, nor is it probable that Hitch would have effectively diminished himself in everyone's eyes by arranging such a callous tactic. More to the point, to presume otherwise is to take for granted that Hitch's order to any and every actor, even regarding off-the-set behaviour, was taken as an imperial command never to be contravened.

There are other explanations. Had Hitch believed that his leading lady was doing a fine job from day one, she might have become too relaxed, and her performance as a frightened little doe would have suffered. To avoid that, he pursued a scheme to insure her utter dependence on him and to prevent her from approaching the other players. 'He seemed to want total possession of me,' she said years later.

> He was a Svengali. He controlled me totally. He took me aside and whispered, 'Now, kid, you go in there and you do this and you do that.' And then he said, 'Do you know what So-and-so said about you today? Well, never you mind. You just listen to me.' Now some of what he told me might have been true, but of course it also made me feel absolutely miserable all the time. To be honest, he was divisive with us. He wanted total control over me, and he seemed to relish the cast not liking one another, actor for actor, by the end of the film. This helped my performance, since I was supposed to be terrified of everyone, and it gave a lot of tension to my scenes. It kept him in command, and it was part of the upheaval he wanted. He kept me off balance, much to his own delight . . . But he didn't give me what I needed most, confidence.

Poor Fontaine did not help her cause when, perhaps desperately, she boasted to a member of the cast, 'My grandmother was the Honourable Lady de Havilland, the first lady of Guernsey!' Hitchcock's whispered response: 'That's like being the first lady of Catalina' – the rocky, sparsely inhabited island off the coast of Los Angeles. As biographer Patrick McGilligan succinctly wrote of Fontaine, 'She was not,

it must be said, all that popular.' Nor could she have much appreciated being paid $166 per day when Olivier's rate was $695 and Judith
Anderson's $291; but they, of course, had far more experience.

Still, the entire emotional weight of the movie depended on
Fontaine's performance, which Hitch had to entice, cajole and coax
from her with painstaking direction. 'She was not a good enough
actress to play in *Rebecca* – she really was not,' recalled Selznick's executive assistant, the perceptive, discreet and efficient Marcella Rabwin.
This realisation even dawned on the once-smitten Selznick: 'I am
aware that it takes time to get the performance out of Joan Fontaine,
but every picture I have ever worked on had some such difficulty . . .
Miss Fontaine requires work.

'I think Joan has been handled with great restraint,' Selznick added
as filming concluded, 'but I think we've got to be careful not to lose
what little variety there is in the role by underplaying her in her
emotional moments . . . [We must not] make it seem as though Joan
is simply not capable of the big moments.' But in fact she was not
capable of the big moments, and Hitchcock had to confer with
cameraman George Barnes to cover some thorny shots when Fontaine
could not provide what was required.

Recalling these incidents with the star, script supervisor Lydia
Schiller said, 'She was practically a puppet,' and Leonard Leff, who
devoted an entire book to the Selznick-Hitchcock years, put it tersely
when he wrote, 'A well-trained actress would have used her reserves
to counter such obstacles as long hours and inhospitable colleagues;
young and inexperienced, Joan Fontaine immediately drew on her
capital, and, at its rapid depletion, became vulnerable to fatigue and
even self-destruction.' At one point, Selznick was so fearful of her
'weakness' that he asked his wife to look at the footage shot thus far
– should the film be scrapped? No, said Irene Selznick, it will be a
fine picture.

But the journey to success was tortuous. Much of Fontaine's speech
had to be re-recorded – 'dozens of isolated lines,' according to Leonard
Leff. And when principal photography was concluded, Selznick himself
had to sit with editor Hal Kern and fine-tune Fontaine's portrayal.
'He often grafted improved line readings onto weak visuals,' Leff
continued, 'and he revised scenes to highlight Fontaine's best moments.
When he had no suitable take of the actress from which to choose,
he neutralised her performance of especially marginal readings by

using (where possible) master shots or close-ups of other actors.' The finished film and Fontaine's performance, in other words, was remarkably enhanced in the editing and dubbing rooms.

'Although Hitchcock is full of kind impulses,' wrote one reporter after visiting the studio, 'he is never happier than when seeing someone writhe. The sadistic cruelty which Mrs Danvers [played by Judith Anderson] manifests toward the second Mrs de Winter is precisely the sort of thing which brings the roses to Mr Hitchcock's rather extensive cheeks.' Leff put it well: 'Many of the actors with whom Hitchcock worked found him endearing, but his humour had a darker side, sometimes abusive and inescapably deliberate . . . Hitchcock's épée was his wit, wielded with grace, speed, and a sometimes unexpected fatality.'

Judith Anderson summarised the atmosphere of the production with polite reticence: 'There were very unpleasant things I prefer not to discuss,' she said years later. Anderson may well have meant the day described by Joan Fontaine as 'unforgettable' – when Hitch (at her own request) slapped her so that she could bring forth the tears required for an emotional scene. Or perhaps Anderson was thinking of another day when Fontaine, alone with Hitchcock and ready for a close-up shot, saw him in his director's chair, facing her. 'Then I saw that he had put the cork of a champagne bottle in his crotch,' Fontaine remembered, 'so that it looked like something else sticking out. He could be very naughty.'

As Marcella Rabwin recalled, Hitch did not hesitate to tell anyone at the studio 'the dirtiest joke in the world, and he never cracked a smile.' Florence Bates, then fifty-one, was receiving her first movie credit for her role as the aggressive and vulgar matron Edythe Van Hopper in the Monte Carlo sequences. Of keen humour and intelligence, Bates was the first woman to receive a law degree in her home state of Texas, and Hitch (who had seen her onstage at the Pasadena Playhouse) recommended her to Selznick. One morning at the studio, just before one of her scenes with Fontaine, Bates stood silently in a corner, facing an off-camera mirror and trying out a gesture. She was not someone easily embarrassed by salty language or manly crudeness, but she was astonished to hear Hitchcock's voice suddenly booming over the studio loudspeaker system: 'Well, Miss Bates – when did you start playing with yourself?' Such coarse double entendres were par for the Hitchcock course.

Lydia Schiller's ordeal as script supervisor lasted longer. Ordered by Selznick to report to him whenever Hitch deviated in any significant way from what the producer had approved, Schiller had of course to follow instructions. This she had done only once when the director learned of what he considered an ambush. 'You're supposed to be working with me, for me,' he told her angrily. 'Instead, you've been spying on me, reporting on me.' With that, Schiller continued, her 'baptism of fire' began,

> and I had no peace from then on. In his very quiet way, as we sat and worked over the script, he said these things to me – they were obscenities. I didn't even know what they meant. It was just shattering to me. Two or three times, I just had to leave. Finally, I was able to overcome that feeling of revulsion and continue with my work.

Rebecca was completed before the end of November 1939 and released in the spring of 1940, just after *Gone With the Wind* was awarded ten Academy Awards, including best picture – for which the statuette was handed to the producer, David O. Selznick. The following year, Selznick again won, for *Rebecca*, and George Barnes won an Oscar for its black-and-white cinematography. Hitchcock was nominated in the directing category but lost (to John Ford, for *The Grapes of Wrath*) – a situation that would be repeated four times in his career and that understandably infuriated him.

During production, Laurence Olivier was uncomfortable with his co-star, his role and his director's apparent diffidence, and in the finished film, he can be seen rubbing his temples, passing his hand over his forehead, and sighing deeply, as if confusing emotional anguish with a sinus headache. 'His pauses are the most ungodly slow and deliberate reactions I have ever seen,' noted Selznick – 'as though he were deciding whether or not to run for president, instead of whether or not to give a ball.'

As for Fontaine, she – like Olivier and Anderson – was nominated by the Academy for her performance. American critics generally, if not passionately, liked her acting, but the British were unsympathetic: 'Joan Fontaine at moments even succeeds in coming, however artificially, alive.' Charmingly awkward in the first half-hour, she then gave what might be called a successful example of a one-note performance – rather like Judith Anderson's, but pleasanter to watch. To be fair, it is difficult to tell if the fault is in the actress or the script, which makes her a Gothic heroine who is just too 'coy and simpering' – precisely what Alma Reville and Joan Harrison found so repugnant in her tests.

Rebecca offers dashing Laurence Olivier in one of his rare indifferent performances, and attractive Joan Fontaine in one of her rare good ones. It remains entertaining hokum, leavened with occasional (but not enough) humour – a Selznick picture more than a Hitchcock one, as the director said. Together, these two men enlivened a prolix and complicated story that seemed to end two or three times, and they created a palpable sense of horror in the notion that someone dead may be witnessing and even controlling one's destiny. To this latter premise, Hitch would return with a vengeance in *Vertigo* and *Psycho*.

For a $54,000 profit, Selznick then loaned out Hitch to producer Walter Wanger for an independent picture made at the Goldwyn Studios on Santa Monica Boulevard. *Foreign Correspondent* was one of the director's warmest and wittiest thrillers – a story short on politics and long on human interest and astounding special effects that are still impressive many decades later. Charles Bennett wrote most of the snappy screenplay; Joan Harrison did some editing and polishing; humourist Robert Benchley wrote his own comic scenes as a tippling journalist; and James Hilton and Ben Hecht contributed to this or that scene – in other words, it was much a collaborative effort, as usual with Hitchcock and Hollywood.

Foreign Correspondent was a massive project, both financially and technically, and its enormous sets and set pieces (central Amsterdam, Waterloo Station, the Dutch countryside, Westminster and the middle of the Atlantic Ocean) required the most creative artists and technicians then working in movies. For his leading players, Hitch could not have his first choices (Gary Cooper and Barbara Stanwyck), and he thought he was settling for B-list talent when the roles went to Joel McCrea and Laraine Day.

In neither of these estimable actors did he demonstrate any interest; that was reserved for the participation of Herbert Marshall (from *Murder!* a decade earlier); for the venerable German immigrant actor Albert Basserman; and for the film's extraordinary special effects, which required 600 carpenters, electricians, plumbers, property men and engineers. For the famous rain sequence on the steps of the Amsterdam Town Hall – built on the back lot – the Colorado River was diverted, an elaborate sewer system was constructed, and water splashed down on hundreds of extras for long hours over three days.*

Laraine Day, a lively twenty-year-old brunette with superb comic timing, was borrowed from Metro-Goldwyn-Mayer to be the leading lady opposite McCrea, an appealing, competent and altogether effective leading man. 'Hitchcock had a habit of drinking a pint of champagne at lunch,' McCrea recalled. 'One afternoon, there was a long scene with me just standing and talking. When the scene was over, I expected to hear "Cut!" but I looked over and there was Hitchcock, snoring! So I said "Cut!" and he woke up and asked, "Was it any good?" I replied, "The best in the picture!" and he said, "Print it!"'

'Hitch was always playing practical jokes on people during production,' added Laraine Day, who had played a nurse seven times in the *Dr Kildare* movies. 'Once, he nailed shut my exit door in a scene – and another time, there was a false wall suddenly put up on the other side of another exit door. This kind of thing threw me off, of course, but Hitch loved to play his gags on actors.' But the actors were apparently spared the cruder and more uncomfortable sort of Hitchcock pranks: neither she nor McCrea could recall foul language, and there was no sign of handcuffs or ill-placed champagne corks. Hitch may have begun to realise that Hollywood was not as patient as London with such shenanigans.

But coarse words, spoken merrily and prodigally, were heard at the RKO Studios in the autumn of 1940, when Hitch arrived there to film – of all things – a screwball comedy starring the popular blonde comedienne Carole Lombard, best known for raucously amusing movies and her liberal use of language that could make sailors blush. She had married Clark Gable the year before, and the Hitchcocks were renting her former Bel-Air home while they sought a permanent residence.

* *Foreign Correspondent* was nominated in six Oscar categories but won none: supporting actor (Albert Basserman), black-and-white art direction (Alexander Golitzen), black-and-white cinematography (Rudolph Maté), special effects (photographic effects by Paul Eagler, sound by Thomas T. Moulton), original screenplay (Bennett and Harrison) and best picture (Wanger). Hitch was again ignored.

The two families socialised from time to time, and Hitch later claimed that, as a personal favor to Lombard, he agreed to direct *Mr and Mrs Smith*, a droll tale of marital mishap. He added that he did not really understand the squabbling American couple of Norman Krasna's screenplay, which concerned a devoted but high-strung married couple (to be played by Lombard and Robert Montgomery) who learn that because of a geographical technicality, their marriage has not been legal. The ultra-thin narrative takes them through a series of jokey sequences until they realise they were meant for each other all along. To direct this and a second film for RKO, executives at that studio borrowed Hitch, in autumn 1940, from Selznick – who, as usual, pocketed an enormous weekly profit from loaning out people he had under contract while continuing to pay them only their stipulated salaries.

Interestingly, the RKO archives tell a story different from Hitch's stated indifference to the project and his mere acquiescence to Lombard's request that he find an idea. The studio had already bought the script for her, and when Hitch learned this, he at once expressed an enthusiastic desire to direct it – not only for the chance to work with her, but because he was more eager to go to RKO than to return to Selznick servitude. The highly paid Lombard made it happen.

After the English story and characters of *Rebecca* and the non-American settings of *Foreign Correspondent*, Hitch wanted to direct a typical American comedy about typical Americans, presumably for a typical American audience. The result, *Mr and Mrs Smith*, was one of the great hits at the Radio City Music Hall, New York, beginning in January 1941. The public loved it, although reviewers were lukewarm – it seemed so anomalous a Hitchcock work – and the critics were soon all but unanimous in proclaiming it a minor and tedious work. Seen almost seventy years later, it is a harmless, faintly amusing bit of moviemaking – verbose, sweet-minded, perhaps too traditionally moral for its own good, but superbly acted by everyone including the bit players.

'I liked [Carole] very much,' Hitch said later. 'She had a bawdy sense of humour and used the language men use with each other. I'd never heard a woman speak that way. She was a forceful personality – stronger, I felt, than Gable.' And he simply could not make her uncomfortable with any salty language or dirty story. After he saw the rough cut of a scene one day, he met Lombard: 'Oh, you've looked at the rushes without me,' she cried. He assured her that everything looked just fine. 'I don't give a fuck about that,' she said. 'How did my new tits look?'

Aware of Hitch's reputation for practical jokes, Carole prepared a few of her own. He agreed to let her direct his cameo appearance – a long shot as he strolls past an apartment building – and, straight-faced and utterly serious, she put him through several hours of exercise, requesting that he walk repeatedly, eight, ten, fifteen times until, she said, she had it just right. A week later, she had another prank ready when Hitch arrived on the set. Were actors really cattle? Carole had set up a pen with three heifers, which stomped and mooed, bearing the names of the movie's three stars on neck tags. Hitch was not inclined to handcuff nor to insult her. As for obscenities, she outdid him every day in that department.

6

Chilling Elegance
(1941–1942)

The next project was to have been the first under the RKO deal, but it was delayed by a chain of thorny script problems and so was temporarily replaced with the less challenging story about the cranky Smiths. The second picture took writers four months to complete their first script, and revisions almost past counting continued even during filming, which lasted from February through July 1941. The production, eventually titled *Suspicion* (a title Hitch disliked but had to accept from RKO executives), was based on a 1935 British novel by Anthony Berkeley Cox, writing as Francis Iles.

Published as *Before the Fact*, this was an experimental psychological tale, told from the viewpoint of a woman who gradually learns that her adored husband is not only a cad, a liar and an embezzler, but also that he plans to kill her for her money. She does not wish to live without him, but also does not wish him to live on through their (yet unborn) child, and so she plans to accept death by poisoning at his hands. Before the fact, however, she writes a letter to her mother, explaining everything and implicating her husband in all his crimes as well as her murder. She then asks her husband to post the sealed letter, and she downs the fatal drink. *Before the Fact* thus explores the psychological extremes of one woman's passionate, obsessive love.

However odd this property, Hitch always claimed this was precisely the story he wanted to film, starring Cary Grant against type. 'He brings his wife a fatal glass of milk. She knows that she is going to be killed, so she writes a letter to her mother: "I'm in love with him, I don't want to live anymore, he's going to kill me, but society should be protected." Folds the letter up, leaves it by the bed, says, "Would you mind mailing that for me?" She drinks the milk, he watches her die. Last shot of the picture is Cary Grant whistling very cheerfully, going to the mailbox and popping in the letter. But that was heresy, to do that to Cary Grant in those days . . . I wasn't in charge at that time. I had to be more or less compromising. I was loaned out to RKO by Selznick and they had the whole thing set up.'

And so, according to Hitch, the studio would not allow the role of a killer to be played by Cary Grant, who had specialised in romantic comedies and whose fans would not accept him in so unsympathetic a role.* This admixture of the sinister with Grant's appeal was, of course, precisely what Hitch had wanted to exploit. RKO's refusal to allow this (Hitch said) was just like the situation with Ivor Novello in *The Lodger*: in both cases, front-office interference ruined a good movie.

Of course, well might we ask why should Cary Grant *not* have appeared in such a role? After all, Robert Montgomery, also best known on stage and screen for romantic comedies, had recently played a lunatic killer in *Night Must Fall*. In that case, MGM did not insist on altering the play and substituting a happy ending; in fact, in the bargain, Montgomery received a best actor Oscar nomination. But apparently RKO could not be persuaded to risk Grant in an unsympathetic role.

For the leading lady, Hitch was eager to have the French star Michèle Morgan, in her American debut. But *Rebecca* had made Joan Fontaine a major Hollywood presence, and RKO borrowed her, too, from Selznick, for the role of the wife. This was to be a variation on her role of the beleaguered girl in *Rebecca*, except that she is a far

---

* During the course of his forty-five-year career in seventy-three movies, Cary Grant appeared with (among others) Jean Arthur, Tallulah Bankhead, Ethel Barrymore, Constance Bennett, Joan Bennett, Ingrid Bergman, Leslie Caron, Doris Day, Marlene Dietrich, Irene Dunne, Joan Fontaine, Kay Francis, Jean Harlow, Audrey Hepburn, Katharine Hepburn, Grace Kelly, Deborah Kerr, Carole Lombard, Sophia Loren, Myrna Loy, Marilyn Monroe, Ginger Rogers, Rosalind Russell, Ann Sheridan, Eva Marie Saint, Sylvia Sidney, Shirley Temple, Mae West and Loretta Young. But not Greta Garbo.

more disturbed little rosebud in *Suspicion*. She is also photographed even more beautifully, which is part of the movie's problem: the wife is a wealthy young thing, and when transformed by love, she becomes more splendidly coiffed and dressed as the picture progresses. This makes it difficult for some viewers to accept an important part of the film: her unbalanced emotional life, an extreme of love that is ultimately fatal.

Typically, Hitchcock's marker of this transformation was his subtle but unmistakable insistence on eyeglasses for his leading lady. In the opening train-compartment scene, Lina's repression is signified not only by her body language but also by her unattractive spectacles. Similarly, Madeleine Carroll's eyeglasses, in her first scene of *The 39 Steps*, fall to the floor when Donat kisses her. Ingrid Bergman wears eyeglasses during her first scenes of *Spellbound*, but once she develops an interest in Gregory Peck – no more of them. Hitch fitted Kay Walsh for eyeglasses in *Stage Fright*; Laura Elliott and Pat Hitchcock had them for *Strangers on a Train*; and Barbara Bel Geddes wore eyeglasses for her role in *Vertigo*. Hitch even insisted that Carol Stevens, his Hollywood secretary and business manager, choose four or five pairs of eyeglasses especially designed for her by a studio optician. 'If I came on the set without my glasses on,' she recalled, 'it irritated the devil out of Hitch. He had a fetish about glasses.' But then he often ordered her to take them off.

What seems to be behind all this? For Hitch, the removal of eyeglasses of course discloses a partially concealed beauty, but the gesture can also render the wearer vulnerable and somewhat isolated, removed from a situation. The glasses, in other words, become Hitch's modern version of the Venetian mask – a kind of prop that both conceals and reveals.

The screenplay had a tangled history. Various scenes were written, sometimes filmed, then removed, then reinserted elsewhere, and different endings were discussed, occasionally filmed and then re-edited. All this has been painstakingly researched more than the texts of any other Hitchcock picture. The project was in a state of chaos even when filming began in February 1941, and all during production, no one was quite sure how the picture would end. This is not a rare dilemma in moviemaking; another example is *Casablanca*, bedeviled by precisely the same situation a year later.

What is clear is that the first draft of the screenplay, and most of what ultimately remained, was written by Samson Raphaelson, author of *The Jazz Singer*, a playwright and screenwriter who had written (among other highly regarded projects) several brilliant scripts for Ernst Lubitsch. According to some scholars, Hitch asked Raphaelson's approval to give on-screen credit to Alma, who was also being paid by RKO. Generously, Raphaelson acquiesced. Hitchcock pressed on, asking if Joan Harrison could also have screenplay credit, which she needed to get other jobs, as she was planning to leave Hitch and strike out on her own. Raphaelson agreed to that, too. Hence the final credits for *Suspicion*:

Screen Play by
Samson Raphaelson
Joan Harrison
Alma Reville

'Hitchcock's material was never very close to mine,' Raphaelson reflected years later. 'I was more comfortable with Lubitsch's style and tone. After I was off the project, Hitch had Alma and Joan work on it, and perhaps this [joint effort] as much as studio interference explains why the picture has less of the Hitchcock insignia than any of his pictures – there's no distinguishing scene of the kind for which he's famous.' And given the changes in studio management that season, the vigilance of the censors, the pressure of Cary Grant's fans and the endless rewrites, it was perhaps inevitable that *Suspicion*, in its final form and as we have it, is not an entirely satisfying picture. Nevertheless (whether by design or accident may never be known), it is, in the last analysis, a movie with a fascinating, distorted treatment of romantic love that was unusual for Hollywood in 1941 – and just the sort of thing that also intrigued the director.

The story was made more complex than the novel, if not more credible. Lina McLaidlaw (Fontaine) is the shy daughter of proper and wealthy country gentlefolk (Sir Cedric Hardwicke and Dame May Whitty) who presume Lina is destined for spinsterhood. But she precipitously elopes with the reckless playboy Johnnie Aysgrath (Grant). Aware of his immaturity, his spendthrift habits, his laziness and his irresponsibility – and eventually convinced that he is guilty of more serious crimes of theft – she nevertheless readily forgives him every time she is confronted with his felonies and lies, for she fears, most of all, that she will lose his love. From this obsession she is not deterred, even when she believes he plans to murder her for her money. But she is wrong about his killer instincts, and at the end it seems as if the couple may rebuild a relationship, after all.

Hitch always claimed that his intention even toward the end of filming was that the glass of milk (highlighted by a light bulb inside the glass) contained poison that she would drink – hence the letter she had written (as in the novel) implicating him, which he un-wittingly posts as she dies. The changed ending, as we have it, with the couple surviving and Lina's suspicions revealed as a chain of neurotic imagination, was not what Hitch wanted but what audiences wanted and RKO gave them. And yet sometimes, in important interviews, he gave the impression that he knew from the beginning that he would be denied his intention and so concocted alternatives. When, for example, François Truffaut asked him if Cary Grant would have refused the role of a murderer, Hitch replied, 'No, not necessarily. But the producers *would surely have refused* [emphasis mine].' As late as 1972, he said, 'The whole subject of the film is the woman's mind – is my husband a murderer?' His remarks suggest that Hitch knew from day one that he would have to provide an ending different from his pref-erence – and he did.

Yet there was evidently another ending screened for a preview audience in Hollywood, and these viewers had rejected it – the woman's acceptance of death-for-love was hooted, and they resented the over-turning of Cary Grant's amiable public image. And so was inserted the last-minute ending in which it is revealed that Johnnie was plan-ning not to kill Lina but himself, but he knew that this was too cowardly a way out of his troubles. He was, therefore, going to deliver her to the care of her mother and then return alone to face the consequences of his crimes. But the final image – a rear viewpoint of Johnnie and Lina driving home in their open roadster – is highly ambiguous, as they seem to return to life as it was. (By the time this last shot was filmed, the leading actors were off the picture and stand-ins were used who are very obviously not Joan Fontaine and Cary Grant.)

Nothing seemed to go right during production. Cinematographer Harry Stradling (who had photographed *Jamaica Inn* and *Mr and Mrs Smith*) had been assigned by RKO to work simultaneously on another

75

project. Informed of this, Hitch stormed into the office of RKO's executive producer Harry Edington and threatened to stop directing unless he could be guaranteed Stradling's undivided collaboration. 'I have a raving maniac on my hands with Hitchcock!' wrote Edington to a colleague. A week later, Stradling was removed from the second picture and turned over to a still pouting Hitchcock.

The problems multiplied. The lack of an ending threw the actors into confusion, for no scene had a sure purpose. For the first time in years, Hitchcock then fell ill, and shooting was suspended for a week. He returned exhausted and depressed, and Fontaine felt that he was uninterested in her as well as the picture. 'Hitchcock does not appear to be giving as close attention to this picture as he should be,' one of Edington's staff reported, 'and we have good cause to worry. As a matter of fact, Joan Fontaine has indicated that Hitchcock has not been so exacting on his requirements for her as he was on *Rebecca*.'

In addition, Fontaine and Grant were not friendly. 'The scenario,' she wrote in her autobiography, 'was one Cary felt would give him a serious acting role – unlike the comedies he'd been making, such as *The Awful Truth* and *Bringing Up Baby*.' She praised his professionalism, his timing, his technical expertise. 'The only mistake he made on *Suspicion* was not realising that the part of Lina was the major role. It was through her eyes that the story unfolded. She had all the sympathy. He was the villain. Cary found this out halfway through the shooting schedule. That, plus Hitchcock's "divide and conquer" technique created . . . tension on the set.' She also recalled Hitch's 'habit of saying "this silly old actor over there", or "that idiot", or whatever it was, and [he] probably did the same about me.'

Much of the tension certainly derived from Grant's unpleasant insistence that Fontaine was 'stepping in [his] lights', which would obscure or overshadow him – an objection that rightly puzzled her, for Stradling and Hitchcock knew what they were doing, and the actress was unable to do such a thing even had she so desired. But Grant could not be dissuaded from his unjustified apprehension: as his authorised memoirist has written, he 'did not feel the rapport with his co-star, Joan Fontaine, that he had with Rosalind Russell or Irene Dunne' on earlier pictures. To muddy the waters further, it was understandable that Fontaine was anxious: although her stock had risen after *Rebecca*, she had not worked on another movie from the autumn of 1939 until she began *Suspicion* in 1941.

Typically, Grant frequently contradicted himself (and Hitch) about *Suspicion* in later years. Sometimes he seemed to have been in favour of Hitchcock's original intention; sometimes he was convinced that it would have been impossible. 'I thought the original was marvellous. It was a perfect Hitchcock ending. But the studio insisted that they didn't want to have me play a murderer.' And contrariwise: 'But I'm sure I didn't do it. My character wasn't that sort of chap at all. He couldn't possibly have murdered her. My character was a rogue, not a rat.'

There is no accounting for public taste, nor can predictions ever indicate the final reception of any entertainment. By early autumn 1941, the movie was complete, a November release date was set, everyone was nervous, and Hitch was ready to disclaim the picture. One New York critic wrote that *Suspicion* was 'far finer than *Rebecca* . . . Hitchcock has made another brilliant film.' Others were not completely enthusiastic: 'The ending is not up to Mr Hitchcock's usual style,' wrote the influential Bosley Crowther in the *New York Times*. 'Still, he has managed to bring through a tense and exciting tale, a psychological thriller which is packed with lively suspense.' That was not generally the sort of encomium later lavished on *Suspicion*: even among Hitchcock's most ardent fans, a large proportion have always agreed with Cary Grant that it is the 'least satisfying' of his four films with Hitch – and, as well, less than first-rate Hitchcock.

Yet *Suspicion* was nominated for an Oscar as best picture of the year, and Franz Waxman for his musical score. Those awards went to others, but Joan Fontaine won the statuette as best actress of the year – an honour judged by many to be compensation for her loss in *Rebecca*. When she turned ninety, in 2007, she was living quietly in northern California, four marriages and her career long since over. Her abilities as an actress were perhaps never as refined or richly nuanced as those of her sister, Olivia de Havilland, who was nominated five times for Academy Awards and won twice. But Joan Fontaine was the only performer in a Hitchcock movie to win an Oscar.

No honours or nominations came to Hitch's next picture, *Saboteur*. This was a disappointing film whose occasionally thrilling sequences cannot make up for its cluttered story about fascists destroying American defence plants and generally planning countrywide havoc. The first of two pictures for which Selznick loaned Hitch to Universal

Studios, *Saboteur* was an obvious but futile attempt to repeat the pic-aresque structure of *The 39 Steps*, but Hitch and his writers (Peter Viertel, Dorothy Parker and Joan Harrison) somehow could not make things work. John Houseman, by now associated with Selznick, went over to Universal with Hitch as a de facto but transient producer.

'I had heard that he was an unappealing man who told filthy stories and cultivated his image as a gourmet and wine connoisseur,' according to Houseman. 'But there was more to Hitch than that. He was also unusually sensitive, and everyone who worked with him found him amusing as well as a brilliant moviemaker. Some of his sarcasm may have owed to the fact that Hitch was still in revolt against the British class system. He was certainly one of the most gifted directors, and I can think of no other filmmaker who was so exquisitely prepared for the day's work.'

For his leading actors, Hitch had hoped to have Gary Cooper and Barbara Stanwyck, who had been a successful team in Frank Capra's *Meet John Doe*. 'But I had to take [Universal's contract player] Priscilla Lane, a blonde who wasn't the right type for a Hitchcock picture. And I was also handed Robert Cummings, who has a comedy face, and so you don't believe the situations.' *Saboteur* was completed in February 1942, and the memory of it always evoked Hitch's criticism. With a weak script and scant interest in his actors, he accumulated scenes, took refuge in a series of jokes, and devised cinematic tricks like the villain's fall from the Statue of Liberty.

By the time the movie was released that spring, Alfred Hitchcock had been told a story that would provide him with the basis of his first American masterwork – and, into the bargain, he would cast a leading lady he not only admired but very much loved.

Gordon McDonell, the husband of one of Selznick's story editors, told Hitch about a 1939 news story concerning a serial killer of rich widows. 'Uncle Charlie', as he called his fictionalised version of the idea, was just an outline for what McDonell planned as a novel about the title character, a homicidal maniac who hides from the police with his sister's family, only to be found out by his beloved niece. Hitch asked the producers at Universal to hire the playwright Thornton Wilder, for he correctly reasoned that the author of *Our Town* would provide the necessary sense of small-town American life. Together, they scouted locations in northern California and expeditiously concocted a masterful first draft script, to which (when Wilder went off to military service after a six-week collaboration) Sally Benson, Patricia Collinge and Alma Hitchcock made subsequent contributions.

Casting was completed in July 1942 for what was now known as *Shadow of a Doubt*. 'This was my father's favourite picture,' Patricia Hitchcock O'Connell said in 2001. But once again, she misrepresented his judgement: 'I wouldn't say that *Shadow of a Doubt* is my favourite picture,' Hitchcock firmly told Truffant.

He assigned the role of the chillingly elegant, apparently kindly but sociopathic Uncle Charlie to tall, courtly Joseph Cotten, who had recently appeared in *Citizen Kane* and *The Magnificent Ambersons*. On advice from Thornton Wilder, the director then asked Universal to borrow Teresa Wright, at that time under contract to Samuel Goldwyn.

Muriel Teresa Wright was born in New York City in 1918 and raised in Manhattan and suburban New Jersey. Her parents separated when she was a child, and she was shuttled from one relative to another. Occasionally she bought a cheap seat for a theatre performance, and at Christmastime 1935, she went with a school group to see Helen Hayes on Broadway in *Victoria Regina*. 'I was seventeen, and although I had seen plays and even acted in a few at school, the idea of being an actress had never occurred to me until that Saturday matinée. From that day, I knew – I felt that my life was being shaped, even while I was on the train going home that evening,' she said years later. (Informed that there was an actress named Muriel Wright, she abandoned her first name professionally.)

In early 1938, when she was nineteen, Thornton Wilder and producer-director Jed Harris selected Teresa to understudy the leading role of Emily Webb in *Our Town* – a part she ultimately assumed when the play toured. She was back in New York in the autumn of 1939, appearing in the historic comedy *Life With Father*, which eventually ran for 3,224 performances and eight years. The senior drama critic of the *New York Times* praised her as an actress of 'uncommon charm and willowy skill'.

Things happened quickly. Lillian Hellman, on the lookout to recommend players for important roles for the upcoming screen version of her hit play *The Little Foxes*, saw *Life With Father* and contacted producer Samuel Goldwyn. Before the end of 1940, Teresa had left Broadway and was preparing for her movie debut as Alexandra Giddens, opposite the formidable Bette Davis, who admired and befriended her.

At the same time, Goldwyn signed Teresa to a contract. But she was wary of certain movie-star traditions and, politely but firmly, she stipulated what she would and would not do as a player in the Goldwyn Studios game. Her requirements simultaneously ridiculed the absurdities of the Hollywood publicity machine.

'I will not pose for publicity photographs in a bathing suit – unless I'm doing a water scene in a picture. I will not be photographed on the beach with my hair flying in the wind, holding aloft a beach ball. I will not pose in shorts, playing with a cute cocker spaniel. I will not be shown happily whipping up a meal for a huge family. I will not be dressed in firecrackers for the Fourth of July. I will not look insinuatingly at a turkey on Thanksgiving. I will not wear a bunny cap with long ears for Easter. I will not twinkle for the camera on prop snow, in a skiing outfit, while a fan blows my scarf. And I will not assume an athletic stance while pretending to hit something or other with a bow and arrow.' Perhaps to everyone's astonishment, Goldwyn acceded to her demands.

Those who worked with Teresa in the theatre, movies and television over her long career were unanimous: her warm and unassuming manner, her humour and gift for mimicry, her unassailable professionalism and enormous kindness were accompanied by an admirable toughness when that was required. Nor was her career impeded by her pellucid beauty, flawless alabaster skin, expressive blue eyes and a radiant, unaffected smile. When *The Little Foxes* was released in the summer of 1941, director William Wyler (not a man for hyperbole) described her as the most gifted and promising young actress he had ever met; he directed her twice more, always insisting he would have liked to multiply those collaborations.

But Teresa did not want to abandon her stage career, and during the summer of 1941, she starred in Molnar's *The King's Maid* at the Bass Rocks Theatre in Gloucester, Massachusetts. Her co-star was Karl Malden, who was also commencing a long and distinguished career; Teresa counted him and his wife Mona among her lifelong friends.

Wyler's judgement was impeccable. The Academy nominated Teresa as best supporting actress for her debut in *The Little Foxes*, and the following year, she was nominated in two categories – as best actress in *The Pride of the Yankees* and again as supporting actress in Wyler's *Mrs Miniver*, for which she won. After less than a year in Hollywood, Teresa was receiving more than ten thousand fan letters a week and was (thus the Associated Press) 'the best actress Hollywood has stolen from Broadway in a good many years.'

Precisely because she projected a rare, unsentimental sincerity and suggested a credible core of strength and purpose, Hitchcock considered for *Shadow of a Doubt* no other actress for the role of Charlotte 'Charlie' Newton. 'When he invited me in to talk about *Shadow*,' Teresa said, speaking of their first meeting in June 1942, 'it was as if he had finished the picture – he had it completely in his mind even before we began. And every sound effect had a reason. If a character was strumming his fingers on a table, for example, it wasn't just an idle gesture – Hitch put a beat to it, like a musical pattern, a sound refrain. If someone was walking or rustling a paper, tearing an envelope or whistling, or if there was a flutter of birds or some outdoor sound – Hitch orchestrated everything carefully.' She recalled, too, his endless word games and puns for the entertainment of the cast and crew. His ideal production company, he said, would consist of a leading lady named Dolly Shot; a leading man called Ward Robe; a villain, Mike Shadow; a German spy known as Herr Dresser; a character designated as Mae Kupp; a cameraman, Otto Focus; a child actress named Fay Doubt; the cutter, Eddie Tor; the designer named Art Director. This was not sophisticated humour, but he loved it.

'I got on very well with Teresa,' Hitch told me in November 1975, when we first discussed some of his important leading ladies; it was as if he were surprised by the memory. 'She was easy to work with, and she made no demands. She seemed very happy.' In fact, that May (just before she met Hitch, and two months before the start of filming), Teresa had married the writer Niven Busch. She was twenty-three, a seasoned professional and neither naïve nor prudish; nevertheless, she sometimes did not know how to react when Hitch – just before he called 'Action!' – whispered something utterly obscene to her, 'usually,' as she recalled, 'having to do with a young bride on a honeymoon.' Hitch also could not resist muttering inappropriate comments about her husband, who was fifteen years her senior. But she coped by simply smiling, as if she did not understand, or as if the remarks were the politest kinds of compliments – hence she deflected what could have been fairly embarrassing.

This was not, of course, the first time Hitch indulged in verbal mischief with a leading lady. Perhaps most of all, he wanted a reaction, a sudden expression of dismay before a certain difficult, emotional scene; such tactics are not unusual among those in charge of actors, singers or dancers. But he was also on a lifelong mission to shock, in person as in art. In this regard, Hitch's professional garb, invariably a suit, white shirt and tie; his calmness during the work day; his refusal to shout or cause a fracas; his deliberate air of bourgeois respectability – all this contrasted with unexpected explosions of the crudest, rawest kind of language.

Shadow of a Doubt offers a virtual textbook in extraordinary film acting. The film was, of course, shot out of sequence – all the location exteriors in Santa Rosa, then the interior studio work in Hollywood. This made especial demands on the estimable Teresa Wright, who created a portrait of a girl enduring a kind of moral education. Not yet twenty-four during filming, she demonstrated in every sequence a natural suppleness of understanding, so that the character's ordeal seems both shocking and inevitable. Her appeal, her credulity and her authentic sweetness are never cloying, her charm never artificial.

In her scenes with veteran performers Henry Travers and Patricia Collinge (as her parents), she is such an acute listener that one listens with her – hence our identification with young Charlie deepens. Opposite the pliant lure of Joseph Cotten – with whom another ingénue might have seemed diminished because his role is so strongly idiosyncratic – Teresa Wright allows the maturing of a young woman to emerge without forcing the issue. This is a lesson in nuanced, exquisitely rendered characterisation. Present in almost every sequence, she gives this masterwork very much of its coherence, force and complexity.

Uncharacteristically, doubtless because he was genuinely fond of her, Hitch followed the chain of successes that accompanied Teresa's later career. Appearing in almost one hundred films and television dramas, she was sought by and worked with directors Fred Zinnemann, George Cukor, Richard Brooks, Francis Ford Coppola and others, and she was chosen to be the leading lady in Marlon Brando's first movie. Her stage work encompassed classic plays by Shakespeare and Ibsen, and modern works by William Inge, Arthur Miller, Eugene O'Neill, Tennessee Williams, Clifford Odets, and Teresa's second husband, Robert Anderson.

'She had a genius for decency,' as one critic wrote, 'and a gentleness of spirit that has gone out of style. Hitchcock often ravished his actresses with horrified open-mouthed reaction shots, but here [in *Shadow of a Doubt*], he was satisfied to let Wright play almost the entire progression of niece Charlie's tragedy in her eyes and face.'

In her fifties and sixties, Teresa was remarkable for the assistance, encouragement and support she gave to young actors, writers, students and scholars. She seemed never to be too busy for her legion of fans and friends, to whom she was utterly devoted. In 1997, when she was seventy-eight, she appeared in what turned out to be her last movie (Coppola's *The Rainmaker*), whose young stars – Matt Damon and Claire Danes – very quickly came to love and admire her. During her calls from location shooting in Memphis, she told me how thrilled she was to be working with Coppola, and with such a serious and gifted cast. 'Matt and Claire are so dear and so full of energy!' she said. 'They give us hope for the future of the movies. And Francis has us all together like a family reunion.'

Teresa Wright died of a heart attack on 6 March 2005, at the age of eighty-six. We had spoken by phone the previous evening, when she was in high spirits, her voice warm, youthful and enthusiastic, as always. 'It has been chilly,' she said, 'but I think the first spring flowers are about to bloom in our garden. Already there are robins here, and daffodils are peeping out – do come and visit!'

7

From Raw Stuff to Poetry
(1943–1944)

After a year of script preparation and pre-production, Hitch's next picture was finally ready to roll at the Twentieth Century-Fox Studios in late August 1943. He set himself a daunting challenge, and the resulting movie is something of a curiosity – all the action occurs in the eponymous *Lifeboat*. Based on an idea by John Steinbeck and developed by several writers, the narrative presents a motley crew of wartime survivors, cramped onto a space only a little larger than a canoe in the middle of the Atlantic Ocean. An enormous studio tank was constructed, into which the cast had to climb by ladders, and there was generous use of rear projection films of sea, sky and storms.

'We were always falling in and out of the water,' recalled actor Hume Cronyn. 'We were covered with crude oil, and when we finished a scene there might be an hour or so of waiting time for a new camera setup. We were soaking wet, there were wind fans and water-spraying machines, and then we waited under hot lights, were soaked again – and as a result, all of us in the cast came down with colds and sore throats, and some got even sicker.' In her memoirs, Tallulah Bankhead – the star of the picture – recalled that she was 'black and blue from the downpours and the lurchings. Thanks to the heat, the lights, the fake fog and submersions followed by rapid dryings-out, I came up with pneumonia early in November.'

Tallulah, then forty-one, was talented, audacious, brash and eventually self-destructive, a casualty of a strange promiscuity, of alcoholism and drug addiction. After a childhood spent with her Southern family (which boasted several members in the United States Congress), she achieved great success on the London stage in the 1920s. Subsequently she played the leading roles in the Broadway productions of *Dark Victory*, *Rain*, *The Little Foxes* and – just before she began work on *Lifeboat* – the new play by Thornton Wilder, *The Skin of Our Teeth*. She had also appeared in a dozen unremarkable films, none of them in the last twelve years. Hitchcock, and Fox's Darryl F. Zanuck, planned to capitalise on her bravado and make her a major wartime movie star.

Difficult, eccentric and unpredictable, Tallulah also had an indefinable star quality, and her baritone voice, raw sensuality and quick humour made her a unique personality in both her career and her social life. 'Have you ever been mistaken for a man on the telephone?' columnist Earl Wilson once asked her. Her immediate reply: 'No – have you?' Her lovers, according to herself and her biographers, were a legion of men and women. One day in New York, she spotted an ex-boyfriend she had not seen in eight years. Rushing up to him, she cried, 'I thought I told you to wait in the car!'

Of all her peculiarities, the most frequently documented was her exhibitionism: Bankhead thought nothing of completely disrobing at a party – her own or another's – and she routinely continued a conversation from the toilet, leaving the door wide open. Trouper though she was during the rigors of filming *Lifeboat*, Bankhead raised eyebrows in Hollywood as elsewhere. 'She had no inhibitions at all,' Hitch said. 'Now some people can take this, others can't.' He could, and he relished her bawdiness and swapped filthy stories with her on the set. But things reached critical mass when Tallulah, drenched like all the players, grew tired of changing her underwear so often. 'We all had to climb ladders to get up into this boat,' Hume Cronyn recalled,

> and to avoid getting her dress wet, she cinched it up above her waist – and there she was, stark naked, no underwear, and exposed for everyone to see. This got to be her regular procedure! One day, a lady journalist from *Good Housekeeping* [magazine] visited the set, and she was outraged. She went off to the front office and raised absolute hell – this was a disgrace, everything she had heard about Hollywood was true, and so forth and so on. Well, the head of publicity at Fox came down to the set and told the

unit manager, 'Look, this has got to stop. You get Miss Bankhead to wear some underclothes or else we close the set. And if we close the set, it's a damn nuisance, because we lose major publicity for the picture.' The unit manager wouldn't risk going near Tallulah with this objection, so he went to Hitch and asked him to speak to her. But Hitch said, 'I always try to avoid getting involved in departmental disputes, and in a case like this it's hard to say where the responsibility lies. You might consider this is a matter for the wardrobe department, or perhaps for the make-up people – or maybe it's for hairdressing.' I don't think anyone ever got pants on Tallulah.

In every way, *Lifeboat* was a difficult and awkward production, and the troubles persisted when it was released in 1944. Some critics openly condemned it as anti-American, misperceiving the picture as an elevation of the Nazi ideal of the superman because the German played by Walter Slezak was inventive and intelligent – but he was also cruel, murderous and deceptive. There was wide astonishment when the film was nominated for three Oscars – including one for best director. No awards were handed out for *Lifeboat* at the Academy's rites of spring, but the nominations helped at the box office.

'I was under contract to Selznick, and so was Hitchcock – and one day at the studio, I just happened to be walking by, and Hitch said to someone, "Well, she could play in my next picture."' Years later, Ingrid Bergman was telling me how she met Hitch, and how they first worked together. It was typical of Ingrid not to exaggerate the circumstances, nor to describe just how important she and Hitch were to Selznick's fortunes; in fact, their meeting and eventual collaboration were not so dependent on mere accident during an afternoon stroll. She was Selznick's most valuable contract player, as Hitch was his most prestigious director. For significant profits, they had both been loaned out to other studios; now, Selznick was actively searching for a project for them to do together, which he could produce.

After his enormous successes with *Gone With the Wind* and *Rebecca*, Selznick had fallen into a clinical depression that was aggravated by both his manic work habits and dependence on various pills. By early 1944, he was regularly consulting a psychiatrist; so was the prolific screenwriter Ben Hecht. At the same time, Hitchcock happened to have the film rights to a 1927 novel he thought might become the basis for a picture to be produced by Selznick, written by Hecht and starring Bergman. He sold those rights to Selznick for a tidy sum, and the necessary deals were made with uncommon speed. But it took more than a year from the first work on the project to the premiere of what was ultimately called *Spellbound*, a title suggested by studio secretary Ruth Rickman.

The book was *The House of Dr Edwardes*, by John Leslie Palmer and Hilary Aidan St George Saunders (writing under the joint pseudonym Francis Beeding). This certainly did not seem suitable for either Hitch or Selznick – nor, indeed, for anyone else. It was a bizarre and complicated tale of witchcraft, satanic cults and murder, all of it set in a European lunatic asylum. But it could be substantially reworked to become a thriller in which a lady psychoanalyst solved a murder mystery and so saved the life of her patient, an innocent man suspected of a murder, with whom she falls in love. Selznick wasted no time in telling Ingrid that this was her next assignment.

Ingrid Bergman's life is often a study in courage and always a tapestry of high achievement. She had lost both parents before adolescence, was raised by relatives who either died or abandoned her, attended drama school in Stockholm and, after a successful career on stage and screen in Sweden, had come to America and to a Selznick contract in 1939. She had then appeared to great success in major films – *Intermezzo, Dr Jekyll and Mr Hyde, Casablanca, For Whom the Bell Tolls* and *Gaslight* (for which she won the first of her three Oscars). In early 1944, she was twenty-eight, highly esteemed by colleagues, admired by the press and idolised by an adoring public. Married to the dentist Petter Lindstrom, who was training to be a neurologist, Ingrid was supporting him and their six-year-old daughter, Pia. 'Lindstrom was terribly tough on Ingrid,' said their friend, the Swedish artist W. H. Dietrich. 'She returned from a day's work at the studio tired but happy, and Lindstrom said, "Well, are you going to do something worthwhile now?" Whatever she replied, he would say, "No, you should do such-and-such instead." I wondered how he could be that way with her – after all, he was not yet set up in practice, and she was bringing in all the money.' Then as throughout her life, Ingrid was committed to doing good work more than she was to amassing wealth, possessions and all the trappings and entrapments of celebrity.

Hitchcock and Hecht outlined their ideas to Selznick, who became, as he said, 'almost desperately anxious to do this psychological or psychiatric story.' Director and writer then visited various mental hospitals in and around New York (convenient to Hecht's suburban home, where they preferred to work), and then they sat down to compose the script – with Hitch, as Hecht observed, 'beaming amid his nightmares'. Hecht, with his experience of analysis, and Hitch, with his experience of loneliness and social isolation, created a new kind of psychological thriller about guilt and tortured romance – all of it interlaced with the images and atmosphere of nightmare.

As the first day of production approached in July 1944, Ingrid met her co-star, another contract player at the Selznick Studios – Gregory Peck, whose first movie was released in June. He was, as the saying went, groomed for stardom. But the script for *Spellbound* troubled Ingrid, who found incredible the mingling of professional psychiatric duty with romance. 'I won't do this movie because I don't believe the love story,' she announced. 'The heroine is an intellectual woman, a doctor, and an intellectual woman simply does not fall in love so deeply, so quickly.'

Selznick could simply have forced Ingrid into the role of Dr Constance Peterson without further ado, but he preferred her to warm to the idea, and so, to dispel her misgivings, he called a meeting with the director, writer and leading lady. Everyone likes a good love story, Hitch said at the outset, and if they wanted to commit to stern realism above all else, they ought to make documentaries. This argument did not carry nearly as much weight for Ingrid as Hitch's thoroughgoing professionalism and his ability to charm her even as he spun the complexities of the plot. As he did, Ingrid sensed the flow of the entire picture. She had admired the bold darkness of *Shadow of a Doubt*; now she understood that the unusual love story and the technical innovations would provide much of the uniqueness of *Spellbound*. In addition, she was fascinated with their plans to have brilliantly disturbing dream sequences designed by Salvador Dalì.

At this point in the meeting, Selznick was called away. 'Don't worry about the psychiatric jargon,' Hitchcock then whispered conspiratorially to Ingrid. 'Just remember, audiences don't know much about that.' He was on the mark: Freud had died only five years earlier, and talk of guilt complexes, father-fixations and dream symbolism was not in common currency, however much it had been fancied by some writers. Hence, what had initially appeared to Ingrid as a simplistic conclusion to the thriller aspect of *Spellbound* could be made fresh and fascinating. It was a lovely story with unexpected twists and turns and (as she later said) 'that touch of art.'

'Before we began to shoot the picture, he invited me and my husband to dinner at his home,' Ingrid recalled.

> He had just bought the house [in Bel-Air] and they were still putting up pictures and selecting fabrics for furniture. There were good food and wine, and after dinner, we rolled back the carpet and danced. I had the impression that Hitch was very exclusive and chose his friends very carefully. Cary Grant was there, and Teresa Wright and her husband . . . Hitch didn't mingle a lot with people – he was polite, but I think there was a little bit of the snob in him, and a fear of social rejection, too. He sat and told jokes and all that, but he wanted to be in control of things. If people got noisy, he would lower his voice – lower and lower until he was pretending he was talking but he wasn't. That's how he got silence, that's how he got people to pay attention to him.

Hitch's tactic for control of the situation was the same on the set of *Spellbound,* which began filming at the Selznick Studios in Culver City on 10 July – Ingrid's seventh wedding anniversary, which he honoured with a huge cake for the cast and crew at the end of the day's work. Everyone was in good spirits.

As usual, script problems arose during production – some from Selznick's interference, some from the effort to integrate Dali's angular, allusive designs, some from the unexpected accidents of filmmaking itself. Hitch may have been a bit surprised that Bergman and Peck took everything with absolute gravity, to the point of requesting discussions with him about scene and dialogue changes. 'Selznick treated his actors like little tin gods,' Peck said years later, 'but he was hard on directors. On the other hand, Hitchcock could be hard on actors, but he learned to take a tin-god producer in stride.'

Ingrid recalled just how the stride was achieved. 'When Selznick came down to the set to inspect progress, the camera suddenly stopped, and Hitch told him the cameraman couldn't get it going again – "I don't know what's wrong with it," he would say. "They're working on it, they're working on it." Finally, Selznick would leave, and miraculously the camera would start rolling again. After this happened a few times, David of course guessed what was going on. They were two strong men, but I think they really had great respect for each other.'

Selznick's respect for Ingrid was another critical element. When he learned that she was sitting for still photos on *Saratoga Trunk* during May 1943, for example, he wrote to Joe Steele, his publicity director. The letter is important for details of Ingrid's professionalism:

> Ingrid is so extraordinarily cooperative that I think we must lean over backwards not to take advantage of her good nature or some day even her wonderful character will rear up and reach against us, just as happened with Garbo at Metro as the result of early lack of consideration of her by their publicity department.
>
> In all the years I have been in the picture business, I have never heard of a girl going through so tough a schedule as Ingrid has had in recent months, and even though this has been entirely by her own wish, I think it behooves us to be very sure that she at least gets her Sundays for rest and her child. *For Whom the Bell Tolls*, with its terribly difficult location trip, alone would have been enough to knock out any average person, and to cause them to absolutely require a rest. And it must be borne in mind that, by Ingrid's wish, she started *Bell Tolls* with literally not even a single day off following the completion of *Casablanca*. On top of this, she started *Saratoga Trunk* without any rest . . . and has worked for over ten weeks without one single day free – something I have never heard of before. I tried very hard to force rest days on Ingrid, but she wouldn't take them, and the very least we can do is to be certain that her Sundays are not cut into. It must also be borne in mind that Ingrid doesn't even take the one day off monthly that is the habit of feminine stars, once they achieve stardom – and as you know, some of them insist on two or three days.

This was the first of a trio of films in which Hitch directed Ingrid; it was also the beginning of a friendship that endured until his death thirty-six years later. However mutually rewarding professionally, it was deeply problematic personally, for Hitch fell passionately in love with her and nursed feelings she did not reciprocate. Ingrid respected his genius and had enormous filial affection for him – but there her sentiments ceased. This made their collaboration both a great joy and a painful trial for them both.

Throughout her personal and professional life, Ingrid Bergman was attracted to intelligent, artistic, dynamic men with good humour and a zest for life – these were qualities she found more appealing than mere good looks. (Later, she had romances with musician Larry Adler and photographer Robert Capa, who could hardly be described in terms of movie-star glamour.) From the first meeting with Hitchcock, she found him irresistible as mentor and father figure, for he put her at ease, explained things clearly but without condescension, and appreciated her European sensibility. She laughed easily, she was charmingly flirtatious, and she liked a good martini at the end of the day. Hitch, alas, mistook her buoyant camaraderie as amorous, and her response as identical with his: he was quickly smitten like a schoolboy. That summer of 1944, *Spellbound* began, as did a tangled, disturbing and finally touching relationship.

'It was sometimes not easy for me,' she said quietly many years after his death,

> because I had to keep things light and not [allow him] to get too serious. This led to some disagreements during *Spellbound*. One day, I said, 'Oh, Hitch, I don't think I can give you that kind of emotion in this scene.' He took me aside for a few moments and told me a story of a man who worked behind the scenes in Hollywood studios. He knew that everything is fake – the beauty is fake, the hair is fake, the teeth are fake, even the food is not what it looks like. So one day he goes to the studio restaurant and asks for a cup of coffee and a piece of pie, and the server says to him, 'I'm sorry, sir, but we're out of pie.' And the man answers, 'Well, then, fake it!' And that was his answer to me when I told him I couldn't do such and such a scene, or I couldn't give him that emotion or walk this way, or whatever was my objection. He sat and listened patiently, and just when I thought I'd won him over to my viewpoint, he said very sweetly, 'Ingrid, fake it.' And that's how he got what he wanted. Usually, of course, he was right.

When they first met for story conferences, Hitch had been fascinated by Ingrid's agile mind and willingness to learn, but by the time they were filming, he was like a helpless romantic. He directed her with wit and tenderness, he provided explanations for her, and he told amusing stories; more to the point, he promised that he would star her in his next picture, which of course was not within his power to provide.

To Gregory Peck, Hitch was markedly different. 'He really didn't give me very much direction,' Peck recalled, 'although I was so inexperienced I felt I needed a good deal of direction. In answer to my questions about mood or expression, he would simply say that I was to drain my face of all expression and he would then photograph me. I wanted more than that – the business was so new to me. But whereas he didn't give me direction, he did give me a case of wine when he found out I was a novice about wine – he was more than willing to improve my education in that regard.'

Leonard Leff rightly noted that 'although Hitchcock meticulously sculpted the performances of many youthful or untrained actresses, he could neglect actors. His superior pose and his preference for medium and close shots over the master shots that gave performers their bearings in a scene could strain relations between director and actor. And if Hitchcock did not like an actor, he could prove alternately sarcastic and distant,' which he certainly was, if only occasionally, with young Gregory Peck.

Regarding Ingrid, Peck was puzzled: 'She was marvellous to work with, but whenever he was with her, I had the feeling there was something ailing him, and it was difficult to know exactly the cause of his suffering, although some of us had our suspicions.'

'Sometimes, to irritate us,' Ingrid told me, 'Hitch said, "Well, all my fun is over now that you actors are here." He insisted that most of his enjoyment was in the preparation, the writing, the planning of camera setups – the fantasy of seeing the picture in his mind – and he regarded us actors as intruders into his fantasy. But he was always very controlled. He never lost his temper or screamed at anyone – yet he always got what he wanted.'

As for the actual direction: 'He watches what you're doing, he tells you what to do, and then he rearranges what he wants for information and stress and speed. Sometimes he acted something out – I have so many photographs of him doing that. He doesn't want you to imitate him, he wants to hear what the intonation is.'

★   ★   ★

A great part of his fantasy concerned his selection of leading ladies like Ingrid. 'He doesn't talk much about acting,' according to Ingrid. 'I think he chose Grace Kelly and Tippi Hedren because of what they looked like, the same with me.'

'I have to consider,' Hitch had said, 'whether she is the kind of girl I can mould into the heroine of my imagination,' and his imagination was amazingly, sometimes alarmingly fertile. About the time of the film's release, for example, Hitch began to tell an elaborate tale, forged in the workshop of his capacious imagination – a fantastic account of what, he said, happened one evening. After a dinner party at the Hitchcock residence, Ingrid supposedly refused to leave his bedroom until he made love to her. If this fiction were not so sad and pathetic, it would be amusing, but Hitch insisted it was the truth. He and Ingrid, so he believed with all his heart, would be the perfect couple, if only . . . if only – well, after all, as he wrote for her to say in *Spellbound*, 'We're all just bundles of inhibitions.'

Quite apart from the fact that their spouses were in the adjoining room, it would have been entirely out of character for Ingrid to behave this way with a man for whom her feelings were never erotic. 'Some people really believed his story,' she said years later, with compassion, and with a gentle, dismissive laugh. 'I never got angry when it came back to me. People will believe what they want to believe – Hitch, just like anyone else. I loved him, but not his way. Well, I wanted to keep his friendship, and I did.'

Indeed, Ingrid did nothing to foster Hitch's amorous inclinations, but, as so often, her restraint had the opposite effect on him. He was courtly and attentive on the set, but never effusive in the presence of others. Disallowing the emergence of his deepest feelings, he added – at the last moment – a telling bit of dialogue (hastily written in his own hand) for Ingrid and actor John Emery, who was playing a colleague whose infatuation, like Hitchcock's, she does not reciprocate:

DR FLEUROT (Emery): You're a sweet, pulsing, adorable woman underneath. I sense it every time I come near you.
CONSTANCE (Ingrid): You sense only your own desires and pulsations. I assure you, mine in no way resemble them.

Hitch took her caution for diplomacy, and so he redoubled his efforts to attach her permanently to his life. To that end, he spun the outlines of this and that story for them to make as films together; more than once, word of this got back to Selznick, who had politely to remind them that he had approval over their future projects.

Just as Ingrid had to live within a world of vivid imagination in order to create credible feelings for her characters, so the power of Hitch's films owed to his unassailable genius as a visual storyteller who worked with the raw material of his own fantasies. All objections notwithstanding, he had no other material with which to work than his daydreams and fantasies – and that, after all, must be said of every creative storyteller and artist; to maintain otherwise is to exhibit a profound ignorance of the creative process. Hitch could not leave himself at home when he went to a studio; had he been able to do so – and if those fantasies had not been more or less recognisable as human possibilities – then we would certainly not have the universally popular Hitchcock movies we have. His pictures are part of him and us: our response to them is, 'Yes, some of life is like this – and all of life is in danger of becoming like this.'

During his long creative life, he existed within a kind of prison. His frustrated passion for several of his leading ladies brought him great pain. The constant struggle with morbid obesity isolated him, making any kind of intimacy impossible; indeed, Hitch created the ultimate physical prison for himself. (During a year, beginning in late 1942, he had lost almost 100 pounds, but that loss did not make him a slender man: at less than five feet eight inches, 225 pounds was still a hefty number. By 1945, the weight was slowly going back on, and by 1951, he was again well over 300 pounds. He then went on another reducing plan, and by 1953 was back down to 200 – and then the reverse cycle continued, a sine curve of gain, loss and gain.)

It was precisely Hitch's separation from others that gave the world a legacy of great films. His art was realised in the kiln of a lifelong pattern of discontent, from which he often sought refuge at the table and the bar. Much of his despondency had to do with the fact that he seemed to long for romance and for true friendship but had the gift for neither – except in his fantasy life, and in this regard, he left a profound spiritual autobiography in his work.

Perhaps when his daughter Patricia denied this aspect of her father's character, as she regularly did after his death, she really (and rather poignantly) believed that there was no connection between Hitch's life and his art. Insisting that his movies had nothing to do with his own life, his own feelings, his own emotions – that they were merely stories – could she have been so acutely unaware of the constant connection that always exists between the storyteller and the story, however transmuted the story becomes?

'Hitch couldn't stand the interference from Selznick,' Ingrid told me. 'David would come down to the set, saying "Hurry up!" or "There are too many mistakes!" or "Don't the actors know their lines?" And he arrived with friends, which made it seem as if Hitch was incompetent.

'But dear Hitch had a way of dealing with this. He went into perfect double-talk. There were words, you could hear them, but none of it made any sense – it was his way of getting rid of Selznick. He'd say to me, so the producer could hear him, "Now, my dear, you see those lights . . ." and then he'd talk about a close-up or a long shot or a focus problem, and in between, there were words that made no sense at all – and you would just die laughing, because you knew what he was doing – driving them off the set, so he could get back to work!'

As the making of *Spellbound* proceeded, Ingrid told her family and friends how much she enjoyed working with her director: 'I have started my new movie,' she wrote in Swedish to her father-in-law on 3 August, 'and all is well. I'm playing a doctor, and this is different from the films I have acted in before. I like it that I can play different roles – and that is seldom done by actors in Hollywood. They usually play the same types over and over again until they die!' On 10 October, she wrote to him again: 'I finished my film, "Spellbound," and I believe it will be an interesting one. I really enjoyed working with Alfred Hitchcock, and I am so happy – it looks as if his next film will also be with me. It is a spy story.'

The enduring appeal of *Spellbound* does not derive from its complicated and incredible plot, but rather from the natural and understated performance by Ingrid Bergman and the vulnerable (if occasionally awkward) characterisation by Gregory Peck. In the delicacy of Ingrid's portrayal of Constance Peterson, in the way she turned her head, folded her hands or stifled an inchoate sob, there was virtually a textbook on allusive screen acting – much of it already part of Ingrid's equipment, and all of it endorsed by Hitchcock. Of all that she learned from him, the most valuable lesson was the significance of her close-up – a simple glance downward, or to the left or the right, could reveal an anxiety, thought, or sudden reflection. Underplaying – what Hitchcock bluntly referred to as 'not acting' – was something Ingrid instinctively comprehended. She did not require guidance, systematic-ally, through a scene: she understood from the first reading what was called for, and any modification was readily effected in a matter of moments, with few words.

Perhaps the most moving example of this occurs when her teacher, Dr Brulov (impeccably played by Michael Chekhov) bids Constance (Ingrid) farewell, and it seems that she has forever lost her beloved (Peck). 'It is very sad to love and lose somebody,' he says (just before the dénouement saves the situation). 'But in a while you will forget and you will take up the threads of your life where you left off not along ago. And you will work hard. There is lots of happiness in working hard – maybe the most.' There is enormous kindness here, and the scene became the perfect representation for the delicate rela-tionship between Ingrid and her director.

Once released, *Spellbound* never lost its popularity, even after its specifically psychiatric elements were parsed as flawed and simplistic. But Hitchcock correctly made a distinction between *psychological films* and *psychoanalytical films*. The latter, stories about illness, doctors, patients and treatment, he dismissed as 'a passing phrase.' But the assertion that he had no interest in *psychological films* can be made only by someone unfamiliar with Hitchcock's career, for human psychology fascinated him; indeed, his pictures are about little else.

'The psychological film is quite a different thing from the psycho-analytical,' he said as early as 1946. 'If, by psychological film, you mean a particular way of telling a story, by trying to get at the characters, then I think it is inevitable that the psychological approach to story will be employed more and more frequently as the screen comes of age.' (The screen came of age at least partly because of Hitchcock films like *Suspicion*, *Shadow of a Doubt*, *Notorious*, *Strangers on a Train*, *The Wrong Man*, *Vertigo*, *Psycho* and *Marnie*.)

Spellbound was a far greater success than anyone could have predicted: it cost $1.7 million to produce and grossed more than $7 million in its first release, thus making it one of the two or three most lucra-tive movies of the 1940s. It also received six Oscar nominations – for best picture, director, supporting actor, cinematography, special effects and musical score; only Miklos Rozsa won, in the last category. This was also the first American film in which Ingrid Bergman received star billing, and Selznick – perhaps to everyone's astonishment – officially called the picture 'Alfred Hitchcock's *Spellbound.*' So it appears in the opening credits, as Selznick said, 'because I think he is entitled to it . . . and due to the fact that Hitchcock secured such remarkable quality with such prompt efficiency and without the slightest set supervision on my part, either.'

8

Desires and Pulsations
(1945–1946)

Even before *Spellbound* was completed in October 1944, Selznick had passed along to Hitchcock and Hecht the basis of a story he wished to turn into a film. One of Selznick's story editors had found the germ of an idea in a piece of short fiction published in the *Saturday Evening Post* in 1921, but as usual, the finished film was different, richer, more complex, more disturbing, more appealing.

According to the earliest studio memoranda about the production, Ingrid was to portray a hard-drinking woman of easy virtue, carefully trained for an espionage assignment in which she is forced to marry a Nazi spy in order to smoke out a dangerous plot. The man she really loves, who has got her into this unattractive game of sexual blackmail, is afraid of her romantically even while he needs her professionally. This premise went through several development stages and was continually altered even during filming (from October 1945 until early February 1946) before it became – only in the final editing – an effective, coherent, taut and, into the bargain, a masterwork of motion picture entertainment.

Notorious, as it was titled, is a testament to Ingrid's enormous, subtle, wide-ranging and deeply affecting talent: never for a moment do viewers doubt they are watching a woman named Alicia Huberman. Ingrid gloried in playing a variety of women, and she was fortunate to have opportunities to do so even when Selznick loaned her out elsewhere for most of her pictures. Before her role as a psychiatrist in *Spellbound*, which was an enormous success and which she was of course delighted to have done, her American films had featured her as a dedicated teacher (in *Intermezzo*); a companion (in *Adam Had Four Sons*); a wife (in *Rage in Heaven*); a bewildered lover (in *Casablanca*); a brutalised girl who finds love amid political terrorism (in *For Whom the Bell Tolls*); an implacable adventuress (in *Saratoga Trunk*); the intended victim of a murderous thief (in *Gaslight*); and a highly unconventional, flesh-and-blood nun (in *The Bells of St Mary's*). The role of Alicia added still another very different jewel to her crown. In addition, her leading man was to be Cary Grant, back for his second Hitchcock movie and, in the role of intelligence agent T. R. Devlin, a role once again contrary to his image.

Notorious is the story of the wounded, cynical but lovesick Alicia and of the emotionally withdrawn Devlin, a man wondering how to become one – and of Devlin's rival, Alexander Sebastian (Claude Rains), who is betrayed by his devotion to Alicia. The element of espionage and its details are Hitch's MacGuffin – his excuse to spin a romance, a profoundly adult exploration of adult confusions. In retrospect, it is astonishing that this movie could be produced and released in 1946: it has blunt dialogue about government-sponsored prostitution; supposedly heroic American intelligence agents who advance the idea of sexual blackmail; and, for its heroine, a morally dubious woman who tries to redeem herself and is brutally exploited for the sake of political expediency. The moral murkiness and the implicit denunciation of American officials were unprecedented storylines in Hollywood circa late 1945, when the Allied victory in war had just inaugurated an era of understandable but ultimately dangerous chauvinism. The conventional wisdom was that the United States government alone was the world's hero and could never be tainted with scandal or corruption – but *Notorious* is not so sure of that.

Hitchcock did something behind the scenes that was atypical in his career thus far: he made Ingrid his closest collaborator on the picture. 'But Hitch,' she said one day, 'the girl's look is wrong in this shot. You have her registering surprise too soon. I think she would do it this way' – and with that, Ingrid did the scene again, her way.

There was not a sound on the set, for Hitchcock did not suffer actors' ideas gladly – he knew what he wanted, and what he did not want was interference from mere performers. But from Ingrid, there came forth some good ideas, and that day – to everyone's surprise – Hitch said, 'I think you're right.' That he was open to her ideas was even more surprising, perhaps because Ingrid was involved in an intermittent, episodic romance with the war photographer Robert Capa.

Hitch, doubtless aware by this time that his own chances with her were impossible, agreed to Ingrid's request that he engage Capa to be the publicity photographer on the set of *Notorious*. Capa took historic still photos of the party sequence, in which Ingrid furtively clasps the wine cellar key – a scene justly famous for its crane shot in which the camera descends without a cut from a vast overview of a grand foyer to a tight close-up of a key clutched in Ingrid's hand. This extraordinary moment was not simply technical wizardry devised by a clever director; it was, on the other hand, crucial for him to emphasise two levels of reality within a single image. The literal key to something dangerous lies within an impressive setting – one spatial continuum, in other words, contains a double reality, just as the expensive bottles of wine contain uranium ore, and just as (elsewhere in the film) affectionate gestures mask multiple realities.

Yet Hitch's engagement of Capa may not be so difficult to comprehend: many unrequited lovers try to please the object of their affections – and if they are going to suffer, they are often intent on real suffering. This, after all, is the core of the romantic fallacy, as the unrequited lover nurtures his anguish: history is gravid with the names of those whose personal pain nourished their public art in music, on canvas, in words and on film.

Seeing Ingrid with Capa must have been a kind of agony for Hitch, even though the photographer's contributions to the movie's publicity were invaluable. This triangular complex of emotions was itself a kind of scenario, alternately ruthless and touching. To make the situation even more byzantine, Ingrid's marriage to Lindstrom was effectively over. But the American movie-going public, who followed such things with religious intensity, read only the devotional articles served up in magazines and newspapers, and so they believed that her brilliant career was complemented by an ideal home life; in reality, she was miserably lonely in her marriage, from which she had sought refuge in a few extramarital affairs. A rueful smile may have crossed her face when she read in an interview that year, 'Miss Bergman just can't help being a good girl on the screen because that's the way she is.'

★   ★   ★

In August 1945, Ingrid turned thirty, but there was still a girlish, callow aspect to her personality; in some ways, she was not the worldly, contented woman the public regarded so highly. Her early life had been spent on unstable ground, with the deaths of her parents and of relatives before she was fourteen. By the time she married (at twenty-two), she was willing to rely entirely on her husband for life's practical decisions, so that she would be free to pursue work she loved. Uninterested in matters financial throughout her life, she readily left the management of them to her three husbands. At the time, then, her career was managed by Selznick and by her agents, all of whom were superintended by Petter Lindstrom.

Ingrid's refusal to prevaricate or to affect airs and graces endeared her to colleagues as much as to the press and public. If people placed her on a pedestal and adored her, the cult was of their own invention – to evoke their loyalty and support, she only worked (brilliantly) as an actress. Admirers prized her beauty more than Ingrid, who was never hesitant to appear plain for the truth of a role, and as she aged, she refused to cling to an unrealistic attitude about eternal youth. 'It's hard for me to find good roles,' she told me when she was fifty-seven, 'because I'm too old to play a young lover and too young to play one of those haggard old grandmothers. You might say I'm at that awkward, in-between stage.' In fact, she undertook the right roles for her age as long as she could work.

At first, marriage had brought her great consolation. Always attracted to intelligent, mature men rather than merely attractive and sporting types, she had found those qualities along with a kind of protective paternalism in Lindstrom, eight years her senior and a man of unassailable probity. But they were creatures of their time and culture, and a husband's supremacy was presumed, which Ingrid very soon resented. Once the Lindstroms had settled in America, she worked constantly to support herself, her husband and their daughter. Soon the marriage was troubled by Petter's overbearing domination of her and his interference in the business of her career. Ingrid's subsequent extramarital romances were not the cause of her irretrievably troubled marriage; they were in fact the result of a union already soured.

Perhaps to show her confidence in him, perhaps to short-circuit any intentions he had, and even to seek some guidance from one she always regarded as a mentor, Ingrid confided her private life to her director. Hitch loved to hear from her (and from others' more spicy and embellished versions) about her brief but intense affairs with Robert Capa, the musician Larry Adler and the director Victor Fleming. Her relations with these men blazed and cooled during the time Hitch and Ingrid collaborated on a trio of films.

Ingrid's liaisons ought perhaps to be regarded as those of a woman of significant inner resources who mimicked love in art but who felt deprived of it in life. It was not, I think, the mere convenience of sex that drew her to her lovers, it was their strong dispositions, their creative lives and their unique outlook, and their lack of any desire to control her. Capa, for example, with his keen eye and Gothic philosophical disposition, swept her away with his energy and his sheer desire for life. 'You have become an industry,' he told Ingrid. 'Your husband is driving you; the film companies are driving you; you let everybody drive you.' In a way, he was correct – but none of this 'driving' continued, for the present, without her cooperation. Capa did not want a life with her in Hollywood, but on the road, in places exotic and distant (especially wherever there was the high drama of war). He desired not the film star but the woman – but not for a wife, and this, along with his heavy drinking and a certain recklessness, put the brakes on the velocity of their affair.

Ingrid met the married musician Larry Adler when she went abroad to entertain troops during the war. 'I fell in love with her immediately,' he told me years later. Ingrid was, Adler thought, the least affected person he had ever met, and the most generous performer who came to the front. He also felt that she was not exactly right for the task: 'The boys wanted comic book humour, burlesque, raw stuff – and there was Ingrid, reading mostly from plays and poems.'

It was her seriousness and her respect for his musicianship that changed his life: 'If it wasn't for Ingrid, I would never have become a composer. She encouraged me to learn to read and write music, not just improvise.' Later, after studies with no less a figure than Ernst Toch, Adler became famous as the virtuoso of the harmonica, which he elevated to concert status. Darius Milhaud and Ralph Vaughan Williams, among other noted composers, wrote works especially for him, and Maurice Ravel was so impressed with his arrangement of the 'Bolero' for harmonica that he asked to keep the holograph as a souvenir. Adler also wrote film scores and played with many of the world's great symphony orchestras. Ingrid's and Larry's brief liaison very quickly became a platonic friendship, and this endured until her death.

Victor Fleming had directed many films (and completed *The Wizard of Oz* and *Gone With the Wind*) before Ingrid's heartbreaking performance for him in *Dr Jekyll and Mr Hyde*. 'By the time that film was over,' Ingrid recalled, 'I was deeply in love with Victor Fleming. But he wasn't in love with me. I was just part of another picture he directed.'

Fleming was a rough-and-tumble racing-car addict with a limited education but infinite arrogance, a craggy-handsome face and a reputation to rival Casanova's. He was also short-tempered. If a neighbour's whining cat or barking dog disturbed his sleep, he simply reached for a rifle and with one clean shot stopped the noise. Twenty-six years older than Ingrid, he was married and a father, but was evidently emotionally accessible only to drinking buddies like Clark Gable and Spencer Tracy. He ordered the word 'love' excised from his marriage ceremony and then, as further witness to his spirit of blithe convenience, refused to bring his wife into his home until she became pregnant a year later. After that, the hapless Mrs Fleming was alarmingly often the butt of sadistic manipulations: he treated her (according to their daughter Victoria) 'like a cat with a mouse'. Of all this Ingrid was unaware at the time.

Notorious, sold as a package by Selznick to RKO Studios when the producer became obsessed with his production of *Duel in the Sun*, re-established Cary Grant as a serious actor with hitherto unexplored depths.★ During production, Ingrid relied on Cary's friendly collaboration. His career was foundering when he was chosen for the part, a man almost pathologically afraid of women – a man who can kiss but not commit, who very nearly sends the heroine to her death. Unlike his experience with Joan Fontaine, Cary Grant worked harmoniously with Ingrid, and they formed a lifelong friendship; wild rumours to the contrary, there was no romance or affair.

In his quiet, proprietary manner, Hitchcock gave Bergman and Grant the impression that he virtually owned them – or at least had

★ Selznick received $25,000 a week from RKO for Hitchcock's services and $20,000 a week for Ingrid's; they, of course, received their usual salary from Selznick, which was slightly more than 10 per cent of those sums.

rented them for the time of his production. As with Fontaine, one way of establishing his primacy was (as Leonard Leff wrote) by 'dominating'. This is not an unusual quality among directors, who must always command respect and attention. But Hitch (as Fontaine said) divided in order to conquer. One day at RKO, before accompanying him to his trailer on the stage, his secretary Carol Stevens

> chatted with several studio employees. Later Hitchcock told her, 'You think everyone likes you – well, Cary Grant hates you!' Stevens reeled, then privately questioned Grant about the remark. 'Good heavens,' he replied, '*you* ought to know how possessive Hitch is!'

Hitch took special, whimsical pleasure in writing the three-minute balcony kissing scene in which Grant and Bergman nibble at one another's lips, ears and neck while talking about their supper plans. (When Ben Hecht saw the pages of dialogue, he told Hitchcock, 'I don't get all this talk about a chicken.') Devised by Hitch in an attempt to circumvent the Hollywood restrictions against prolonged kissing, the scene, he said, gave the public

> the great privilege of embracing Cary Grant and Ingrid Bergman together. It was a kind of temporary *ménage à trois*. I felt that they should remain in an embrace and that we should join them. So when they got to the phone, the camera followed them, never leaving the close-up all the way, right over to the door – all in one continuous shot. The idea came to me many, many years ago when I was on a train going from Boulogne to Paris. There's a big, old red brick factory, and at one end of the factory was this huge, high brick wall. There were two little figures at the bottom of the wall – a boy and a girl. The boy was urinating against the wall, but the girl had hold of his arm and she never let go. She'd look down at what he was doing, and then look around at the scenery, and down again to see how far he'd got on. And that was what gave me the idea. She couldn't let go. Romance must not be interrupted, even by urinating. [Grant and Bergman] told me they felt very awkward in that scene in *Notorious*. But I told them not to worry, it would look great on film, and that's all that mattered. It's one of my most famous scenes.

While filming *Notorious*, as Ingrid recalled, 'Hitch could be a little shocking sometimes. It wasn't so much what he said as how he said it and the moment he chose to say it — it was sometimes inappropriate, and people could feel embarrassed. But he was absolutely a genius.' The inappropriate remarks were generally of the schoolboy type, mixing a little British toilet humour with a risqué allusion.

Hitch was justifiably proud of the scene in which Ingrid goes to the office of the American intelligence agents in Rio to tell them that Claude Rains has proposed marriage and wants an answer before lunch. 'You might think,' Hitchcock told me in July 1975, 'that I would concentrate on the reactions of the men in the room — what they thought of the idea, what their expressions would be, and so forth. But I didn't do that. I kept the camera on Grant and Bergman, because it was their glances and expressions that carried the emotional weight of the scene. The other people in the room were incidental — what the audience needed to feel was the tension between Grant and Bergman. Would he break his silence? What did he feel about her? Here she was, wondering if he would let her do this — so I concentrated on close-ups of them and ignored the rest.'

Throughout, Ingrid was brilliant, and Hitch, who had few criticisms for her, routinely kept her a few moments at the end of the day's work. Never given to praise any actor, he offered her a drink, smiled and said, 'It was very good today, Ingrid — very good.' In fact, every day was good, and they both knew it, as would the critics. 'Ingrid Bergman's performance here is the best that I have ever seen,' wrote James Agee, who was not easily pleased, and the *Film Bulletin* summarised the critical consensus, praising 'Ingrid Bergman's brilliant portrayal, [which] again makes her a candidate for an Academy Award' (for which, amazingly, she was not even nominated — nor was anyone connected with this masterwork).

In any case, Ingrid was more concerned with the quality of her work than the accumulation of awards. 'I really don't know much about acting,' she said. 'As for my one year of [drama] school [in Stockholm], I'm sure I learned about using the voice, using the body, listening to others. But instinct is what I go on. The only thing I go for is simplicity and honesty, because if something isn't simple and honest, then it doesn't reach people. It's lost.' Regarding the role of Alicia in *Notorious*, she added, 'I like to portray characters whose lives have been irregular, or sometimes even a little abnormal – people who have been affected by unusual circumstances, or who have been reared in unusual environments.'

As for the undercurrent of tension between actress and director, she ensured that their friendship would remain intact, and she encouraged him to think of future projects for them to share. 'He was very exclusive with me all during production,' she said. 'All of us were like his pieces of chess on a board. As long as we held to our assigned place on the board, we had a lot of range – with our expression, for example. But if he thought we were getting something wrong, or going away from our place on the board, he said so at once. Hitch and I were good friends and worked very closely together. He was very controlled – he knew that he had to be, and that I had to be. The most awful things were going on for both of us in our lives, but he kept his temper. I never heard him raise his voice or yell or scream – even when I was stubborn and demanding!'

The basic concern of *Notorious* is a twofold redemption – a woman's need to be trusted and loved, which will enable her to transcend a life that has become empty of affection and riddled with guilt; and a man's need to open himself to love, which will enable him to overcome a life of severe emotional repression. Aptly, Hitchcock and Hecht chose to locate this romance about trust and its betrayal within the package of an espionage thriller, for spies are characterised by their exploitation of trust. Going one step further, the motif was represented in the image of drinking. Instead of standing for unity, toasting health or celebrating prosperity, all the drinking in *Notorious* is either socially empty or downright poisonous – thus the opening whiskey-soaked party; Alicia's pattern of camouflaging emotional rejection by pouring herself a drink; the ingredient for the bomb hidden within a wine bottle; and the poisoned coffee.

There is an actress in *Notorious* about whom little has been written in recent decades, but whose role is central to the picture; her performance is unforgettably, deliciously villainous. The mother of Claude Rains was to have been played by Ethel Barrymore, but she turned down the role. RKO then suggested Mildred Natwick. But the role of the spidery, tyrannical matron demanded a stronger, older presence. To the rescue came Reinhold Schünzel, who portrayed the surprisingly benevolent Nazi scientist of whom Alicia becomes genuinely fond. Schünzel, an actor and director perhaps best known for the original *Viktor Viktoria*, proposed one of the great actresses of pre-war Germany, Leopoldine Konstantin. Tall, aristocratic and speaking English with a clearly enunciated Teutonic accent, she was at the time fifty-nine years old, but audiences had no trouble accepting her as the mother of Claude Rains, who was fifty-six.

Konstantin came from a wealthy Austro-Hungarian family who were horrified when she expressed a yearning to go on the stage; in fact, they all but disowned her until she had triumphantly acted with Max Reinhardt's great Deutsches Theater. Her specialty was, of all things, light drawing-room comedy, in which she excelled and for which she was much loved and admired. Eventually, she formed her own touring repertory company and continued acting in films (which she had done since 1910, when she was twenty-four). In 1937, Konstantin fled Hitler and settled in Hollywood – and, she thought, into permanent retirement. When her only son died in a London air raid early in the war, she lost all interest in acting.

Hitchcock, frustrated in his search for the perfect 'Madame Sebastian,' heard that Konstantin was living quietly in Hollywood. He remembered seeing her onstage in Munich twenty years earlier, and he sought her out. Encouraged by friends and reassured by Hitch, she accepted the role. 'I almost frightened myself,' she recalled after completing the picture. 'Never before have I attempted such a role. When I saw it, I thought, "My God, I'm a female Boris Karloff! What will my friends ever think of me?"' Nothing at all like the role she played, Konstantin was a woman of quick wit and enormous warmth – and was so absolutely convincing in the role that (like Karloff) she feared losing friends and frightening children.

Notorious was her only American film. In the early 1950s, she returned to Austria, settled unpretentiously in Vienna, and died there in 1965, aged seventy-nine. Leopoldine Konstantin's single and singular performance in the picture won for her a richly deserved American legacy.

The final moments of the picture are remarkable for Hitchcock's ability to evoke power from camera movement, lighting and perform- ances. Perhaps rarely in the history of the movies has an actress been so delicately, adoringly photographed as Ingrid in the final bedroom scene. As a woman sick unto death, she was rendered in shadow and half-light. A radiant tenderness envelops her. Hitch disallowed any accompanying music for the scene, whose whispers and muted gestures lead to Devlin's final admission to Alicia that he loves her. 'Oh, you love me!' she whispers. 'Why didn't you tell me before?' As the camera encircles her and Grant, he replies, 'I was a fat-headed guy, full of pain. It tore me up not having you.'

It's usually easy, watching movies, to recognise the difference between, on the one hand, a director's aesthetic distance, a simple celebration of an actor's beauty, and, on the other hand, a deeply personal emotional involvement. The former attitude characterised, for example, the appreciative detachment of D. W. Griffith's approach to Lillian Gish and F. W. Murnau's to Janet Gaynor. But the senti-mental attachment was obvious in Josef von Sternberg's rendering of Marlene Dietrich, and Hitchcock's presentation of Madeleine Carroll and of Ingrid Bergman. In this regard, all the motifs of *Notorious*, and all the tangle of emotions that comprised the relationship between Alfred Hitchcock and Ingrid Bergman, coalesce in the final sequence, wherein he created perhaps the tenderest and most deeply felt love scene of his career.

Straight from the pages of a fairy tale – the Prince saves Sleeping Beauty – it remains every romantic's ultimate fantasy: to save the beloved from the jaws of death. That it remains so compelling many decades later is a tribute to the talents and sentiments of its director, his writer, his leading man – and perhaps most of all to Ingrid, the closest actor-collaborator in Hitch's career.

9

Breaking and Entering
(1947–1948)

David O. Selznick liked to think of himself as a star-maker. He brought Vivien Leigh to America and assured her international celebrity when he cast her in *Gone With the Wind*. He enabled Joan Fontaine to graduate to A-status in Hollywood when he gave her the leading role in *Rebecca*. He believed that Phylis Isley, a deeply insecure girl with a slight speech impediment, could be turned into a star, and so he made her over as Jennifer Jones and married her. In 1946, he decided to create another new star.

For years, *The Paradine Case*, a Robert Hichens novel published in 1933, had fascinated Selznick. That year, the producer had just gone to work at MGM, and at his urging, the studio bought the film rights and hoped to interest Garbo in the leading role. But she had no liking for it, and there the project lay, undeveloped and unscripted. At one point, MGM announced that John and Lionel Barrymore would co-star with Diana Wynyard. Finally, in 1946, the now independent Selznick bought the rights from MGM and showed the novel to Hitchcock, who took it on with considerable enthusiasm – not with indifference, as he implied. Everyone knew that the book would require wholesale cutting, reshaping and simplification, and that its transformation into a movie was an enormous challenge. Still, Selznick and Hitchcock warmed to the task.

A complex thriller of more than 525 pages, *The Paradine Case* is essentially a chain of interlocking character studies. In England, Mrs

Paradine murders her husband, Colonel Paradine, a military hero. Her defending lawyer jeopardises his marriage when he falls in love with her. Acquitted of the crime, she then takes her own life. Other lawyers figure in the case, and there are a judge and his wife and ancillary characters that illuminate the plot and one another.

Hitchcock liked the English setting, the courtroom drama, the sense of romantic obsession and the murky psychology of just about everyone in the book. He was also at the end of his contract with Selznick and was planning to produce his own films, alternatively in London and Hollywood. This he would do through Transatlantic Pictures, his newly formed partnership with his old acquaintance Sidney Bernstein, a founding member of the British Film Society and the head of Granada (the film, television and publishing combine). Travel costs for preparatory meetings with Bernstein in London, Hitch reasoned, could be borne by Selznick when Hitch went over for some background shooting for *The Paradine Case*.

The success of the new picture depended, first, on casting an appealing British leading man in the role of the married but obsessed lawyer, Anthony Keane. Hitchcock voted for Laurence Olivier or Ronald Colman; Selznick gave the part to Gregory Peck, who was under contract, and from day one Hitch made no secret of his displeasure with the choice. Of even greater importance was the casting of Mrs Paradine. Garbo again passed, and Selznick hoped for Ingrid Bergman, but her contract with him, too, was expiring, and she had her own plans for the future. Dozens of other actresses were considered.

Among the last players to be cast in the film, the Italian star Alida Valli was signed to a contract as soon as Selznick saw one of her recent European pictures – such was his version of what happened. But that was mere Hollywood hype, and it conveniently ignores the far more interesting story of how this fine actress got the part and began a short but memorable American period in her long international career.

As early as June 1945 – eighteen months before filming began, without Alida Valli – an executive of Selznick's production company saw one of her Italian pictures in Paris and arranged an introduction to her in Rome. 'Whatever Miss Valli thought of us at that first meeting,' recalled a journalist who acted as interpreter, 'we doubted that she was a film star. She was good-looking, all right, and her eyes had that photogenic something, but she was dressed simply, almost plainly, and she had none of the gaudy, glamorising patina that an American comes to associate with a movie star.' As they were instructed by another Selznick rep in Paris, the Roman contingent told Valli that the producer might be interested in employing her if his European representatives could send good photos and a recommendation; she was politely non-committal. Meantime, would she like to come to the local American officers' club to see a Hollywood movie?

The screening for which she showed up consisted of a newsreel of the 1944 Army-Navy football game, along with a dreadful musical. 'Miss Valli thanked us as though she had seen the ten best pictures of the year,' according to the journalist, and then she and her husband, the composer Oscar de Mejo, departed. Soon after, the Selznick staff – still unaware of her European career – sent for a few of her movies; there were over twenty from which to choose. They watched . . . and they watched more . . . and by September 1945, they excitedly contacted Selznick with the news that Miss Valli would be another Greta Garbo, or another Ingrid Bergman. Negotiations to sign Valli to a Selznick contract took a year – not because she was difficult, but because Selznick was occupied with other projects, and then he temporised, simultaneously wishing and fearing to create a new star. When he finally decided to do so, he stipulated that she was to be known only by her surname, as Valli – like Garbo. It took some time before anyone in Hollywood did some homework and appreciated the significance of the firmly established stage and screen actress Selznick was getting.

Alida von Altenburger, Baroness of Marckenstein and Freuenberg, was born 31 May 1921, in northern Italy's Istria region (now part of Croatia). Her father, the baron, was a professor and music critic, her mother a culturally sophisticated Slovenian-Italian housewife. From the age of eight, Alida took part in amateur and charity perform-ances, and at nine she appeared in a seventeen-minute musical called *Gypsy Land* – produced by, of all people, Michael Balcon. After her father's death, the teenage Alida and her mother moved to Rome, and the girl enrolled at the Centro Sperimentale di Cinematografia. She appeared in a dozen Italian film comedies in the 1930s, aban-doning her German surname and presenting herself as Alida Valli (taking the new name from the telephone book, she said). Turning to serious film dramas, she had great success, and in 1941 was hailed as best actress at the Venice Film Festival for her performance in Mario Soldati's *Piccolo Mondo Antico*. In her next picture, her co-star was Rossano Brazzi, and with him, she began to work with anti-fascist resistance groups against the Mussolini regime.

In 1943, the government ordered her to appear in fascist propaganda films; to avoid this she went into hiding. In a tragic accident, her beloved mother was shot and wounded by her anti-fascist colleagues, who mistook her for a collaborator. While in virtual seclusion, Valli continued her fight against fascism. She married the painter and composer Oscar de Mejo, and they had two sons. At five feet, five inches, with luxuriant dark hair, high cheekbones, fine skin and intense, widely spaced green eyes, Valli in her twenties had an austere, patrician beauty and was photogenic in virtually any light and from any angle. At the end of the war, when she met Selznick's scouts, she was one of Italy's most popular and respected actresses, equally successful in light comedies and serious dramas.

As an Italian national, she was officially designated an enemy alien by the US Department of State when her agents applied for her to travel to Hollywood for Selznick. Falsely identified as the mistress of Joseph Goebbels, she had a gruelling time clearing her name of this charge, which was singularly repellent in light of her anti-fascist activities. Finally, in January 1947, with *The Paradine Case* already in production, Alida, her husband and son arrived in America. 'On the train ride from New York to Los Angeles, I read the script they had sent me – and when I arrived at the studio, I found that it had very little to do with the film they were making!' That was easily explained: after discarding the scenario prepared by Hitch, Alma, Ben Hecht and a team of writers, Selznick was drafting the screenplay himself – page after page, day by day, while filming continued.

This was Valli's first English-language picture, and in addition to that challenge, she was subjected to a typical Hollywood makeover. Selznick thought she was overweight, so she quickly slenderised; Selznick thought her teeth were uneven, so they were capped; Selznick thought her hair needed colouring, and so it was done. With all this and the daily memorising of new script pages, Alida felt overwhelmed, but she was a thoroughgoing professional. 'I never heard a whisper of complaint from her,' said Gregory Peck.

New to the vast and complex conditions of American moviemaking,

Valli was, as she recalled, 'shaking all over at first — I just couldn't stand still, I was so nervous. But really, everyone was very kind and helped me out.' In fact, Hitchcock was enormously gentle and patient with her and spent extra hours, explaining and preparing her for her long and difficult scenes. Theirs was a good collaboration, without confusion or conflict.

Hitch had to cope with the new pages of script rushed down to him and his actors each morning. 'This, of course, drove him to distraction,' recalled Gregory Peck.

> Selznick was totally disorganised but essentially a lovable man, while Hitchcock, whose manner was not quite so lovable, was totally organised. This created an unavoidable tension between them, and it clearly affected Hitchcock's attitude during production. He seemed bored with the whole thing, and often we looked over and he would be — or pretended to be — asleep. Something was troubling him even more than during *Spellbound*. He was never sadistic or cruel or openly unkind to anyone on the film, but he was obviously suffering terribly over something during the shooting of *The Paradine Case*.

Indeed, this was an anxious time in Hitch's life. He was directing a troubled project. He was uncertain of his future, as the security of his Selznick era was ending. He was unsure he could make a success of his own inchoate production company, which had to deal with risky post-war economies. And he was sorely disappointed that *The Paradine Case* was being torn to shreds, diluted and turned into an enamelised Selznick vehicle.

Despite the fact that any studio would have signed him to a lucrative contract, Hitch was, as always, terrified of poverty. He was one of the most highly paid and secure directors — but money was an obsession, and obsessions know no logic. As colleagues like John Houseman noted, 'Hitchcock [had a] lifelong and highly neurotic preoccupation with money.' He was a collector of modern art, he purchased oil stock and cattle ranches, he grew richer by the year — and yet 'he drove us crazy,' as his secretary said, recalling his demands for frequent accountings of his net worth.

Despite all his worries, Hitch was unfailingly polite and even paternal with Valli, who was both respectful and willing to learn.

He genuinely liked her; he sympathised with her uneasiness in English and her occasional awkwardness amid the oddities of Hollywood – and he consistently put her at ease. Years later, recalling his courtesies to her, she still felt that 'he was not a director of actors. He dealt more with the technical aspect of things. He left actors to themselves, but he had precise instructions for the camera.'

Decades later, Alida Valli's performance in *The Paradine Case* seems richer, subtler, and more complex than it did for audiences in 1948, just as the picture itself is arguably a far finer one than even Hitchcock's partisans have allowed.

Also playing a major role in *The Paradine Case* was the British actress Ann Todd, who was making her American movie debut, too. In 1930, Hitch had seen her onstage in *Honour's Easy* and had told a journalist, 'In the right part, she would do extremely well.' He now thought that the role of Gay Keane, the lawyer's wife, was the right part. At thirty-nine, she was a strikingly elegant, cool blonde with a warm smile, expressive eyes, and a restrained technique; she had been in films since 1931, and had made a huge success most recently as a troubled pianist in *The Seventh Veil*.

'He took the trouble to study his actors quite apart from what we were playing,' Ann Todd recalled years later, 'and so he was able to bring out hidden things. But he was also very puckish – he waited for silence on the set before he called "Action!" and then he whispered the naughtiest things to me, just before he took a close-up shot. Later, I learned that he did this with many of his leading ladies, in England and in America. I think he wanted to pull us down, in a way – it gave him a feeling of domination.' (This was not something Hitchcock tried with Valli, perhaps because he thought she wouldn't understand the language, and perhaps because her husband was never far away; Ann's husband, on the other hand, was at home in London.) Hitch was also, Ann realised,

> a very complex man – an overgrown schoolboy, really, who never grew up and lived in his own special fantasy world. He had a schoolboy's obsession with sex that went on and on in a very peculiar way. He had an endless supply of very nasty, vulgar and naughty stories and jokes. These amused him more than they amused anyone else, but I think he was really a very sad person.

I feel that he wanted to be what he was not – a good-looking man, like Cary Grant – and he never came to terms with what he himself was.

While filming *The Paradine Case*, Hitch's way with Ann, on one occasion at least, was more physical than verbal. 'There was a scene with Greg [Peck], and I was reclining on a bed, wearing an elegant dressing gown. Suddenly, Hitch took a flying leap, ran across the set, jumped on me and shouted, "Relax!" For a moment, I thought he might have broken my bones.'

Greg and Ann may have been the players who most clearly understood the conflict between Selznick and Hitchcock. 'I think power was very important to Hitch,' she said years later.

> That was perhaps the most basic thing, beneath all the masks and veils he wore – power over his cast, power over his leading ladies, power with studio executives. Perhaps this compensated for his feeling that he was ugly and unpresentable in polite society. But his desire for power clashed with David's. For example, Hitch prepared an elaborate five-minute take early in the picture. Greg was to come in the door of the house, climb a staircase, meet me on the upstairs hallway and go into a room, with both of us talking all the while. We rehearsed it with all its complications, then shot it perhaps thirty times to get it exactly right. But when Selznick heard about it, he came down to the set and demanded that the whole thing be done in the ordinary way, in short takes and with cuts. 'We're not doing a theatre piece!' he cried. Of course, Hitch had to give in – he knew whom he could bully, but he also knew whom he had to obey.

After the conclusion of *The Paradine Case* in the spring of 1947, Ann Todd returned to England. Two years later, she became the third of David Lean's six wives, and he directed her in three pictures before they divorced in 1957. Her career continued virtually without interruption, and in the 1960s and 1970s, she directed impressive travel documentaries in Egypt, Nepal, Greece, Iran, Australia and Jordan. She published her autobiography (*The Eighth Veil*) in 1980 and, in her late seventies and into her eighties, was a handsome, spry and intellectually curious woman. In person, Ann Todd had none of the aloof chilliness many of her roles required. 'I have written 200 pages of my novel,' she wrote to me late in her life, 'and it seems to be turning out as a story for a TV series – it's much harder work than writing about myself!' Declining health prevented her from finishing the task, but not from welcoming friends to her modest but cosy flat in Kensington. She died of a stroke in 1993, at the age of eighty-six.

After four more English-language films, Alida Valli returned to Europe – without her husband, who had found a career as an artist in America. At the age of thirty, she resumed a busy career in Italy, France and Germany, but unfortunately, she was tangentially involved in a scandal in the spring of 1953. Divorced from de Mejo, she was visiting the producer Carlo Ponti at his Amalfi villa with the composer Piero Piccioni when Piccioni was charged with involvement in a notorious drug murder. Valli never wavered in providing details of his alibi, but the ugly media exposure severely hindered her career for several years. A second marriage, to director Giancarlo Zagni, ended after less than a decade.

When she resumed working after the Piccioni affair, Valli was triumphantly in demand for another fifty years. In addition to movie thrillers and romances, she excelled on stage in the works of Shakespeare, Ibsen, Pirandello, Williams, O'Neill and Miller. As she aged, she accepted supporting and even minor roles and often worked in television melodramas.

According to many journalists, Valli was a shy, rather distant woman who refused to talk about the past. But when I met her in Los Angeles, about the time of her seventieth birthday, she seemed a warm Italian *mamma* with a ready smile and bright eyes, speaking respectfully but realistically of her limited time in Hollywood. 'Hitchcock was very kind to me – everyone in *Il Caso Paradine* was kind to me when I was a newcomer in America,' she recalled, 'but maybe I was not right for movies here. Anyway, I was happy to go home.'

At dinner that spring evening, she seemed pleased that some Hitchcock fans were re-evaluating the generally negative criticism of *The Paradine Case*, and she was glad to be remembered after so long an absence from Hollywood – pleased and glad, but not to the point of excitement or rapture. Alida Valli's niche was always in Europe. She knew it and made the most of it; she could count many awards from Italian and French cultural institutions and universities, and later, she was especially proud of her 2001 'Vittorio de Sica Award,' presented by the president of Italy. She died in Rome in April 2006, a few weeks before her eighty-fifth birthday, having appeared in more than 130 films, sixty TV shows and over forty plays. 'I had so much,' she said a few months earlier. 'Maybe I have had more than I gave – but I tried to give something.'

Hitch's next picture was the first of only two films he directed for Transatlantic Pictures, his business partnership with Sidney Bernstein. *Rope*, also his first colour movie, is best categorised as an experimental movie, filmed almost completely in ten-minute takes.

Based on a play by Patrick Hamilton, the film concerns two young men (Farley Granger and John Dall) – who may or may not be lovers but certainly seem perversely gay. They strangle a friend for the sheer excitement of feeling superior over matters of life and death, and then they conceal the body in a piece of furniture. That same evening, the men host a dinner party, at which their college professor (James Stewart) is present along with other guests; the suspense derives from the gradual revelation of the macabre truth.

As for what Ann Todd had called Hitch's 'schoolboy obsession with sex,' the playwright Arthur Laurents, who wrote the screenplay for *Rope*, thoroughly agreed. 'We never discussed the homosexual element of that script,' Laurents recalled,

> but Hitchcock knew what he wanted to get away with. He was intrigued by the varieties of sexual life and conduct as he was by the varieties of moviemaking methods – in fact, he was like a child who has just discovered sex and thinks it's all very naughty. He might have been indirect in dealing with sexual things, but he had a strong instinct for them. He thought everyone was doing something physical and nasty behind every closed door – except himself. He withdrew; he wouldn't be part of it.

Laurents added that Hitch

> lived in the land of kink. Initially, I thought he was a repressed homosexual. The actual word *homosexuality* was never said aloud in conferences on *Rope* or on the set, but he alluded to the subject so often – slyly and naughtily, never nastily – that he seemed fixated if not obsessed . . . It tickled him that Farley

[Granger] was playing a homosexual in a movie written by me, another homosexual; that we were lovers [in real life]; that we had a secret he knew; that I knew he knew . . . Sex was always on his mind; not ordinary sex, not plain homosexuality any more than plain heterosexuality. Perverse sex, kinky sex, that fascinated him. He himself didn't strike me as ever having much sex or even wanting sex.

The perverse and the kinky made their way into social chatter, too, as in a new cocktail recipe Hitch said he devised for Laurents: 'a new martini – gin and menstrual blood.'

Hume Cronyn, on friendly terms with Hitchcock since *Shadow of a Doubt*, worked on the treatments for *Rope* and the film that followed. Hume recalled the director's tendency for risqué stories, which were 'not very amusing, actually – the kind of jokes schoolboys tell, sniggering and childish.'

Obsessed with perfecting every one of the twenty-five to thirty camera moves in *Rope*'s every shot, Hitch lost touch with his cast: 'The really important thing here is the camera, not the actors!' complained James Stewart, who asserted that he would never again work with this director. Years later, Hitch agreed: 'I realise that it [the ten-minute take] was quite nonsensical because I was breaking with my own theories on the importance of cutting and montage for the visual narration of a story . . . No doubt about it – films must be cut. As an experiment, *Rope* may be forgiven, but it was definitely a mistake when I insisted on applying the same techniques to *Under Capricorn*.'

That picture – the final Transatlantic project – was equally ill fated, and after the film's eventual commercial failure, he always insisted he had directed it only as a favour to Ingrid, who loved the book. In fact, Hitch had known Helen Simpson, the author of the novel; she had also co-written the literary basis for his film *Murder!* in 1930. Selznick had bought the rights to *Under Capricorn* for Ingrid, and it was on Hitch's list of potentials since 1944.

He directed the movie during the summer of 1948, in London; seen years later, the picture has much to recommend it that mysteriously escaped reviewers in 1949. It has the luxuriantly morbid atmosphere of its setting, which is nineteenth-century Australia, and it has glorious Technicolor – and Ingrid Bergman, in her third outing with Hitch. But the long, fluid takes once more made Hitch's cast miserable.

'He got such pleasure out of doing those camera tricks,' Ingrid recalled,

> but of course the continuous shots and the moving cameras were very hard on everybody. We rehearsed for days, and then at last we put on make-up and had a try at a reel. We had perhaps six minutes just fine, and then suddenly something went wrong, and we had to begin the whole reel again. Hitch just insisted – he wanted those long uninterrupted takes. Then the prop men had the job of moving all the furniture while the camera was rolling forward and backward – and the walls were flying up into the rafters as we walked by, so that the huge Technicolor camera could follow us. It just drove us all crazy. A chair or a table for an actor appeared the moment before an actor needed it. The floor was marked with numbers, and everybody, and every piece of furniture, had to be on the cued number at the right moment. What a nightmare! It's the only time I broke down and cried on a movie set. I think Hitch did all this to prove to himself that he could. It was a challenge only to himself, to show the movie industry that he could accomplish something so difficult.

There was one glorious exception to her objections – Ingrid's nine-minute-long confession scene, when the camera never left her as she rose from a chair, walked around the room, leaned over a table and sat down again. After one rehearsal, Ingrid delivered the speech without a cut, and the effect was like a Richard Strauss aria. She began the speech quietly, smiling as she recounted happy memories of the character's early years in Ireland. Then she became resolute, recalling her marriage to a stableman, against the wishes of her aristocratic family. From this, she rose to the climax, the dramatic description of her shooting of her brother. From there, she dipped to a coda, the tearful expression of gratitude to her husband for assuming the guilt for her crime and for his fidelity over the years.

Technically, getting the speech on film was a nightmare for Ingrid and the crew.

> We rehearsed a whole day, and the next day we put on the make-up and had a dress rehearsal, and then after lunch we shot

one take. We had six minutes and then something went wrong – the fly-away walls creaked, or someone's slippers squeaked. Then I had to time my words for the right moment for a man who was crawling with a table or chair on his back for you. If he was a little late – stop! So we stopped. Six minutes, five minutes, seven minutes filmed. Then something else would go wrong and we had to start over again, from the beginning. So much technique and so much for Hitch to show off, and that became very, very difficult. And the curious thing was that when it was finished, I asked Hitch if the speech was any good, and he said, 'How do I know? I couldn't see you for the huge camera! I hope it was good, Ingrid – we rehearsed it!'

In a film not generally regarded very highly even by most Hitchcock partisans, Ingrid's uninterrupted speech has been studied for years by apprentice and accomplished film actors. In 1975, when she won her third Academy Award (as best supporting actress for her role in *Murder on the Orient Express*), Ingrid told me, 'Really, it was very nice, but I didn't think I deserved it. People were so impressed because I did a long dialogue [with Albert Finney] in a single take – but that was not nearly so long or demanding as my big nine-minute monologue for Hitch in *Under Capricorn*!' On the evening of the Oscar presentation, she was typically generous in accepting the award:

Thank you very much indeed. It's always nice to get an Oscar, but in the past he has shown he is very forgetful and has poor timing, because last year, when [Truffaut's film] *Day for Night* won, I couldn't believe that Valentina Cortese [one of the players in it] was not nominated, because she gave the most beautiful performance. And now, here I am, her rival because she is nominated this year, and I don't like it at all. Where are you, Valentina? [She spotted her friend in the audience, and Cortese rose and blew Ingrid a kiss.] Ah, there you are! Please forgive me, Valentina, I didn't mean to win!'

As in *Rope*, the problem with the long takes in *Under Capricorn* was a lack of subjective viewpoint; more to the point, long takes are essentially anti-cinematic. Hume Cronyn put the matter succinctly: 'I think this method led him astray. He became so fascinated by [the long takes] that the line of the narrative got lost, and there was an awkward-ness telling the story.' Indeed, Hitchcock himself summarised the basis of all good filmmaking when he said, 'The best way to do it is with scissors.'★

Ingrid had to agree. 'He did this sort of thing in order to prove to himself that he could – it was a challenge to himself, and a chal-lenge to show the movie industry what he could figure out. But the audience couldn't care less. If he had cut to a close-up or a medium shot and just told a good story and cut it as usual, the audience would be just as happy as if the camera was rolling up and down hill and keeping focus, going under tables and all that!'

In some ways, *Under Capricorn* continued themes in Ingrid's previous Hitchcock films, as she was the first to understand. From *Spellbound* came the motif of the secret and the transfer of guilt from childhood to a neurotic adulthood; from *Notorious*, there was the theme of a woman's alcoholic intemperance and the attempted poisoning of her. Most of all, however, *Under Capricorn* is the story of a face – Ingrid's. Her first appearance is indicated by a close-up of her bare feet at a dinner party, a neat marker of the film's dual themes of enslavement and lost manners. After that, the film is virtually a study of her tortured, confused, haunted but exquisite features – in mirrors, in medium shot, in close shot and from every angle. 'Ah, yes,' Hitch had Joan Chandler say in *Rope*, 'Ingrid Bergman! She's the *Virgo* type – I think she's just lovely!'

As did he, and it may be that his obsession with technical matters for this film was his way of avoiding a new and unpleasant reality. On the weekend of her thirty-third birthday, which fell on Sunday 29 August 1948, Ingrid went to Paris to discuss making a film with the Italian director, Roberto Rossellini.

As the saying goes, the rest is history. Eventually, after returning to Los Angeles when *Under Capricorn* was complete, Ingrid Bergman left for Italy; made a movie with Rossellini on a volcanic island called Stromboli, which gave its name to the first of their five movies together; bore their son out of wedlock; and was vilified from the floor of the

---

★ This remark was the whole of his response to the applause at the gala in his honour, tendered by the Film Society of Lincoln Center, New York, on 29 April 1974. Moments before, the audience had seen the killing with scissors in *Dial 'M' for Murder*, and, as so often, Hitch's comment had a double meaning.

United States Senate as 'a free-love cultist . . . an apostle of degrad-
ation' and 'a force of moral evil'. Her films were banned all over
America, where she was threatened with arrest and imprisonment if
she returned. Those were the days.

Americans felt betrayed by the woman who had recently played
Joan of Arc on Broadway and in an epic movie. 'The devil himself
is at work,' fumed the *Boston Pilot*, the official Catholic newspaper
of that diocese. 'Some people have tried to make romance out of a
cheap, sordid, immoral affair. Miss Bergman has openly and brazenly
flouted the laws of God, and decent, moral Americans should stay
away from these practitioners of moral filth.' Similar sentiments were
printed in Catholic periodicals all over the country, and were heard
from far too many pulpits. Even beyond the Catholic realm, 5.5
million American clubwomen voted to boycott all of Ingrid
Bergman's movies – *The Bells of St. Mary's* included. Alas, such
condemnations (and they proliferated from Maine to California)
were an egregious symptom of a corrupt religious sensibility, not
to say an outrageous social hypocrisy.

It is worth adding that in Europe, Catholic clergymen and lay folk
minded their own business; they had, after all, far more pressing problems after the war than condemning movie stars and directors, and
they considered the Bergman-Rossellini affair a private matter. In
Rome, *Il Popolo*, the newspaper of the Catholic Party, considered the
American condemnations 'a preordained plan of cannibalistic aggres-
sion against Miss Bergman'. The official Vatican newspaper printed
no denunciation. And even in the United States, the National Legion
of Decency (sponsored by the Catholic Church to monitor films),
which wielded such power that it could ruin a film's financial success
by condemning it, issued an astonishing statement: 'It is our policy
to judge the film itself, not the actors in it.' And with those words –
would wonders never cease? – they rated *Stromboli* an acceptable
motion picture for public viewing. Perhaps the last citation on the
matter should be the remark from an elderly Italian priest, who had
no patience with merely human judgements: 'Why do they talk about
a scandal, when God has been so good and blessed their union with
a child?'

'Nobody could have lived up to that unreal image people had of
me during the 1940s,' Ingrid told me years later. In a way, that image
began with Selznick: 'I wanted to put Ingrid on a pedestal, and I

insist upon keeping her on that pedestal.' But she wanted nothing of the sort:

> When people saw that I did not perfectly fit that image, they felt betrayed and all hell broke loose. They decided that I had planned so much deception all along, and that when I left my husband and daughter I had no intentions of ever coming back – that I had wanted to go to Italy and be a star there, and to hell with everything else. But why would I have gone to Italy and to Rossellini if I wanted to be a big star? That would have been the worst possible place for that! In Hollywood, I was being offered the best scripts and the best directors in 1949 – Hitchcock, Huston, Wyler, Mankiewicz, they all wanted to work with me. But I wanted something else. I wanted a different environment and a simpler kind of moviemaking. I wanted to expand my talents, and the Italians were making the kinds of movies that deeply impressed me.

When she returned to London to resume work on *Under Capricorn* after her first meeting with Rossellini, Hitch asked about her weekend. 'I met a director from Italy, that's all,' she replied. 'Hitch resented her going off with Rossellini,' said Arthur Laurents, reflecting an impression common among those who knew Hitch well. 'His resentment was not caused simply by the fact that he adored Bergman. It was also because she was leaving him for another director.' Indeed, Hitch implied as much: 'I am still,' he said years later, 'in mourning for the films I would have made with Ingrid Bergman, the films that never were. When she left for Italy and stayed there, it was a loss to me, to the world, and to her.'

'I remember it very clearly,' Ingrid told me at lunch one day in May 1975. 'Hitch looked down on me when I left Hollywood for Rossellini, to do neo-realistic films. He said, "What for?" I told him that I wanted a change of movie styles – I wanted to do something different, something new. I was so fed up always to play the same people in the same background, with the same extras – it was always the same people, wearing different clothes. But Hitch couldn't accept that.' Hitch's relationship with Ingrid, as poignant and painful as it sometimes was, had been professionally beneficial for both of them, and it was eventually transformed into a lifelong friendship, thanks to her loyalty, goodwill and common sense. 'But he never forgave Ingrid Bergman for having left him for Rossellini,' according to no less an authority that François Truffaut.

Over the next five years, Alfred Hitchcock could not find the right leading lady for any of his films. To stir up the creative and emotional embers within him, he had to wait for a new alliance, another historic partnership like the one he had enjoyed with Ingrid Bergman. Finally, that happened, in the summer of 1953, with the entrance into his life of twenty-three-year-old Grace Kelly.

10

The Lure
(1949–1950)

In any consideration of the important women in Alfred Hitchcock's life and career, the names of his wife and daughter must be included. He was dependent on Alma for approval because he respected her talent and intelligence. He gave them attention and gifts. Otherwise, with Alma and Pat as, it seems, with everyone in his life, he was a product of his time and place – that is, he was a typical Victorian-Edwardian bourgeois who did not think that emotions need be expressed, simply felt. He was not demonstrative in public, nor, as far as we know, did he praise his wife or daughter to the press. This did not make him a psychological freak; in fact, he was one of countless millions from an era in which propriety required a kind of extreme reticence concerning the expression of sentiment.

In 1952, Pat married Joseph E. O'Connell, Jr. Her subsequent acting career was most notable for two more roles in her father's films and several on his television programmes, and she happily devoted herself to her three daughters and, later, to their families, too. In 1975, I spoke with her about her brief and witty performance as an office girl in *Psycho*. She had great fun during that one day's work.

Of Pat's devotion to her mother, there is no question – she wrote a book to demonstrate that. But Hitch and Pat remain, as father and daughter, enigmatic – which may be what they finally were to each other. This could have been the consequence of their background and culture, too, but I think there are sadder undercurrents. Her conversation with me about Hitch, four years before his death (on Thanksgiving Day 1976, at the home of Peggy and Doug Robertson), indicated that she was certainly dutiful.

Alma was a sometime contributor to the films, a permanent in-house critic and Hitch's co-conspirator in dealings with producers, writers and studio executives. She was also his one true strength and support. Mary Stone, Pat's eldest daughter, said of Alma, 'My grandmother really had the upper hand of the relationship, as small and petite as she was. He deferred to her whether it be in personal [matters] or in his business.' Indeed, Hitch's regard for his wife's estimation, her judgement and even her minor opinions, extended deeply into their private lives. 'She was the only person he was really afraid of,' according to Charles Bennett; production designer Robert Boyle, who knew the couple from 1942, agreed that Hitch 'relied on Alma – well, it was partly reliance, partly fear.'

Why the 'upper hand' – and why 'fear'? These seem completely incongruous with the impression of independence that Alfred Hitchcock wanted to project.

He was certainly aware of his talent – even of his genius – and he struggled constantly to create his fame, to make his fortune and to establish his primacy as a respected and respectable artist. As early as 1926, he had reminded a group of colleagues that 'the name of the director should stay clearly in the mind of the audiences.' Like Dickens, he was his own best publicist – hence the cameo appearances, the regular, prudent and completely controlled interviews, and the cultivation of a proper image of bourgeois normalcy. But the dark suit and tie, the almost expressionless monotone and the dry humour were a convenient cover for a man who admitted that he was frightened not of this or that but of everything and everyone. This is not surprising, for no man responsible for such a body of work as his could possibly be so common, so irksomely flat, so unflappable as the man he marketed. In a culture that shines a light on everything, he worked hard to keep us in the dark.

There can be no question that he was a brilliant artisan and a dedicated artist. Despite his private demons and lifelong fears, his obsessive privacy and his sense of being an outsider provided the conditions for a remarkably prolific life. He had an extraordinary ability to locate and diagnose a lot of the psychological suffering of the twentieth century and much of the delusion and sickness just below the surface of polite society. He spun stories – powerfully visual stories appropriate for a visually oriented century – that touched the universal sense of guilt, anguish and obsession with violence, sex and the detached machinery of death. An anxious man, he was a poet of anxiety and a doomed romantic in spite of himself. These are but a few of the reasons why most of his movies never seem dated, obscure, or parochial. Decades after his death, they appeal to audiences worldwide.

Very little is known of the Hitchcocks' life at home, and no famous couple ever coveted privacy more – hence this is a matter almost impossible to address with anything like certainty. Some observations are not unwarranted, however, and they may have to do with fear as a powerful and sustained component of one's system. Fear because of isolation, of loneliness, of a deeply rooted insecurity. Fear and a frustrated desire for security that can lead a person to depend on *one other* for a lifetime.

Hitch completely lacked social self-confidence and forever considered himself a marginal man, an outsider. This is not uncommon in the case of highly creative people. Hitch was a true genius, and the genius lives at the fringes of polite society, seeing things with a clarity denied to those who can and wish to conform. Hitch preferred order to chaos and serenity to turbulence, and he had a positive horror of argument or confrontation. But he was *different* – as a genius and as an artisan working in the most collaborative form of entertainment. He had not the gift of friendship, and those who called themselves his friends over many years had to admit how little they knew of him.

Hitch was not a man to sit back, exhale, kick off his shoes and confide in people. Except, it seems, for Alma. Sidney Bernstein, whom he knew for most of his life, was fundamentally a business partner; privately, they were little more than the entertainment equivalent of golf buddies. Hitch's agent and later his boss, Lew Wasserman, made Hitchcock rich – and Hitch made Lew rich – but that relationship (so unrealistically described by people who knew better) later came to a shameful conclusion. Otherwise, Hitch not only felt himself to be a permanent outsider, separated from just about everyone: he also seemed to do everything to maintain that status. This is not a flaw in character – indeed, in Hollywood it may sometimes be cause for high praise. Alma knew him, knew how to control him, cook for him, and cushion him from the discomfort he felt in public.

He did not, for example, do all the social and political things a director and his managers do to jockey for an Academy Award, and the result was that he never won an Oscar for directing. On 10 April 1968, at the Academy Awards ceremony, he received the honorary Irving G. Thalberg Award, presented to 'creative producers whose bodies of work reflect a consistently high quality of motion picture production.' But his colleagues never specifically acknowledged his genius as a motion picture director.* When Hitch stepped to the microphone to receive the award, everyone expected a witty, ironic little discourse – the kind familiar from his television programmes. 'Thank you,' he said without expression, and with those two words, he left the stage. Some thought his brevity betokened lightly veiled contempt, and they were probably correct.

Several factors early in his life were responsible for his marginality. He was Catholic, he was Cockney, he was clever, and his father was 'in trade' – not a 'gentleman' in the British class system. As he matured, his overindulgence in food and drink became a serious problem. His weight embarrassed him, but he was unable or unwilling to deal with it on a permanent basis – indeed, it is surprising that he lived to mark his eightieth birthday. In 1943 and again in 1953, he adhered to a rigid diet and each time lost over 100 pounds, but as so often with the problem of morbid obesity, the weight returned.

Although Alma received no credit for any of her husband's productions after 1950, she was no absentee. Her copious notes on every aspect of each film supplemented her continuing involvement, however casual, with writers, designers and sometimes actors.

Pat wanted to be an actress from her youth, and her self-confidence (in addition to her father's name and connections) helped her to achieve early success. On 27 January 1942, she appeared on Broadway in John van Druten's play *Solitaire*, in the role of a precocious, well-to-do eleven-year-old girl who befriends a poor homeless man. In a long and demanding part, thirteen-year-old Pat acquitted herself 'with childish innocence, sincerity and spontaneity', according to the *New York Times*.

---

* Hitch was nominated five times, for his direction of *Rebecca, Lifeboat, Spellbound, Rear Window* and *Psycho*. 'Always a bridesmaid, never a bride,' he muttered to a few people in private; in public, he shrugged and asked, 'Who needs another doorstop?' But he loathed the disregard for his work.

Oddly, the producers put out the word that Pat was twelve years old, and this the press accepted. Perhaps the little subterfuge was created because Pat seemed younger and smaller than her actual age; or perhaps it was thought that more praise would be forthcoming if a year were subtracted from her true age. Whatever the reason, this curious fiction persisted for the next several years, but without any positive impact on her early career. The recent attack on Pearl Harbor and America's sudden entry into World War Two altered everything in American life, Broadway fortunes included, and *Solitaire* closed after twenty-three performances. Those who recall it assert it was a good play, well written, staged and acted.

As the title character in *Violet*, Pat appeared on Broadway a second and final time almost three years later, beginning on 24 October 1944. Written and directed by Whitfield Cook and based on his magazine stories, the play and sixteen-year-old Pat (still billed as a year younger) were dismissed as 'monotonous'. *Violet* vacated the Belasco Theatre on 11 November, after precisely the same number of performances as *Solitaire*. Alma Hitchcock was with her daughter in New York for both these early professional excursions, but Hitch was otherwise engaged: in early 1942, he was detained in California while directing the problematic *Saboteur*; in autumn 1944, he was completing *Spellbound*.

After the final curtain of *Violet*, Pat returned to Los Angeles and graduated from the Marymount School in 1947 a few weeks before her nineteenth birthday. Still eager to act, she won over her parents, who enrolled her at the Royal Academy of Dramatic Art, London. At the end of her studies two years later, Hitch offered Pat a small role in *Stage Fright*, which he was directing in England during the summer of 1949. An inventive romantic-comic thriller, the picture concerns a drama student forced to play roles in real life in order to discover the identity of a killer.

The team of screenwriters for *Stage Fright* included Whitfield Cook, now a Hitchcock family friend – and, on the word of one writer, apparently more than that. Whit and Alma, wrote Patrick McGilligan, had a love affair, or a reasonable facsimile thereof. 'It appears that, on October 1 [1948], after a cosy dinner at a restaurant, they began making love,' McGilligan wrote. This is an extraordinary statement, and one wants to know precisely why 'it appears' so. (As written, the assertion also improbably suggests that a public dining room was the scene of a passionate encounter; surely, this was not the case, even for the wife of a gourmand.) The only source for McGilligan's inexplicably coy report is (or was) *something* in the journal of Whitfield Cook, to which McGilligan claimed access but of which he cited only one phrase – about the lovemaking being 'complicated by an overseas call'. It's disappointing not to have anything clearer, by indirect or direct citation from Cook's journal; nor is there any ancillary statement from anyone about so astonishing an inference.

If indeed this was a consummated love affair, Hitchcock's reaction to it has never been recorded. In the event, he may have been surprised, not least of all, because Cook was (thus McGilligan) 'a bachelor with homosexual friends . . . [who] spent as much time with men as with women.' This is maddeningly vague: by 'spending time', McGilligan clearly means 'in bed'. And does the phrase 'a bachelor with homosexual friends' mean 'Cook was gay'? Perhaps McGilligan was constrained by the fact that Cook was still alive at the time – but since he claims to have had access to the journals and to have conducted an on-the-record interview, why the double-talk?

It's unlikely that Hitch would have been unaware of romantic commotion between his wife and his screenwriter – if such was the case. He may have been complaisant, or indifferent, or grateful that someone was offering her what he could or would not; the possibilities are legion. 'You never knew quite what Hitchcock was thinking,' said Frank Launder, 'because he always played his cards close to his chest.' Later, George Cukor concurred: 'Hitch was so perverse! He'd never tell you what he really thinks – never, never!' Whatever did or did not occur, it seems that no one had the confidence of either Mr or Mrs Hitchcock in this doubtful matter.

These extended reflections on Pat and Alma are important toward an understanding of Hitch's mood and his attitude toward women during the summer of 1949. For the much-maligned *Stage Fright*, which (unjustly) has never had a substantial fan base, he had two very different leading ladies, both of whom, he claimed, gave him headaches.

Prior to filming, however, Hitch, Whit Cook and Alma decided to include a unique element at the beginning of the picture – a flashback that tells the audience not the truth but a lie. Critics seized on this as a fatal flaw in *Stage Fright*: a flashback, it was proclaimed, must always tell the truth. But this objection can only be made by a careless viewer, for at the conclusion of the flashback, the narrator casts a sinister gaze at one of the leading ladies, grins malevolently and presses her hand down on a blood-stained dress, the incriminating evidence of the murder he has just described as committed by someone other than himself. Thus, Hitch clearly indicates that the flashback we've just seen is not to be trusted from the lips of this hostile character – who of course turns out to be the real killer. Nevertheless, the so-called 'lying flashback' annoyed some injudicious critics, and Hitchcock found his reasons – the actors – to discount the movie when it failed commercially.

On 7 March 1949, Warner Bros had announced that their contract player, Jane Wyman, would appear in a new film, to be directed in London by Alfred Hitchcock, whom Jack Warner had signed for a four-picture deal. Two weeks later, Wyman won the best actress Oscar for her touching portrayal of an assaulted deaf-mute in *Johnny Belinda*. In early May, she sailed for England, whence she received news of her final decree of divorce from the actor Ronald Reagan.

Jane had appeared in no fewer than sixty-three films since 1931. An adaptable and engaging talent, she was equally clever in comedies, mysteries, melodramas and musicals. With an irony Hitch may have appreciated, she had once been compelled to be a blonde in comedies, but she eventually reverted to her natural brunette colour and to serious professional goals, of which she was entirely capable.

When *Stage Fright* failed to win critical or public approval, Hitch was sharply ungracious about her, despite her fine performance in a complex and difficult role. 'I was stuck with her,' he said.

> I had lots of problems with Jane Wyman. In her disguise as a lady's maid, she should have been rather unglamorous . . . But every time she saw the rushes and how she looked alongside Marlene Dietrich, she would burst into tears. She couldn't accept the idea of her face being in character, while Dietrich looked so glamorous, so she kept improving her appearance every day.

This was not quite the case, but the eventual commercial failure of the film forced Hitch to offer an explanation of what went wrong, and, as usual, he preferred an actor to take the blame. It was certainly true that Wyman resented the attention lavished on Dietrich. But when she 'kept improving her appearance every day', she did so with the collaboration of the make-up and wardrobe crew, who were of course following instructions. This deserves some elaboration.

Jane's role as Eve Gill, a witty and resourceful drama student, required the character to assume the disguise of Marlene Dietrich's substitute maid, a myopic Cockney frump. As Eve prepares her make-up and outfit to pass herself off as 'Doris', the scene is hilariously played, with Jane's thick eyeglasses, stringy hair, worn clothes, crude accent and a dangling cigarette. But even Eve's mother (played by the great Dame Sybil Thorndike), sans spectacles, recognises her daughter beneath this cover – and so Eve puts away the exaggerated homeliness. Charlotte Inwood (the Dietrich character) would, Eve rightly reasons, never accept so unkempt, graceless and homely a personal maid as the phoney Doris. The memorable Kay Walsh, who played the full-time maid Nellie Good, was presented as plain and bespectacled, but not repellent. Hence, Eve's disguise had to be softened. All this is reflected in the production notes and files.

In fact, Hitchcock agreed to this improvement in Wyman's appearance, for the story requires Jane/Eve to play many subsequent scenes as the phoney maid, and neither the 1950 audience Hitchcock wanted to win over – nor, more to the point, Jack Warner himself, back in Burbank – would accept Jane's unattractive appearance for the rest of the picture. As for the actress, she never responded to Hitch's charge, nor did she speak about him in any but the most admiring and grateful phrases.

Hitch's real difficulties occurred with Marlene Dietrich. 'She adopted me,' Jane said of Dietrich, years later. 'She decided to take me under her wing that summer, and she told me what I should demand on the film and in my career.' Famously called 'the world's most glamorous grandmother' that year, when she was forty-seven, Dietrich insisted on a Dior wardrobe for herself, just as she required absolute control over how she was made up and photographed; indeed, she arrived at the studio early each morning to instruct cinematographer Wilkie Cooper on the proper lighting for herself. 'Marlene was a professional star,' Hitch said later. 'She was also a professional cameraman, art director, editor, costume designer, hairdresser, make-up woman, composer, producer and director.' It is not going too far to say that this was an Alfred Hitchcock movie except for Marlene's scenes, when it became a Dietrich movie.

The problems began prior to Dietrich's arrival in London at the end of June. Before she agreed to the dates of production, she had to consult her American astrologer, Carroll Righter, for approval. She then paid Righter to draw up the astrological chart for co-star Richard Todd, who was signed to play the killer in *Stage Fright*. As he recalled, 'When she heard that I was engaged to be married, she asked me for details of my birth date and also [his fiancée] Kitty's, saying she would send for a horoscope for us. It was just as well I did not share her obsession, because when the horoscope reached us, it was a terrible one, forecasting no good at all for Kitty and me.' In fact, the Todds remained happily married for twenty-one years. 'She wouldn't do anything on *Stage Fright* until she consulted her astrologer,' Hitch said of Dietrich. 'He should have received a credit!'

Hitchcock was also none too pleased when Dietrich took for her real-life lover the other leading man in the picture, Michael Wilding, who had been admirable with Ingrid in *Under Capricorn* and now played the detective in *Stage Fright*. Peggy Singer, the continuity assistant on *Under Capricorn* and *Stage Fright*, recalled that the Dietrich-Wilding affair was raucously carried on in the stars' dressing rooms and often delayed a scheduled scene.★ Handsome, artistic and sophisticated, Wilding was married to actress Kay Young when he became Dietrich's new conquest – a list that already included the names of Josef von Sternberg, Douglas Fairbanks Jr, John Wayne, Jean Gabin, Maurice Chevalier, Gary Cooper and James Stewart. (She rarely saw Rudolf Sieber, her husband since 1924, who managed a chicken ranch in Southern California.) Hitch knew of Dietrich's spicy reputation, but he had expected rather more professional behaviour on his sound stage.

'We became inseparable,' Wilding said of his affair with Dietrich. 'In fact, she would not move a step without me. She insisted that I accompany her everywhere, and she took as much interest in my appearance as she did in her own. But close as we became, there was an unfathomable quality about Marlene, a part of her that remained aloof. Sadly, our relationship came to an abrupt end.' When she learned of his marriage to Elizabeth Taylor in 1952, Dietrich was shocked: 'What's she got that I haven't got?' Well might she have asked.

★ Peggy Singer worked for other producers and directors after *Stage Fright*. In 1957, after marrying the film editor Douglas Robertson and moving from London to Hollywood, she rejoined Hitchcock as his assistant and eventually became his de facto associate producer, although he never accorded her that credit. Peggy Robertson worked for Hitch to the end of his career.

For all these reasons, the mere memory of *Stage Fright* evoked an unusually angry animus in Alfred Hitchcock. Unable to establish a positive working relationship with Jane Wyman (who noted with annoyance that the cinematography favoured Dietrich), and virtually powerless to correct Marlene Dietrich's control over everything related to her appearance, Hitch turned his venom on the entire British film-making system. Of good taste, he wrote to Jack Warner, 'there is exactly none here whatsoever. Believe me, they have some pretty crude people. I don't want to bother you with the sordid details. They are my affair, really, and all I have to do is deliver you a picture. As soon as I'm finished shooting and I have the picture rough cut, I'm going to get the hell out of here.' Rarely had he expressed himself in writing with such undiluted, irate misery.

'Hitchcock was a very distant man – cold and professional,' recalled Richard Todd of his experience on this movie. 'He was a strange man, and not a lot of help to his actors. He didn't rehearse, he just gave his first assistant a diagram of what he wanted and then went off to his office. Once we had rehearsed together and worked out our moves, he would come down to have a look, say if it was OK or not, and then shoot it.' Hitch's cool aloofness and distance from the cast of *Stage Fright* was unusually apparent in 1949 – doubtless because of his feeling of estrangement from England and the English, and perhaps because of tensions within the family. (Pat's small role was cut down to less than a minute.) A decade earlier, in the words of his later scenarist, Samuel Taylor, 'He and Alma had shaken the dust of England from their shoes when they set sail for Selznick and Hollywood.' They may have expected the return to be a triumphant or at least an amiable experience, but it was neither. When Hitch left London with his wife and daughter in autumn 1949, he had no immediate idea of the next project. He knew only that he needed to revive a career that, to some critics, seemed blocked.

Strangers on a Train did just that for him, and its success began what might be called a golden age of Alfred Hitchcock masterworks. From 1950 to 1964, he directed thirteen remarkably varied films and, with the inauguration of the decade-long Hitchcock television series in 1955, he became a worldwide phenomenon.

Whit Cook wrote the treatment and Raymond Chandler the first drafts of the screenplay for *Strangers*, based on the novel by Patricia

Highsmith; the final scenario came from the typewriters of Czenzi Ormonde (Ben Hecht's assistant) and Barbara Keon (Hitch's assistant), who worked closely with the director each day.

Produced during the last four months of 1950, the picture gave Robert Walker the role of a lifetime as the wealthy, epicene sociopath who meets tennis champ Farley Granger on a train and suggests that each commit a murder convenient for the other. More subtly than in the book but just as evident, there was a subtext of gay courtship in *Strangers on a Train*, and both the narrative and the accumulated scenes favour Walker and Granger. The leading lady was a Warner contract player, Ruth Roman, who was cast as Granger's fiancée, the daughter of a senator. She had appeared in over twenty movies but was credited in only three, and was best known for her turns as Lothel, The Jungle Queen. In 1949, she appeared in the gritty drama, *Champion*, and Warner set her up for stardom. Their expectations were unmet, although Roman later had a long career in television.

Farley Granger recalled that Hitch drove himself, his crew and his actors with unusual zeal that autumn. But the director had a marked lack of interest in Ruth Roman. 'He was quite critical and harsh with her. Hitch was great fun, but in each film, he had to have one person he could harass.' During the difficult filming of *Rope*, fifty-two-year-old Edith Evanson (as the housekeeper) was the object of Hitch's curious, unaccountable disaffection; now, however improbably, it was an actress favoured by the studio who received his verbal daggers – perhaps because she had not been his choice.

He offered his daughter Pat the role of Roman's outspoken sister; this was the most memorable of Pat's three roles in her father's films, and she dispatched it with a keen mix of cynicism, humour and terror. She was especially effective during a terrifying scene in which her resemblance to the woman he murdered almost causes the psychopathic Bruno (Robert Walker) to repeat the crime and to strangle a party guest.

The motif of strangulation (or attempted or implied strangulation was carefully rehearsed and dramatically rendered in *Strangers on a Train*, as in so many other Hitchcock films: *The Lodger, Secret Agent, Young and Innocent, The Lady Vanishes, Jamaica Inn, Shadow of a Doubt, Notorious, Rope, Stage Fright, Strangers on a Train, Dial 'M' for Murder, Rear Window, To Catch a Thief, Torn Curtain* and *Frenzy*. In social situations, too, Hitchcock delighted in showing friends 'how to strangle a woman with just one hand'. A famous photo sequence by Philippe Halsman shows Hitchcock doing various things to a sculptured bust of his daughter. The final gesture: strangling her.

11

Anne, and a Year of Grace
(1951–1954)

During the four years after Ingrid Bergman appeared in her third and final film for Hitchcock, he had not found anyone like her, nor anyone remotely approaching his ideal of a leading lady. Nevertheless, by summer 1952, he had to proceed with his next picture for Jack Warner – *I Confess*, based on a French novel and play whose premise had intrigued Hitch for years. This was the story of a Catholic priest, wrongly accused of murder, who cannot exculpate himself because the killer confessed the crime to him in a formal act of sacramental confession. Further complications to the plot derive from the fact that the murdered man was blackmailing the priest's former (and now married) girlfriend.

Deeply talented, darkly handsome and exceedingly popular, thirty-two-year-old Montgomery Clift was cast as the taciturn, tortured cleric. Before he became a movie star, Clift had a successful stage career from the age of fourteen, with exceptional notices in Broadway plays by Robert E. Sherwood, Thornton Wilder, Lillian Hellman and Tennessee Williams. At twenty-eight, in 1948, he went to Hollywood and began working with first-rate directors – Fred Zinnemann (*The Search*), Howard Hawks (*Red River*), William Wyler (*The Heiress*) and, most recently, George Stevens, who cast him in *A Place in the Sun* (which marked the start of Clift's lifelong friendship with his co-star, Elizabeth Taylor). With unfailing, discreet loyalty, she listened to his obsessive guilt over his homosexuality, for which his remedies included a dangerous consumption of drugs, washed down with copious amounts of alcohol.

'There are some actors I've felt uncomfortable with,' Hitchcock said, 'and working with Montgomery Clift was difficult because he was a method actor and a neurotic as well.' Karl Malden, in the role of the detective inspector, had known Clift for years. 'Monty was a friend, but he was already a sick man, in the grip of terrible addictions to drugs and drink. As a person, he was wonderful, a great talent, good enough to have been a protégé of the Lunts and Wilder – but he was an accident waiting to happen.'

To play the married woman who is still in love with her former boyfriend (now a priest), Warner believed he had achieved a coup. The Swedish actress Anita Björk had been highly praised for her performance in a film version of *Miss Julie*, and she was eager to meet Hitchcock and to appear in *I Confess*. But the actress arrived in Hollywood with a baby in her arms and a lover at her side. Warner, doubtless thinking of the American public's recent outrage over Ingrid Bergman, dismissed Björk forthwith.

Two weeks remained before the start of location shooting in Quebec that summer, and the picture still lacked a leading lady. Then Warner told Hitch that he had managed to sign the estimable Anne Baxter, a stage and screen actress since the age of thirteen. She had been a major contender to play Scarlett in *Gone With the Wind*, and had appeared in more than thirty films; that year, she was twenty-nine, had won an Oscar for *The Razor's Edge* in 1946, and had co-starred in *All About Eve* in 1950. The granddaughter of Frank Lloyd Wright, Anne was a highly intelligent, greatly respected player who earned the affection and loyalty of her colleagues and fans. She had known the Hitchcocks from the time of *Lifeboat*, in which her husband John Hodiak played the male lead, and so she anticipated a pleasant experience in *I Confess*.

In this, she miscalculated. First, Hitch let it be known that he was displeased with Warner's choice. 'He gave me the impression that I wasn't attractive enough to be in his film,' Anne recalled, 'and so he ordered my hair to be dyed bright blonde, and he merely had Anita Björk's costumes quickly altered to fit me. I didn't object to any of that, but there was a lot of Pygmalion in him – he was very proud of his practice of transforming actresses in order to fit them into his rather fixed ideal. There was also a terrific duality about him. He wanted to be thought of as calm and unflappable, but he could suddenly leap up with alarming speed – it was like lightning encased in the figure of Buddha. Moments like that usually occurred when he had ideas about the "acting" of his camera; the work of the actors interested him much less' (an opinion shared by James Stewart during *Rope*).

As production commenced, he was again fortunate to have the collaboration of Robert Burks, the cinematographer of twelve Hitchcock films from *Strangers on a Train* through *Marnie* – every production except *Psycho*. 'Bob Burks gave Hitch marvellous ideas, and he also had a very tense time with Hitch,' said screenwriter John Michael Hayes, who wrote four Hitchcock scripts during the 1950s. 'He worked long hours, and by the end of every picture was emotionally worn out. He was a painstaking craftsman and contributed greatly to every picture during those years.'

Hitch's cool attitude toward Anne Baxter began an unending chain of difficulties for her. She had complex emotional scenes to perform with Clift, 'but he was so ill and distraught that his eyes wouldn't focus. I needed something from him – some response – but there was nothing, just a blank and distant gaze. He was so disturbed and unhappy.' In addition, there were physically challenging sequences.

The storm scene in the long flashback was extremely difficult – crew members hosed down Monty and me with blasts of cold water, and there were wind machines blowing the piped-in rainwater at the same time. We had to run across a field toward a house in this 'storm' – more hoses, more wind – and Hitch called for repeated takes. He thought actors had it too easy and ought to be roughed up every so often. He was a genius, but he had a bit of the devil in him, no question of that!*

To make the enterprise even more frustrating for everyone, Clift would play no scene without the presence, approval and, effectively,

* The storm sequence and the actors' ordeal in *I Confess* recall similar moments in *The Skin Game, Jamaica Inn, Foreign Correspondent* – as well as anticipating the near-drowning of characters played by Kim Novak in *Vertigo*; Tippi Hedren in *Marnie*; and Julie Andrews, with Paul Newman, in *Torn Curtain*.

the direction of his acting coach, a Russian immigrant named Mira Rostova – a woman of no noticeable talent for either performance or teaching, who had somehow attached herself to this insecure, unhappy actor. She had not appeared on stage or screen in America, but somehow Rostova created the impression that she had a mystic insight into performance art. 'She stood just off camera, nodding her endorsement of everything Monty did, or withholding it,' Anne recalled, 'and this of course enraged Hitchcock.' Karl Malden agreed: 'Monty was absolutely dependent on Rostova – no one could understand why – and this created constant tension for everyone.'* Two years later, Mira Rostova appeared with Clift in her only theatrical outing – an Off Broadway production of *The Seagull*. 'As Nina, she is handicapped by a florid style alien to the whole spirit of Chekhov,' wrote the senior drama critic for the *New York Times*.

As Anne said, there was a 'duality' in Hitchcock, who resented Clift's Method acting and reliance on Rostova but was simultaneously intrigued by the actor's evident self-laceration. Having dealt with gay actors and/or characters in *Rope* and *Strangers on a Train*, Hitch relished the gossip about Clift's private life and that of the German actor O. E. Hasse, who played the killer.

Then an unfortunate incident turned Hitch's behaviour toward Anne from merely cool to downright gelid. One Sunday afternoon, she invited Alma to join her for a drive out to the Canadian countryside. Alma accepted, reminding Anne that she would have to return to Quebec by dinnertime, for Hitch never dined without her. But unusually heavy traffic snarled the roadway on their return, and they arrived at the hotel over an hour late. 'Alma ran through the lobby and into the dining room, where Hitch sat, a look of cold fury on his face. She tried to explain and to lighten the tone, but he would not be placated. I saw then how completely dependent he was on her, and I think she liked that dependence. He needed her to be with him at the dinner hour, and she hadn't been there. I apologised, but he never forgave me, and our relationship was permanently damaged.'

---

* At precisely the same time, the vulnerable Marilyn Monroe was also under the useless tutelage of a Russian acting coach – Natasha Lytess. The 1950s was a period of dangerous Cold War sentiment between the USA and Russia, but it was also notable for a curious idolatry about anyone who claimed even a remote connection to the traditions of the Moscow Art Theatre.

As she was to many actors and directors, Anne could have become a valued friend to the Hitchcocks, but this he would not permit. To François Truffaut, Hitch spoke with singular (and undeserving) asperity in 1963: 'When you compare Anita Björk and Anne Baxter, wouldn't you say that was a pretty awkward substitution?'

The critics were chilly when *I Confess* was released in 1953, but their mostly negative reactions later seemed shallow and blinkered; more than a half-century after the fact, this movie is more often rightly regarded by Hitchcock admirers as both important and rewarding.

As for Anne, she subsequently appeared in no fewer than seventy movies and television programmes and enjoyed enormous success on stage in musicals, dramas and comedies. When she married a second time in 1960 – to entrepreneur Randolph Galt – she acceded to his precipitous, eccentric desire to manage a cattle station in the Australian outback. To say that her life there was austere would be to glorify it: she lived in a tin house that had electricity only two hours daily. She and Galt had two daughters, and Anne endured a miscarriage. Then one day, her husband simply walked out. The result of these formidable years was a remarkable book, *Intermission: A True Story* – 'written with inner eyes and a dramatic sense', according to an astute reviewer in 1976. 'She has balanced beautifully the internal and external "plots" of her story. Had she transformed the material into fiction, someone would have compared Anne Baxter to Doris Lessing. Read this serious book and pray its author is at work on another.' In February 1977, Anne married stockbroker David Klee, with whom she undertook the redesign and enlargement of a home in Connecticut – but Klee died suddenly eight months after their marriage.

When I visited her in 1980, she was busy preparing several new roles. A woman of many interests and talents, of consummate charm and immediate warmth, she was uninterested in mere celebrity: 'I just want to improve myself with every new project,' she said. In early December 1985, she collapsed, suffering a massive stroke while walking along Madison Avenue in New York City; on the twelfth of that month, without regaining consciousness, she died. Anne Baxter was sixty-two.

'I have to consider whether my potential heroine is the kind of girl I can mould into the heroine of my imagination,' Hitchcock had said earlier. 'She must have real beauty and real youth.' In late spring of 1953, seeking a leading lady for his film version of Frederick Knott's successful play *Dial 'M' for Murder*, Hitch finally found the heroine of his imagination. Twenty-three-year-old Grace Kelly came from a wealthy Philadelphia family, had attended the American Academy of Dramatic Arts and performed in a number of live television plays in New York and Hollywood. Her movie debut was little more than a cameo in *Fourteen Hours*, and in Fred Zinnemann's *High Noon*, she seemed awkward as the Quaker wife of Western lawman Gary Cooper, who was twenty-eight years her senior, looked every day of it, and dominated the film. 'When I saw the first cut of that picture,' she told me, 'I raced back to New York from Hollywood and begged [the noted drama teacher] Sandy Meisner for acting lessons.'

That had been the extent of Grace's experience. Although she was under contract to Metro-Goldwyn-Mayer, the studio executives seemed oddly lukewarm toward her, showed no interest in promoting her, and blithely loaned her out for bargain prices. But when Hitch saw a preview of John Ford's still unreleased African adventure *Mogambo*, in which Grace was a supporting player to Clark Gable and Ava Gardner, he saw the indefinable conjunction of elegance and sexuality that convinced him she could be transformed into a major star. Very few shared his intuition, but Jack Warner was eager to get on with *Dial 'M'*, to be photographed in 3-D; besides, she came to his studio cheaply.

3-D was one of Hollywood's gimmicks, a reaction to decreased movie attendance in the early 1950s, when television was invading the American home. The process, which required movie-goers to wear special disposable eyeglasses, did not interest Hitchcock at all, who saw it as fundamentally anti-cinematic, with its constant reminder to the audience that they were 'out there' merely to be assaulted by visual tricks.

'Hitch felt frustrated and annoyed at having to use the cumbersome 3-D process,' Grace told me years later. 'And poor Bob Burks had to tell him, "Oh, no, Hitch – with this 3-D camera, you can't do this and you can't do that." Almost the entire movie was filmed in a single set, and things would have proceeded much more easily in a traditional format, but we had endless rehearsals and were always doing an awkward dance around the enormous machine, which seemed to me the size of a room. Hitch was right when he said that most movie-goers would not see the picture in 3-D – the fad would soon be over, and most theatres screened it flat, which was no detriment to the film's effect at all.'

Grace's co-stars were Ray Milland, Robert Cummings and (from the Broadway production) Anthony Dawson and John Williams. Filming began on 30 July 1953 and concluded on 25 September; the release, however, had to be delayed until the conclusion of the New York run of the play, almost a year later. Despite the technical inconveniences, challenges and general nuisance, Hitchcock was in high spirits, thanks to Grace. He planned her hairstyles and wardrobe with her cooperation, and he accepted some of her important suggestions. As so often, he also tried to shock her with his crude jokes, sexual innuendoes and toilet humour. 'I said I heard worse things when I was in convent school, and he loved that.'

He also relished the reports of Grace's private life. At twenty-three, she was playful, athletic, popular and freewheeling. A devout Roman Catholic, Grace was nevertheless sufficiently independent to allow for love and its facsimiles without a burden of neurotic guilt. Her lovers (among them designer Oleg Cassini and actors Gene Lyons, Jean-Pierre Aumont and William Holden) made up an impressive platoon of men. She and her parents of course presumed she would eventually marry – preferably a Catholic, but certainly not a divorcé. Meantime, her youth, beauty, wit and talent were powerful attractions; she was, in other words, firmly in the Hitchcock tradition of Madeleine Carroll and Ingrid Bergman.

During the production of *Dial 'M' for Murder*, Grace and Ray Milland (twenty-five years her senior) became ardent lovers, to the point that his two-decade-long marriage was seriously jeopardised. 'Hitchcock the voyeur couldn't have been more delighted,' wrote one biographer. Such a reaction was another example of what Anne Baxter called the duality in the director. He adored Grace; he was in love with her the way a schoolboy develops a hopeless crush on an unattainable object of desire; he was already planning a second and third feature for her, and he hoped for more after those.

Hitch marked his fifty-fourth birthday during production that summer. He seemed content with cosseting Grace, creating an image of apparently cool, chic sensuality whose inspiration was at least partly the woman herself, and partly Hitch's intuition of what she might be or become under his tutelage. Decades later, her performances are remarkable for a quiet, cautious refinement and warmth that forestalls remoteness. By projecting a credible hybrid of elegance and sex, Grace might for ever belong professionally to Hitch, in roles created for her that were variations on herself. He even spoke to her of his long-cherished hope of one day making a film of James Barrie's delicate, mystical romance *Mary Rose*.

Not only because of Grace's attractive suitors like Milland and others, Hitch clearly knew that any notion or attempt at frank sexual activity between them was more than unlikely, it would be disastrous. If she would only remain his willing and winsome Galatea, and she did, he might never lose her – but this was the height of improbability, the repetition of the Ingrid fantasy. Hitchcock was simultaneously a mature artist and something of an unseasoned, awkward and still socially insecure adolescent, resentful of the impulses that were paradoxically at the very source and centre of his visual genius.

It is precisely this complex of elements that gives the life and character of Alfred Hitchcock such poignancy; that must evoke our compassion; and that in some marred, marvellous way for the better, still shares something of our common humanity. Were that not so, it would be impossible to explain his enduring worldwide popularity and his legacy of sleek entertainments.

The sexual revolution that exploded in the 1960s in America was being quietly but audaciously prepared by a few directors like Hitchcock in the 1950s – the era of another Alfred who was pre-occupied with sex: the notorious Dr Kinsey, who had already published *Sexual Behavior in the Human Male*. Just when Hitch and Grace were at work on *Dial 'M'*, Kinsey brought out a companion volume, *Sexual Behavior in the Human Female* – a topic that was all but taboo. At the same time, movies were pushing the boundaries of the permissible – like 3-D, a gradual new frankness in dialogue and dress was partly a response to the threat from television.

The often lazy sprinkling of four-letter words and the easy exploit-ation of sex in movies were some years ahead, but things began to percolate when director Otto Preminger released his movie *The Moon Is Blue* in June 1953. Clark Gable had told Vivien Leigh that he didn't 'give a damn' what happened to her at the end of *Gone With the Wind*, but fourteen years on, Preminger's characters used – for the first time in an American movie – the proscribed words *seduce, mistress* and, most offensive and therefore most publicised, *virgin*, a word that presumably could only be uttered with reference to one woman in religious history.

With that, the lid was off, and there were dire predictions about the imminent collapse of morality in America. Atomic and hydrogen bombs were being tested; there were signs of both dangerous and aggressive isolationism and imperialism; and the death penalty was routinely used as state-sanctioned murder. But the country's pulpits and classrooms thundered with imprecations against sex, particularly as it involved the feelings and needs of women. There was, therefore, a schizoid attitude in popular culture, a potent sign of which was the amalgam of affection and condescension with which Marilyn Monroe was regarded.

One of the oddest means taken to protect less frankly physical movie stars from any connection to sexual activity was by casting them opposite men old enough to be their fathers. Watching *Sabrina*, movie-goers somehow accepted that Audrey Hepburn would reject dashing William Holden in favour of Humphrey Bogart, who was thirty years older than Hepburn; that she would be romantically involved with Henry Fonda (twenty-four years older) in *War and Peace*; with Fred Astaire (Bogart's age) in *Funny Face*; and with Gary Cooper (twenty-eight years Hepburn's senior) in *Love in the Afternoon*. Watching these pictures decades later, perhaps only Cary Grant was credible as her romantic leading man, and to hell with the twenty-five-year age difference between them in *Charade*.

Audrey Hepburn was lithe and lovely, entirely feminine but with a faintly boyish aspect, for she had no figure, much less curves; 'gamine' and 'elfin' were most commonly used to describe her – words that could never apply to Marilyn Monroe. Audrey was also insistently European, and she evoked a somewhat protective, romantic reaction from some in her audiences. But she was more of a fragile, stained-glass-window figure than a sex symbol. This may be why her profoundest performance was in *The Nun's Story*, and her least credible was as a Manhattan prostitute in *Breakfast at Tiffany's*.

Grace was exactly Audrey's age, and her leading men were also her elders: Gary Cooper, Clark Gable, Ray Milland, James Stewart, Cary Grant, Alec Guinness and (twice) Bing Crosby. Hence, the odd asymmetries in casting leading men opposite Grace and Audrey ought to be understood in light of radically shifting notions about sex in America, which was still in the stern grip of its Puritan roots.

As complicated as the 3-D process was for Hitch, his crew and cast, there was an even greater challenge during the week of rehearsals and multiple takes for the attempted strangulation of the heroine by the hired killer and her stabbing him with scissors. 'This is nicely done,' he said after one shot, 'but there wasn't enough gleam to the scissors, and a murder without gleaming scissors is like asparagus without the hollandaise sauce – tasteless,' which is a typical Hitchcock analogy, linking violence with food, a recurring motif absolutely central to his penultimate picture, *Frenzy*. The finished sequence, awkward and difficult even for the pliant, patient and cooperative Grace, remains one of the most explicitly disturbing in the Hitchcock catalogue. The attempted murder is a kind of sexual conflict, with inserted shots of Grace's legs – visible through her diaphanous negligee – pushing up against her attacker, and her gradually stifled whimpering recorded to resemble erotic moaning.

According to Grace, Hitch was able to sustain the demands of the picture because he was already preparing his next one, from a witty and suspenseful script by John Michael Hayes (the first in Hitch's lucrative, multi-picture deal with Paramount Studios). 'He described all the details of the fabulous set for *Rear Window* – the apartments of the characters opposite Jimmy Stewart's, and their little stories. Hitch was thinking about it all the time, and when he had a moment to himself he went off to confer with Mr Hayes or the production designers.' The result would be one of Hitchcock's indisputable master-works and a perennial crowd pleaser.

'The stamp of Hitchcock's genius is on every frame of the finished film,' recalled Hayes, who wrote three more scripts for the director.

> But the impression he gave everyone – that he did every bit of it alone – is utter nonsense. Reading Hitchcock's interviews, it's possible to have the impression that *he* wrote the scripts, developed the characters and provided the motivations. I knew that he liked my script for *Rear Window* when he told me that *Alma* liked it – that was the only way he could offer a compliment. He also said that because I was receiving such a low salary, he thought I deserved a bonus. Then he said we ought to wait and

see if *Rear Window* would look as good on film as it did on paper. And when it did, he said the bonus would have to wait for the reactions of critics. By that time, it was clear that he kept putting me off because he wanted me to do his next picture at the same salary. When we disagreed on some points in the script for *To Catch a Thief*, Hitch told me, 'Don't get me angry, or you won't get the bonus for *Rear Window*,' and I replied, 'Hitch, don't ever mention that imaginary bonus again.' He didn't, and I never got it.

But Hitch could also be surprisingly thoughtful toward Hayes: 'When he learned that I'd never been to the south of France, he arranged for me and my wife to go, at studio expense, so that I could research the locales [for *To Catch a Thief*].The trip was, of course, very welcome.'

Despite his unpleasant recollections of working on *Rope*, James Stewart quickly signed on for *Rear Window* after reading the script and learning the identity of his co-star. He had new toupees created and called in expert cosmetologists, the better to deflect recognition that he was twenty-one years older than the leading lady.

Meanwhile, Hitch proceeded with his meticulous, deliberate construction of Grace's image. 'She was rather mousy in *High Noon*,' he said, 'but she blossomed out for me.' Accordingly, the costume designer for *Rear Window* recalled that Hitch was virtually clinical in his precise ideas for Grace's wardrobe. 'Every costume was detailed in the finished script,' according to Edith Head. 'There was a reason for every colour Grace wore, every style, and he was absolutely certain about everything. For one scene, he saw her in pale green, for another in white chiffon. He was really putting his dream together in the studio. Hitch wanted her to appear like a piece of Dresden china, something slightly untouchable.'

For reasons more significant than costumes and the most elaborate set in Hollywood history, *Rear Window* may properly be assessed as a film of unusual wit, surprising depth and appealing warmth. Both thriller and romance, it has not a moment to spare. 'It was a satisfactory experience,' Hitch told me, 'because it was the epitome of the subjective treatment. A man looks, he sees, he reacts – to a woman even more than to a situation. Thus, you construct a mental process. *Rear Window* is entirely a mental process, done visually.'

The cast list for *Rear Window* was considerably longer than that of

Dial 'M'. Georgine Darcy, in the role of the curvaceous young dancer dubbed 'Miss Torso,' recalled 'Grace was very sweet. Without make-up, you wouldn't know it was Grace Kelly. She wore glasses, and she was very unassuming, very much a lady, very quiet.'

To Darcy's surprise, Hitch asked her what kind of pie she liked. Apple pie, she replied – and maybe cherry pie. 'But I hate pumpkin pie, Mr Hitchcock – ugh!' Next day, he shot the scene in which a neighbour's dog is found strangled. 'I want you to look over there and throw up,' Hitch said. 'I didn't need to throw up, but that was the look he wanted from me. So he brought in a pumpkin pie, and he did the scene several times.' Her filmed reaction close-up is more dismay than disgust – perhaps, as she remembered, because her director served the hated pumpkin pie with a dollop of crude Cockney jokes.

Hitch would have been delighted to begin *To Catch a Thief* immediately after the completion of *Rear Window* in January 1954, but Grace was still under contract to MGM. Executives there noted her increasing popularity and decided to loan her out for three films, to be made in less than four months – *The Bridges at Tōko-Ri*, *The Country Girl* (for which she won the best actress Oscar) and *Green Fire*, in which she coped with the discomforts of the South American jungle. In May, exhausted after less than one day to herself, she joined Hitch, Cary Grant and the crew on the French Riviera for location work on *To Catch a Thief*.

The movie is magnificent to look at (and won for Robert Burks an Oscar for best colour cinematography); it also has a collection of unerringly right American and Continental actors with considerable charm, and some astonishingly risqué double entendres that escaped the censors' pencils. But despite all its prettiness, it is perhaps like a pleasant journey with handsome travel companions and a picnic lunch, and something of a disappointment after the brilliant combination of humour and suspense that characterised *Rear Window*.

The cat burglar sought by French police in *To Catch a Thief* was played by a winsome actress and acrobat named Brigitte Auber, then twenty-six and appearing in her first English-language film. Later, Hitchcock occasionally invited her to fine restaurants when he travelled abroad, on the apparent pretext that he had a starring role in mind for her. One evening, after dinner in Paris, they were seated in her car near the apartment she shared with her boyfriend. Auber was shocked when Hitchcock lurched toward her, attempting to kiss her 'full on the mouth'. She protested, and Hitchcock 'appeared mortified by the incident.' Over the years, he contacted her a few times, asking if they might patch up their friendship, but the bond was broken. The actress told Hitchcock she felt betrayed. 'One never imagines that someone like that has a crush on you,' she said. 'It was an enormous disappointment for me.' No such incident marred the friendship of Alfred Hitchcock and Grace Kelly.

Grace had completed eight films in less than three years, and for a year beginning September 1954, she called a halt to this breakneck schedule to consider her future. She marked her twenty-fifth birthday that November, and she travelled and manoeuvered various romantic entanglements. Her Academy Award for *The Country Girl*, presented in the spring of 1955, made it difficult for MGM to exact retribution for ignoring their increasing demands that she appear in whatever productions they lined up for her, no matter how frivolous, tedious or offensive. During this hiatus – on 6 May 1955, to be exact – she was shipped off to represent MGM at the Cannes Film Festival. As part of the extended activities, Grace agreed to meet Prince Rainier III for a photo session celebrating the principality of Monaco and the kingdom of Hollywood.

Grace Kelly made her last two movies between autumn 1955 and early spring 1956; that April, she married Rainier and became Her Serene Highness, Princess Grace of Monaco. She and Ingrid were the only women who had three leading roles for Hitchcock, and when she departed Hollywood for a new life at the age of twenty-six, he told the press he was pleased she had found the role of a lifetime. Privately, he was less cynical, as François Truffaut observed. 'The former Cockney lad was rather awed by the title of "princess" that the beautiful Philadelphia society girl acquired when she left Hollywood for the cliffs of Monaco.'

12

Women Who Knew Too Much
(1954–1957)

'From the days of the silent movies right up to the present time,' Hitch said at lunch one day in the autumn of 1976, 'I have never had any interest in motion pictures that I call "photographs of people talking". These have nothing to do with cinema whatsoever. When you just position a camera and photograph an actor or two or a group, and then do the close-ups and the two-shots – well, I find that all very boring indeed. Of course, you've got to have dialogue – after all, in the silent pictures, no sound came from the mouths. But at least then the emphasis was on the pictorial and the visual.'

His remarks provide an essential explanation of why his next movie, begun, in October 1954, immediately after the completion of *To Catch a Thief*, may be regarded as an exercise in tedium. *The Trouble with Harry* is little more than ninety-nine minutes of actors talking (and talking some more), with only the repeated action of the burying and unburying of a corpse for action. 'The plot itself is too tenuous for a screen comedy,' wrote a Paramount story editor. 'Not recommended.'

But Hitchcock could do as he pleased, and he went ahead. The result was a film entirely anomalous in his entire catalogue: it is impossible to care much about anyone or anything, for the director seemed to put aside every one of his rules – nothing *happens*. The movie debut of twenty-year-old Shirley MacLaine (playing the mother of a six-year-old boy) was, in the fullness of time, considered auspicious, although in interviews and books, MacLaine has but rarely and paren-thetically mentioned Hitchcock's name.

Decades later, some academics have taken up the critical sword on behalf of *The Trouble With Harry*, claiming to find in its rambling and tortured dialogue all sorts of philosophical and theological depths. 'Well, jolly good luck to them,' as Dr Hartz (Paul Lukas) says, watching a trainload of Britons escape his gunmen in *The Lady Vanishes*. Anguished literary-philosophical tracts should be unnecessary in defending a Hitchcock picture; his genius, after all, was to entertain a mass audience *and*, remarkably often, to deal with consequential matters. In this rare case, he fell wide of the mark. (There was one happy outcome, however: the movie was the first of eight historic collaborations between Hitch and composer Bernard Herrmann.)

Then things happened quickly, and very much for the better. For years, Hitch had tried to find a way of improving and remaking his 1934 British thriller *The Man Who Knew Too Much*. At last, with the new year 1955, he had his chance, thanks to a dazzling, suspenseful and emotionally vivid script by John Michael Hayes, and a superla-tive cast headed by James Stewart and Doris Day. Hitchcock admired Doris's emotional range, and for years, he had promised to find the right project for her. Now he had it, in the story of a family, on foreign holiday, whose son is kidnapped to secure their silence when they become unintentionally involved in a plot to assassinate a foreign dignitary. After the languid restiveness of *The Trouble With Harry*, *The Man Who Knew Too Much* is Hitchcock back at the top of his form, directing a picture remarkable for its frank depiction of love lost and regained and a threatened family restored to safety. It remains one of the most emotionally complex and satisfying pictures of his career.

At thirty-one, Doris Day much anticipated working with Hitch, but she had never been outside the United States and had a lifelong terror of air travel — hence the requirement of location work in London and Marrakesh forced her to travel by train and ship. During her first meeting with Hitchcock in his offices at Paramount, he made it clear that he was (as she recalled) 'very precise about exactly what he wanted for my wardrobe.' But if his concern for her appearance repeated his approaches to Ingrid and Grace, nothing in his manner with Doris exceeded cool cordiality. She did not expect an immediate friendship, but she found him remote and uncaring about her performance.

From that day, 'Hitch and Doris Day did not get on too well,' according to the script supervisor, Constance Willis. Doris did not expect flattery, praise or social intimacy, but she was a serious professional who wanted to please her director, and throughout the filming, she had no indication that she was succeeding. For one thing, recalled cast member Bernard Miles, Hitch 'always seemed more concerned with technical matters than with the actors. And he didn't like having anyone else on the set but himself to tell a joke – so he used to sulk or retire into himself if Jimmy Stewart or another player really made me laugh.'

From April through July, when *The Man Who Knew Too Much* completed interior shooting back in Hollywood, his leading lady spent each day trying to determine just where she was miscalculating, just how she was disappointing the great master.

'He didn't direct. He didn't say a word. He just sat there, and all he did was start and stop the camera. Hitch never spoke to me before a scene to tell me how he wanted it played, and he never spoke to me afterward. "Well, that's the way he is," said Jimmy Stewart.' Throughout production, 'not once did A. Hitchcock say a word to me that might have indicated he was a director and I was an actress.' Her anxiety increased daily.

> I was convinced that I must have been the worst actress he'd ever had – he just never said anything to me about my work, and I had the impression that he felt saddled with an actress he didn't want. I felt I should try to get out of the picture long before we did most of the interiors back in California, and so finally I arranged a meeting with Mr Hitchcock. I told him I knew I wasn't pleasing him, and that if he wanted to replace me with someone else, he could. He was astonished! He told me it was quite the reverse, that he thought I was doing everything right – and that if I hadn't been doing everything right, he would have told me.

The finished film may be the finest of Doris Day's fifty movie and television performances, but this was not a collaboration she wanted to repeat. 'Hitchcock never gave actors any real direction,' according to Reggie

Nalder, who played the hired assassin in the Albert Hall sequence. 'You really didn't know where you stood with him. He told very crude and dirty stories like a schoolboy, and he stared right at my crotch whenever he talked to me, never once looking me in the eye.'

Days before Hitch departed Hollywood for the foreign work on *The Man Who Knew Too Much* in April 1955, he saw an actress on television's *Pepsi-Cola Playhouse*. She was twenty-five-year-old Vera Miles, and he immediately summoned her to a meeting, announcing big plans to turn her into the next Grace Kelly. This was evidently irresistible, for within days, Vera signed a five-year, three-picture deal with Alfred J. Hitchcock Productions. Her contract specified that she was never to appear in advertisements for swimsuits or lingerie and that Edith Head would design not only her wardrobe for films and television but also for general wear in private life – 'so she wouldn't go around in slacks looking like a Van Nuys housewife,' he said.

Hitch was about to launch his own TV series, and he promised her the starring role in the premiere episode, which turned out to be 'Revenge', a kind of curtain-raiser for her first Hitchcock feature, *The Wrong Man*. Her somewhat severe beauty and slightly neurasthenic gaze were perfect for the part of an emotionally disturbed woman. In 'Revenge', her husband returns from work and she tells him she has been attacked by an intruder. As they drive in their car, she sees a man and cries, 'That's him! That's the one who did it!' The enraged husband follows the stranger and kills him. He then returns to his wife, and they resume their journey – until she points to another man and cries out, 'There he is! That's the man!'

'I feel the same way directing Vera that I did with Grace,' Hitch told a reporter. 'She has a style, an intelligence and a quality of understatement.' Hitchcock seemed to disregard – or felt he could soften – the absence in Vera's photos of the single most important quality that gave Grace's image so much nuance and appeal: warmth. His plans for Vera moved along at a rapid gallop: more clothes and make-up tests, more discussions about projects, more talk about her personal wardrobe, and more considerations about where and with whom she must and must not be seen publicly. 'Vera Miles is the girl who is going to replace Grace Kelly,' Hitchcock told the editor of *Cosmopolitan* magazine.

He also chose to discount the fact that Vera had a full life, with two young children by her first husband and a recently contracted second marriage. But she was to be completely made over – as if turned into a new creation without a past – and to this enterprise he gave himself with obsessive fascination. 'Hitch had an obsession with her, sure,' according to his associate producer Herbert Coleman. 'But it never went beyond imagining.'

'He has never complimented me,' the actress said while they were filming *The Wrong Man* in New York during the late winter and spring of 1956, 'or even told me why he signed me.' If he had hoped his attitude would keep her alert and docile, he miscalculated. To begin with, as costume designer Rita Riggs observed, 'Vera was a lovely girl, too independent to be anyone's Trilby [to Hitchcock's Svengali].'

She worked carefully and effectively with Hitch and Henry Fonda on *The Wrong Man*, a disturbing black-and-white movie based on a true story of a man falsely accused of armed robbery. As the victim's wife, Vera gave a haunting performance of a sensitive woman's descent from depression into madness, her expression becoming gradually more distant and affectless, as she loses faith in everything – the judicial system, her husband and herself.

After delays due to script problems and illness, Hitchcock was finally ready to begin production on *Vertigo*. 'Vera's wardrobe, hair and make-up tests had been completed,' Hitch told me, recalling the events of autumn 1956. 'Everything had been very carefully planned and prepared, and Jimmy [Stewart] was ready and waiting. Then she got pregnant, and in the spring, she withdrew – and this was going to be the part that would make Vera a major star, a real actress.' He considered her departure a defection from their mutual best interests.

'Over the span of years,' Vera Miles reflected later, 'he's had one type of woman in his films – Madeleine Carroll, Ingrid Bergman, Grace Kelly. I tried to please him, but I couldn't. I was stubborn, and he wanted someone who could be moulded.' As for *Vertigo*: 'He got his picture – and I got a son.'

She remained under contract to him, appearing in a few of his television programmes and later assigned a supporting role in *Psycho*. 'I lost all interest in her, and I couldn't get the rhythm with her going again.' When Hitch and I discussed *Vertigo* at some length in the autumn of 1976, I suggested that Vera might have given him the performance he wanted, but that her replacement, Kim Novak, was born for the role of a Kansas girl (like Vera) twice refashioned by exploitative men into the image of another. 'Vera walks on the ground' was my analogy during our conversation, 'while Kim seems to float – she's the ghostly figure you wanted for *Vertigo*.' His quiet response: 'Perhaps. At least I got to throw the new girl into the water.'

And so Hitchcock had to force the actress finally cast in *Vertigo* to be a surrogate – to substitute for the one he had initially chosen for the role. This, of course, is the major theme of the picture.

Just twenty-four, Columbia Studios' Kim Novak had dispatched a few uneven screen appearances, but *Picnic* had established her as a major new star – physically opulent, frankly carnal and rumoured to be difficult. She was also splendidly photogenic in Technicolor, and she had a breathless quality suggesting that she was simultaneously available and remote. But she required what is sometimes called special handling.

Kim Novak was no last-minute compromise for Hitch; indeed, she was the only other serious candidate for the challenging role in *Vertigo*. She was also an established commodity, had appeared on the cover of *Time* magazine, was one of Hollywood's two or three bankable stars, and justified the presence of James Stewart in a way that the uncertain and still widely unknown Vera Miles never could. Hitchcock, however, could never let go of his resentment that his plans for Vera had been stymied. 'The majority of actors are stupid children,' he said more than once, particularly in the context of *Vertigo*. 'Think of Kim Novak. In the second part of *Vertigo*, when she's dark-haired and looks less like Kim Novak, I even managed to get her to act. But the only reason I took her was because Vera Miles was pregnant.'

Connie Willis, the script supervisor for the northern California location filming of *Vertigo* before Peggy Robertson assumed those duties permanently in Hollywood, was forever grateful to Alfred Hitchcock for all she learned from him during their work on *The Man Who Knew Too Much* and *Vertigo*. 'But I did see in Hitch that suppression of natural, instinctive feelings which the Victorian era demanded,' she told me, 'and that meant that all sorts of fantasies would emerge – not to mention fetishes, and with Hitch, it was black high heels and blondes.'

In fact, the shoes provided the first sticking point. 'Kim said she couldn't possibly wear them,' Edith Head recalled, 'because they would exaggerate what she thought were her rather fleshy calves.' Virtually the entire wardrobe Hitch and Edith Head had prepared for her became points of conflict for Kim Novak (shades of Nita Naldi).

Many years later, Novak acknowledged, 'Before shooting started, [Hitchcock] sent me over to Edith Head, who showed me a set of drawings. When I saw them, the very first thing I said was, "I'm sorry – I don't wear black shoes." She said, "Alfred Hitchcock wants you to wear these shoes," and I said, "I'm sure he doesn't mind." I didn't think it would matter to him what kind of shoes I wore. I had never had a director who was particular about the costumes, the way they were designed, the specific colours. The two things he wanted the most were those shoes and that grey suit. When Edith Head showed me that grey suit, I said, "Oh, my God, that looks like it would be very hard to act in – it's very confining." Then we had the first fitting of the black dress, and that was even worse, and I said, "This is so restrictive." And she said, "Well, maybe you'd better talk to Alfred Hitchcock about all this!"'

'Miss Novak arrived with all sorts of preconceived notions that I couldn't possibly go along with,' Hitchcock said. 'I don't like to argue with a performer – there's no reason to bring the electricians in on our troubles. So I went to her dressing room and told her about the dresses and hairdos that I had been planning for several months.'

She was not easily convinced. 'I'll wear anything,' Kim Novak said, hastening back to Edith Head's office for refuge, 'so long as it isn't a suit – and any colour, so long as it isn't grey.' Edith then showed her the relevant pages of the script: 'This girl must look as if she's just drifted out of the San Francisco fog' – hence her pale colouring, the formally swept blonde wig, the grey suit, the white gloves. 'She walks and drives a car in San Francisco,' Edith explained to her, 'where everyone wears suits – and the script specifically calls for a *grey tailored suit.*'

'If it has to be a suit,' continued Kim, 'I like *purple* suits, or white suits.'

'Handle it, Edith,' said Hitchcock when he heard of this ongoing contretemps. 'I don't care what she wears – as long as it's a grey suit.'

In *Vertigo*, Kim Novak wore a grey suit, black shoes, a black evening dress, a capacious white coat, and everything else mandated by the director – and when she saw the finished film, she must have realised that he had been right all along, that few actresses have ever been more gloriously dressed and photographed. Very much to the point, her outfits seem undated fifty years later. Like the film itself, her wardrobe was timeless.

From pre-production through filming, tensions mounted. 'I never sat down with him for dinner or tea or anything,' she recalled – 'except one cast dinner, and I was late to that. It wasn't my fault, but I think he thought I had delayed in order to make a star entrance, and he held that against me. During the shooting, he never really told me what he was thinking.' Like many of her predecessors (most recently, Doris Day and Vera Miles), Kim was never sure 'if Hitchcock ever liked me.'

For many years, Kim Novak's few documented remarks about Hitchcock were cool. With time and the establishment of *Vertigo* as one of the great motion pictures of all time, she was more sanguine: the role and the movie were 'so much of what I was going through already at Columbia. We'd be told, "You're special, you're different, we want you," and then someone would say, "We want you, but we want you to look like somebody else."' Which, of course, was precisely the case with both the actress and her role in *Vertigo* – which she later acknowledged. 'It was almost as if Hitchcock was Elster, the man [in the film] who was telling me to play a role – here's what I had to do and wear . . .' James Stewart agreed: 'I could tell it was a very personal film even while he was making it.' So did Samuel Taylor, who wrote the final screenplay for the picture: 'Anyone who saw him during the making of it could see, as I did, that this was a story he felt very deeply indeed.'

Vertigo was the high mark of Kim Novak's career, and she was never again offered anything remotely as significant. Retiring from film and television at the age of fifty-seven, she withdrew from Hollywood to manage an animal farm with her second husband, a veterinarian.

Vertigo is a testament to Alfred Hitchcock's lifelong fascination for making over actresses according to his dream-ideal of blonde perfection. He supervised everything about their presentations on screen, from hairstyles to wardrobes, from make-up to shoes, from camera angles to the final cut.

'He made you over, didn't he?' Stewart shouts at Novak at the finale, referring to the man who 'created' Madeleine from Judy. 'He made you over just like I made you over – only better. Not only the clothes and the hair, but the looks and the manner and the words. And then what did he do? Did he train you? Did he rehearse you? Did he tell you exactly what to do and what to say? You were a very apt pupil, weren't you? You were a very apt pupil!' So much could be (and was) said of the director and his leading ladies. But this close template between the artist and the art is neither rare nor surprising, for the artist, after all, has no other raw material with which to work than his own inner life, however much it is to be treated and transmuted.

To call *Vertigo* a masterpiece of moviemaking is no longer considered a peculiar judgement. It has something of the myth of Pygmalion and Galatea, and something of Tristan and Isolde – and everything of a greatly inspired, greatly troubled and terribly lonely fantasist. Throughout his life and career, Hitch strove to realise his dream ever more fully, but that involved a conflict between brutal, repressed sensuality and fastidious refinement, between reality and art. 'I made the film in order to present a man's dreamlike nature,' he told me at our first long meeting in 1975. The man, I later understood, was Hitch himself. Like Stewart in *Vertigo*, Hitchcock chose fantasy over reality, and for this, the medium of film was perfect, for the carefully designed beauty of an actress is itself illusory. But from that art and artifice derive deeper realities that have nothing fake about them.

And what of Hitchcock and men? He cultivated actors like Cary Grant, Joseph Cotten, James Stewart and Henry Fonda for what they could provide him in his films – precisely the reasons they cultivated him. But there were never solid friendships. 'He was never deeply friendly with any of his famous [male] stars,' according to Hitch's authorised biographer, 'even if, as with Cary Grant and James Stewart, he liked them and worked with them as often as possible' – four times each, in fact. But Hitchcock made no attempt to conceal his discomfort and even his resentment of men like John Gielgud, Michael Redgrave, Laurence Olivier, Gregory Peck, Rod Taylor, Sean Connery and Paul Newman – most of all, perhaps, because they had the confidence that comes from good looks and the adulation of fans.

It is true to say of Alfred Hitchcock what biographer Leon Edel wrote of Henry James: a 'spiritual transvestism' (which fascinated Hitch in both its literal and figurative senses) paradoxically protected a sense of masculine integrity. It was also true of Hitchcock what Edel wrote of James, that all his life he harboured 'within the house of the [artist's] inner world the spirit of a young adult female, worldly-wise and curious, possessing a treasure of unassailable virginity and innocence. For this was the androgynous nature of the creator and the drama of his [art]: innocence and worldliness.'

This goes a long way toward a compassionate understanding of perhaps the greatest conflict and pain in the life of Alfred Hitchcock: that he recoiled from what he most desired, that he knew the deepest meaning of romantic vertigo, the simultaneous desire to fall and the fear of falling in love. In *Vertigo*, we learn as much about Alfred Hitchcock from the complex dualities of Novak's character as from the tormented, doomed lover portrayed by Stewart, for she is both victim and victimiser. She appears cool, remote and aloof, but she yearns to express a raging passion. 'It was actually his heroines that he identified with,' continued Hitchcock's authorised biographer.

In this regard, Hitchcock's mature films poignantly explore the nature of absence and of loss. In *The Man Who Knew Too Much*, it is the loss of family security abroad; in *The Wrong Man*, the loss of innocence and family unity at home; in the trilogy *Vertigo–North by Northwest–Psycho*, the loss of identity itself, for there is no living person at the centre of these three great works. Madeleine Elster, George Kaplan and Mrs Bates are the quintessential MacGuffins.

The emotional landscape of *Vertigo* is both heartbreakingly personal and disturbingly universal – Hitchcock's ultimate statement on the romantic fallacy. He much resembled his countryman Ernest Dowson (1867–1900), whose one loving relationship, with a London waitress, was almost certainly an invention of his fervent imagination. Never convinced that he could find real love, Dowson wanted to kill off all its possibilities in advance and lament the loss forever after. All the stories in his collection *Dilemmas* (1895) tell of frustrated love, of a man's melancholy retreat into the solitude of the disturbed romantic.

In Dowson's most famous poem, 'Cynara,' the impassioned lover cries out for madder music and stronger wine, even as he grieves in the shadow of his lost love. *Vertigo* begins with a tight close-up of an anonymous woman's face, from whose right eye the credits spiral outward. From there to the uncompromisingly tragic ending of *Vertigo*, Hitchcock (like Dowson, in *A Comedy of Masks*) was gripped by the contrast of mask versus face – a common currency in Victorian allegories. As Samuel Taylor recalled, 'Hitch knew exactly what he wanted to do in this film, exactly what he wanted to say, and how it should be seen and heard. It was his story from first frame to last – and every moment of it revealed him.'

13

No One at the Centre
(1958–1960)

'Hitch's main purpose in life,' according to Ernest Lehman, who wrote the screenplay for *North by Northwest*, 'was not the one that might seem obvious – namely, the making of movies. He had to make them, of course, to keep the franchise on his reputation, his fortune and his lifestyle. But making movies was hard work and produced considerable anxiety in him. His greatest pleasure was just to feel comfortable, to sit and spin tales with a writer, and to play with ideas – to be at ease, eating and drinking, without stress.'

The production of the great comic thriller *North by Northwest*, made from mid-summer to late autumn 1958, took the company from New York to Mount Rushmore, South Dakota, and from the scrub brush flatlands of central California to the MGM studios in Culver City. No Hitchcock movie up to this time had required so much travel since the remake of *The Man Who Knew Too Much*.

A fast-paced comic thriller about an innocent man trying to clear his name of murder, about political depravity and sexual blackmail, *North by Northwest* differs sharply in tone and style from the several films preceding and following it, but it shared some of the same sober concerns: great comedy is not frivolous, after all. But after the obsessive and unwittingly self-revelatory romanticism of *Vertigo*, Hitch evidently wanted breathing space. Just when some critics were complaining that he had lost his comic sense after *To Catch a Thief*, Ernie Lehman provided him with means for a response.

With *Vertigo* and *North by Northwest,* Hitchcock concluded two quartets of films – four each with Cary Grant and James Stewart. From *Rope* through *Vertigo,* Stewart had become a kind of surrogate representative of Hitch; only Sean Connery would come that close, in *Marnie.* Admired and celebrated as one of America's exponents of the ordinary man as hero, Stewart became in a way what Hitchcock *considered* himself to be: a theorist of murder (*Rope*); a chair-bound voyeur drawn to and fearful of love (*Rear Window*); a protective but manipulative husband and father (*The Man Who Knew Too Much*); and the passionately haunted pursuer of an impossible ideal (*Vertigo*).

These four roles provided the actor with the most substantial opportunities of his career and Hitchcock with an alter ego acceptable enough to engage the audience's sympathies. Of course, none of this was deliberate on Hitchcock's part – the works would not have their own energetic lives and inner logic if they were schematic movie memoirs. But seen after the fact, the allusive autobiographical elements provide another window through which their richness may be appreciated; and as always, the artist could not leave himself outside the studio doors. The images and stories came from him or were at every turn shaped or approved by him. Given his control and approval, his rejection of this suggestion or his acceptance of that one; given his attention to every detail of music and sound effect, wardrobe and cameras placement, the pictures *were* him.

Cary Grant, on the other hand, may have represented not what Hitch considered himself to be, but what *he would like to have been*: the suave, irresponsible playboy (in *Suspicion*); the ultimate prince charming to a blonde he nearly destroys (in *Notorious*); the innocent hero who wins the glamorous Grace Kelly (in *To Catch a Thief*); and, in *North by Northwest*, the theatre-going advertising executive whose frantic, perilous journey ends with the blonde lifted up from espionage to bed.

For his leading lady opposite fifty-four-year-old Cary Grant, Hitch chose thirty-four-year-old Eva Marie Saint, a happily married wife and mother in private life. After a prolific career on television, she had won a best supporting Oscar for her movie debut in *On the Waterfront* and had completed three more films before Hitch signed her to play the role of the deadliest blonde in his long catalogue. Delighted to be working with him, she presented no problems and their collaboration succeeded without tension.

'I acted just like a rich man keeping a woman,' he said of his pre-production work with the actress –

> just as Stewart did with Novak in *Vertigo*. I watched every hair on her head. I had two wardrobes made for her, and then I saw that for half of it she was being dressed as a waif, as in *On the Waterfront*. So I took her along to Bergdorf Goodman's [in Manhattan] and I sat with her as the mannequins paraded by. I chose the dresses and suits for her – a basic black suit, a heavy black silk cocktail dress with wine-red flowers; a charcoal-brown, full-skirted jersey and a burnt orange burlap for action scenes. I took a lot of trouble with Eva Marie Saint, grooming her and making her appear sleek and sophisticated. Next thing you know, she's in a picture called *Exodus*, looking dissipated!

Toward this straightforward and cooperative actress, Hitch had no romantic inclination – there was nothing like the knotty relationship with Vera Miles, nor was there any of the Novak dust-up. Eva Marie Saint was only docile and cooperative.

Of Alfred Hitchcock's fifty-three motion pictures, the most famous is certainly *Psycho*, a landmark in American movie history and the film that quickly made him a man of great wealth and power (not to say influence). Based on a slim novel by Robert Bloch that was itself inspired by a grisly series of killings, the screenplay was certainly the best of Joseph Stefano's work.

Janet Leigh was the thirty-two-year-old wife of actor Tony Curtis, mother of two girls and a seasoned performer – but she still lacked an enduring or memorable credit on her long résumé. 'My camera is absolute,' Hitch told Janet when they met. 'I tell the story through that lens, so I need you to move when my camera moves, stop when my camera stops. I'm confident you'll be able to find your motivation to justify the motion. I'll be happy to work with you, but I will not change the timing of my camera.' And that was the extent of their first pre-production meeting in autumn 1959. To costume supervisor Helen Colvig, Hitch said of his small *Psycho* cast – perhaps thinking of Novak – 'Either they wear the clothes and do the part the way I want, or they're not going to be in it.'

Janet worked fewer than twenty days on *Psycho*, but for the rest of her life, she was identified with this film in a way that perhaps no other actress has ever been immediately linked with a movie. Indeed, her international fame derived from six damp days of work that December, when she stood in a shower for long hours, with Alfred Hitchcock never far away.

'It was challenging for everyone,' she recalled years later, speaking of that week.

> I had to repeat the same gestures and actions over and over, taken from different angles. Then there were delays due to the moleskin coverings I wore, so as not to be completely nude on the set. And there were the usual problems with cameras and lenses – and my skin was puckering like a prune from all the shower water, so we had to stop for make-up retouches. The finished scene is brilliant, but we had no idea of that while we were doing it. Hitch thought of this as a little thriller he was making with his TV crew, and for a while he even thought of trying to release it on television – but of course as he planned it, the shower murder couldn't have gone out on TV in those days.

Janet always insisted that Hitchcock never asked her to perform the shower sequence in the nude, but that was not the recollection of his staff, the crew and studio executives. Make-up supervisor Jack Barron, for example, recalled Hitchcock saying he was working on Janet to do the sequence naked, but she adamantly refused. Later, Hitch asked if she would yield to him for a few shots intended for the European release version of *Psycho*, but she was not to be moved.

Experimenting with various forms of the desiccated skull to be used for the corpse of the late Mrs. Bates, Hitch tested them out on his star. 'Some hair-raising screams emanated from behind my door when I walked in on these hideous, shrivelled monstrosities sitting in my make-up chair. Looking back [in 1995], I puzzle over whether this was just a gag or an effort to keep me a bit on edge, thus in [her character's] jittery state of mind. Knowing Mr. Hitchcock, it could have been.' Hitchcock added that he wanted to keep the tone on the *Psycho* set from becoming sombre or depressed ('We were dealing with unusual material'), but he also needed to sustain a sense of disquiet and unpredictability.

Hence he supplemented his usual jokes, limericks and sight gags with extraordinarily detailed direction of Janet Leigh, which certainly gave an air of gravity to the proceedings. No aspect of her performance was left unplanned or unsupervised, as Hitch provided detailed on-the-spot drama coaching for her, which was extremely rare for him to do. 'Before every shot, he went to her very quietly and really gave her direction,' recalled script supervisor Marshall Schlom.

A different tone accompanied the huddled whispers before they filmed the movie's first scene, for which Hitch wasn't getting the desired sexual sparks in the lunchtime hotel-room tryst between Janet Leigh (wearing only a bra and half-slip) and John Gavin (bare-chested) as her lover. Hitchcock took Janet aside and instructed her to be bold: she ought to fondle Gavin (whom she had met for the first time only ten minutes earlier), as if the couple were involved in real sexual foreplay – 'See what you can do about it, Janet.' She agreed, and Hitchcock said that he would give Gavin a similar direction. A moment later, just millimetres away from the actors, Hitch beckoned to a young crewman, murmuring in his ear, 'Mr Gavin has an ee-reck-shun.' Later, Janet learned that Hitch had given Gavin no warning: 'I was the one Hitch had used,' she said. 'I adored him, but he did have that mischievous mind.'

Anthony Perkins was forever after associated with *Psycho*, too. Twenty-seven, tall, attractively odd and edgy, he had performed terrifying scenes of emotional breakdown in a picture called *Fear Strikes Out*. This achievement had convinced Hitch that the young actor – agitated, somewhat delicate and hypersensitive – would be perfect as the monstrous but somehow boyishly sympathetic Norman Bates. 'Norman's not just a monster,' Perkins told me after one of his performances in *Equus* on Broadway in 1975. 'He's tortured.' For much of his life, so was Tony, mostly because he was never able to accept and integrate his homosexuality. His lovers (Tab Hunter and Grover Dale, among others) brought him little serenity, and, like Montgomery Clift, he ineffectually sought to become heterosexual through psychotherapy.

Working with Hitch, Janet was anxious to please, and Tony was pleased to be anxious. Up to the time of her death in 2004 at the age of seventy-seven, she never again enjoyed anything like the success or notoriety of *Psycho*, with which she is forever linked – just as he was forever imprisoned by the persona of Norman Bates until he died at sixty in 1992. They may have sometimes quietly resented the ironclad associations, but the movie guaranteed immortality.

Vera Miles was the only participant not to benefit from this historic motion picture. Summoned to play Janet's sister in fulfilment of her contract, she was given an unflattering wardrobe and fitted with a cheap and obviously artificial blonde wig, her head having been completely shaved for a recent picture. 'Vera was very angry throughout the filming of *Psycho*,' according to Rita Riggs. 'Mr Hitchcock made her look like a dowdy, old-maid schoolteacher . . . [and] for most of the film, we saw a lot of the back of her head. But it was Mr Hitchcock's choice. He was very disappointed with Vera, on whom he invested a lot of time, thought and emotion in preparing *Vertigo*. Now, with *Psycho*, this was some of his perversity coming through.'

Rightly studied for its technical virtuosity and rich thematic imagery, *Psycho* is a grimly brilliant study in perversity. It also marked the sharpest stylistic and thematic break in the history of the Hitchcock catalogue. 'He truly thought that he never got angry,' Ernest Lehman told me. 'In fact, he said he didn't believe in anger, that it was a foolish and wasteful emotion. But there were times when he was seething with anger – all of it carefully repressed.'

That *Psycho* followed the wounded romanticism of *Vertigo* and the genial cynicism of *North by Northwest* is not so surprising. All three films have as their emotional focus a desperate, duplicitous blonde; all three films have at the centre a person who is unknown, nonexistent or dead. However different their tones and styles, these films were a triptych of pain, created amid Hitchcock's own loneliness, illness and fear of death. *Vertigo* was, as all his associates knew, a very personal film. The cool and witty adroitness of *North by Northwest* could not disguise the fact that it was a bitter-sweet farewell to the era of glamour and romance. And with *Psycho*, the content, style and tone of Alfred Hitchcock's films changed forever.

14

Obsession
(1961–1962)

'I prefer a woman who does not display all her sex at once,' Alfred Hitchcock said in 1962. 'I like women who are also ladies, who hold enough of themselves in reserve to keep a man intrigued. On the screen, for example, if an actress wants to convey a sexy quality, she ought to maintain a slightly mysterious air.' At the time, he was editing *The Birds* for a 1963 release – an apocalyptic thriller (very loosely based on a du Maurier story to which he owned the rights) in which those creatures attack humans, for reasons deliberately never explained.

'I seem to have developed a reputation for preferring blonde leading ladies in my films,' Hitch continued, naming Madeleine Carroll, Joan Fontaine, Grace Kelly and Eva Marie Saint (but not, unaccountably, Ingrid Bergman). 'And now, in *The Birds*, I am introducing another young lady who happens to be blonde – Miss Tippi Hedren. A woman of elegance will never cease to surprise you.'

During the early autumn of 1961, Hitch and Alma were sipping morning coffee in their kitchen, watching the *Today* news programme. A black-and-white commercial for a liquid diet supplement was broadcast. This product did not interest him, but the lady of the brief narrative did – a blonde model with a good figure, sensual but not brassy, and obviously so successful on her Sego regime that men and boys alike whistle as she strolls along. Before leaving home for his office, Hitch was on the phone to his agents at the MCA agency, instructing them to find 'that girl' and bring her in.

Tippi Hedren had been a successful model for over a dozen years and was then living in Los Angeles. She lacked both training and experience as an actress, but it was immediately evident that she was enormously photogenic, with bright eyes, an unaffected smile and remarkable poise in front of a camera.

On instructions from the studio executive who reached her, she brought her portfolio and some commercial reels to a meeting at Universal Studios on Friday 13 October. They pored over her photos, chatted briefly with her and then asked, to her astonishment, if she would like to sign a seven-year-contract, beginning at $500 weekly. Thirty-one and divorced, with a four-year-old daughter, she felt at the time that this was 'a wonderful opportunity, a life-saving gift to have a guaranteed income for myself and my child.' Without knowing anything more, but presuming that she would be employed on television or in studio commercials, she signed the contract after a quick consultation with her agent, Noel Marshall.

'Would you like to know who this person is?' asked the agent when the ink was dry.

'Oh, that would be very nice.'

'Alfred Hitchcock.'

The following Tuesday, 17 October, Tippi was asked to return to Universal. She was shown into Hitch's private office, where he sat with folded arms, looking content and pleased with himself: after all, the terms she accepted had been a great bargain for him. They chatted for much of the afternoon — about things like travel, food and wine, but there was not a single reference to anything about movies or TV. At the end of the day, she was convinced that Hitch simply wanted talent available for his television series, but that he had nothing special in mind for her. 'I had been a model, and I had no thought of becoming an actress — much less a star.' Subsequently, they were joined by Edith Head, Robert Boyle, Peggy Robertson and others on the director's team, and things began to happen quickly. As Boyle recalled, it was clear that Hitch was once again undertaking 'the Svengali approach to his leading lady. It was love at first sight.'

★   ★   ★

Nathalie Hedren was born on 19 January 1930 at a hospital in tiny New Ulm, Minnesota, near the family home in the hamlet of Lafayette. Dorothea and Bernard Hedren already had a four-year-old daughter named Patty; the girls' mother was a dedicated rural schoolteacher, and their father operated a modest general store. In infancy, Nathalie was nicknamed 'Tupsa' by her father – a Swedish adjective referring to a 'cute' or 'adorable' little girl; soon the child was called Tippi, and so everyone addressed her for the rest of her life.

As everywhere, the Great Depression affected the Hedrens harshly. Bernard lost his store, and Tippi's beloved dog died for lack of money to pay for distemper injections. 'From that time on,' recalled Patty, 'Tippi wanted to raise dogs and cats.' But times were so harsh that new pets were out of the question, and Tippi remembered one Christmas when she gratefully received one present – a coveted bar of soap.

By the time she was in secondary school during World War Two, the shy child had blossomed into a cheerful, vivacious teenager, industrious at school and attentive to her family. One day, as she got off a streetcar in downtown Minneapolis, a woman handed her a business card: 'Tell your mother to bring you down to Donaldson's Department Store, young lady – I think you could model teenage fashions for us on Saturday mornings.' So began a modelling career, and by 1947, Tippi was in post-war New York, working hard but happily for Eileen and Jerry Ford at Ford Models. Among many glossy magazines, she appeared on the covers of *Glamour*, *Seventeen* and *McCall's*, and her photo was all over New York when she was a finalist in the popular Miss Rheingold beer contest – a distinction she lost (as did her contemporary, a model named Grace Kelly).

Soon she was appearing regularly in television commercials, 'and that's where I first met photographers and cameramen who really delighted in embarrassing, insulting and rude behaviour.' She learned to cope, ignoring what she could and walking away from what she could not. During a fleeting appearance on the TV comedy *The Aldrich Family* in 1951, one of her co-players was a good-looking eighteen-year-old named Peter Griffith. They married the following year, and in August 1957, their daughter, Melanie Griffith, was born. By this time, Peter was producing commercials, and eventually he turned to property management. 'But our marriage broke up. I think Peter [three years her junior] should have done a lot more dating before we got married.' The Griffiths were divorced in 1961, and Tippi, hoping for work in West Coast commercials, took Melanie and headed for Los Angeles. She rented a home in the neighbourhood known as Westwood, and there, in October, she took the telephone call from the agents for an unnamed Hollywood producer.

With his trainee firmly under contract, Hitchcock set about directing her in three days of elaborate and expensive screen tests. Wardrobes and hairstyles were prepared for her, and Hitch and Alma coached her in scenes from *Rebecca*, *Notorious* and *To Catch a Thief*. Speaking of Tippi's trial run, actor Martin Balsam (the detective in *Psycho*, brought back to play opposite her in the tests) said, 'It was evident that she was very nervous and unsure of herself, but she had studied every line and every move that was asked of her, and she tried to do everything just right, everything Hitch asked of her.'

'I signed her to a contract because she is a classic beauty,' Hitchcock told a reporter that season. 'Movies don't have them any more. Grace Kelly was the last.' At the same time, Hitch asked Edith Head to design clothes for Tippi's private life, and, as a subtle but proprietary step toward changing her identity, he required that her first name always be printed in single quotation marks (a gesture he left unexplained). By the time of the end-of-year holidays, Hitchcock was tutoring Tippi on the fine points of wine and food.

She had heard that Hitch was working with writer Evan Hunter on the screenplay for *The Birds*, but that project was never mentioned in connection with plans for her. 'Every actress in town wanted that part, and I really never thought of myself as a candidate.' After four months of daily private tutorials on a wide variety of polite topics, Tippi was told to arrive at Chasen's Restaurant one Thursday in February 1961, where Lew Wasserman also joined the Hitchcocks. At her place was a small gift box from Gump's, the prestigious shop in San Francisco; inside was a gold-and-seed-pearl pin with three birds in flight. 'We would like you to play Melanie Daniels in *The Birds*,' Hitch announced solemnly.

Wasserman said little, for he had led the campaign to deter Hitchcock from what he considered the foolish notion of casting a novice in a

Directing Ingrid Bergman, in *Spellbound*

Ann Todd, in *The Paradine Case*

Alida Valli, in *The Paradine Case*

With Tallulah Bankhead, during production of *Lifeboat*

Ingrid Bergman,
in *Under Capricorn*

Jane Wyman, in *Stage Fright*

Marlene Dietrich,
in *Stage Fright*

Anne Baxter,
in *I Confess*

Directing Grace Kelly, in *Dial 'M' for Murder*

Vera Miles

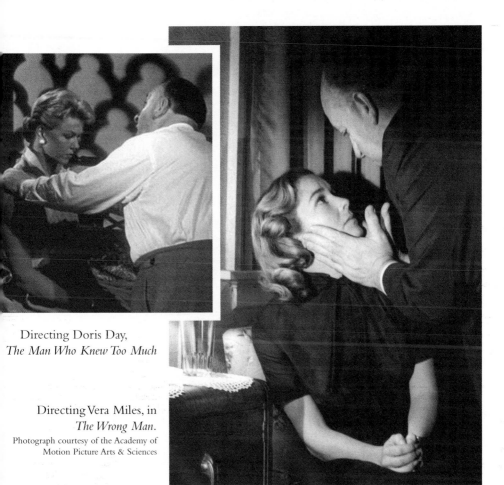

Directing Doris Day,
The Man Who Knew Too Much

Directing Vera Miles, in
The Wrong Man.
Photograph courtesy of the Academy of
Motion Picture Arts & Sciences

Directing Kim
Novak, in *Vertigo*

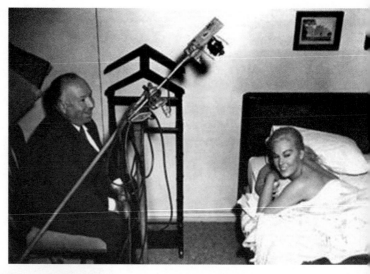

Directing Kim Novak, in *Vertigo*

Directing Eva Marie Saint,
in *North by Northwest*

Directing Janet Leigh,
in *Psycho*

Tippi Hedren, during the
final ordeal of *The Birds*

paring Tippi Hedren for a scene in *Marnie*

Presenting Tippi Hedren to the press

Diane Baker,
in *Marnie*

The Hitchcocks

leading role that would include unprecedented physical demands. 'The studio did not back me,' Tippi recalled, 'because I had no experience. The men at Universal asked him, "Hitch – what are you doing? Are you *crazy*?" But he told them that he had complete confidence in me, that he would enable me to do it. From that evening, I felt terrific responsibility, terrible pressure, and my focus in life was trying to do everything I could to justify his faith in me. If he thought I wasn't doing exactly what he wanted, every day during preparation for *The Birds*, he would sulk or pout or seem hurt or disappointed.'

From that evening, she was instructed to attend every meeting Hitch had with the screenwriter, cinematographer, wardrobe super- visor, production designer and sound technicians – she was receiving, she felt, 'years of technical education in a few months.' Unusually for him, Hitch discussed the script with her, her character's motivations and those of the others, the point of each scene to the whole. For her every appearance in the picture (which meant almost every moment), he had points to make. 'At this stage, he was fantastic to work with as my director, mentor and drama coach. I could never have had this kind of preparation from anyone else, anywhere.' As Peggy Robertson, Evan Hunter, Bob Boyle, Edith Head and others confirmed, Tippi was a remarkably quick study and a willing, affable colleague. 'Well, she has nothing to unlearn,' said Hitch.

Slowly but deliberately, the makeover of Tippi Hedren began and continued each day. Hitch thought the string of pearls she wore to their first meeting was 'too large for the afternoon colour' of her clothes, and so the proper length was purchased for her. He then supervised the precise colour for the wigs and the style of her own hair, and for each subtle element of her make-up. He altered the line and cut of the green suit she wears in the picture (six of them would be required for the five months of production); he took weeks to select accessories and jewellery appropriate for a spoiled, wealthy but resourceful San Francisco socialite; and he laboured over the choice of the character's mink coat. (At the end of production, with a great gesture of generosity, he presented her with the coat as a gift from himself; she later learned that in fact the cost had been charged to the picture.)

'Once we began filming,' Tippi recalled, 'he rarely directed me or anyone else.' But the fact is that he had little interest in the other players and left their questions or problems to his assistant director, James Brown. To the cast were added the honoured stage actress Jessica Tandy; leading man Rod Taylor; thirteen-year-old Veronica Cartwright, already a seasoned player with impressive credits; Suzanne Pleshette; and a complement of skilled character actors. Filming began in late March 1962 in the towns of Bodega and Bodega Bay, about sixty miles north of San Francisco; work in the studio interiors at Universal concluded in early July.

'Tippi Hedren is really remarkable,' Hitchcock told Associated Press reporter Bob Thomas, who had known him for years and was surprised to hear such lavish praise (or any at all) from the master about an actor. 'Get a look at that girl – she's going to be good. I gave her the leading role, a big part. Svengali Hitch rides again!' To a team from *Look*, a popular national weekly magazine, Hitch went further: 'Tippi has a faster tempo, city glibness, more humour [than Grace]. For her scenes, she displayed jaunty assuredness when I asked for that – a pertness, an attractive throw of her head. And she memorises and reads lines extraordinarily well and is sharper in expression [than Grace].'

As usual, Hitchcock relished all the specialised practical challenges and complexities inherent in realising *The Birds*. 'Technically, this was the most difficult film I ever made,' he told me years later. 'We [i.e., Ray Berwick, an experienced bird wrangler] trained birds for close-ups, and we got them to fly here and there on command. But we also had to superimpose images of thousands of other birds, artificially stripped in on separate pieces of film, for many scenes.' The budget for *The Birds* quickly climbed over $3 million.

But things began to change.

'Hitch was becoming very domineering and covetous of Tippi,' according to Rod Taylor,

> and it was very difficult for her, because this was her first movie, and she had no basis for comparison with any other director or production. She was like a precious piece of jewellery he owned, and little by little, no one was permitted to come physically close to her during the production. 'Don't touch the girl after I call "Cut!"' he said to me repeatedly, which was difficult because we had so many scenes together. As he became more and more

possessive, he wouldn't let me or anyone else ride in the studio cars with her, which we often shared for the sake of convenience during location work up north. He was very firm about that – oh, no, I must not ride with her, as if that would taint his goddess. He was putting a wall around her, trying to isolate her from everyone so that all her time would be spent only with him.

As Tippi recalled, 'He was developing this obsession for me, and I began to feel very uncomfortable because I had no control over him. I had to be very careful, very watchful.' Hitchcock started to observe and study her constantly, to stare at her on the set, to listen in when she spoke to others or made a phone call. Flowers, wine, gifts and handwritten notes characterised by schoolboy sentiment arrived at her home and in her dressing room. 'He tried to control everything – what I wore and ate and drank.'

He then had his assistants occasionally pilfer samples of her handwriting, which he sent to a graphologist for analysis. Most alarmingly: 'I was stalked. First, he wanted to know which friends I was seeing during my own private time away from work – and where I was going. He never thought anyone was good enough for me; he simply disapproved of everyone in my life. Then I realised that sometimes I was being followed to events, to restaurants or social occasions – and I *was* being followed, and some of his staff and studio executives *were* receiving reports and relaying them back to Hitch, all about my ordinary comings and goings.' At the same time, her young daughter Melanie realised that 'Hitch was taking her away from me, and suddenly I wasn't allowed even to visit my mom at the studio.'

Tippi began to feel that she had to do her best to avoid him, 'but that was almost impossible. Everyone – from [Hitch's assistant] Peggy [Robertson] to [studio chief] Lew Wasserman and the men in the front office, were covering for him. I told them I was becoming very unhappy with all this, but he was Alfred Hitchcock, the great and famous director, and I was Tippi Hedren, an inexperienced actress who had no clout.' This was emerging as a tale of raw, unchecked power in the days before charges of harassment could be considered; this was nothing less than an episode in which an abusive employer exploited his dependent employee, ignoring her feelings and leaving her without recourse. 'I couldn't just resign or quit my contract – there

173

would have been a major lawsuit, and I was a single mom with a little girl to support. I would have been blacklisted all over town – would have been unable to find work anywhere. So I tried to cope.'

Further resentment arose over Hitch's frequently indelicate conversation. 'He told me dirty jokes and filthy limericks, especially after he learned that I really didn't like that sort of thing. I guess he thought it kept me off-guard, uneasy.'

The history of music, painting, sculpture, theatre and movies is long with the names of creative artists who are entirely dedicated to moulding a career, shaping their presentation of a subject, controlling a performance. Many good directors have done that. But now, after decades of sublimation and suppression, Alfred Hitchcock was overstepping a line. Not content with setting forth his dream or ideal, he was acting like the owner of another's life. But Tippi was under contract, and for the present, she felt she had no recourse but to finesse an increasingly awkward environment. 'It isn't always like this,' Suzanne Pleshette told her by way of reassurance, but that was cold comfort in 1962.

As tensions increased, Alma came to visit Tippi at the end of one week. '"Oh, Tippi, dear," she said to me with real concern in her voice, "I am so sorry you have to go through all this – I am *so* sorry."'

This is a remarkably difficult statement to comprehend. The fact is that the actress was *forced* to endure it, as if it were little more than an alteration to her wardrobe, or additional time in a make-up chair or on a publicity tour. 'Alma was like Hitch's mom,' Tippi said. 'She looked out for him, protected him.' Everyone knew about Alma's influence over her husband, and Alma knew very well that circumstances were becoming more and more problematic. Why didn't this little powerhouse of a woman tell her husband to desist, to stop this sort of destructive behaviour, to cease humiliating himself? There may never be satisfactory answers – or the only answer may be that she tried and could achieve nothing. Whatever transpired between the Hitchcocks on the matter of Tippi Hedren, Alma's effective lack of control resulted in a kind of unwitting collusion, however uncalculated, heedless or ill considered.

Late one afternoon that spring, as she recalled, 'Hitch and I were in the back of a limousine returning from Bodega Bay to the motel where the cast and crew were staying for several nights. When we drove into the parking lot, some of our co-workers were there waiting for us. And when he saw that *they* saw us, he reached over and violently embraced me in the back of the car, to make everyone think that we were in a romantic clinch! I pushed him away and got out of the car, and I thought I would give him the benefit of the doubt – maybe he was just trying to make me nervous, to keep his control, to show me off.'

As Robert Boyle said years later, 'In all the films I had anything to do with' – over a quarter-century, as art director for *Saboteur* and *Shadow of a Doubt* and production designer for *North by Northwest*, *The Birds* and *Marnie* – 'he was always pressing the problems. I suspect he had a certain fear of elegant blondes. His behaviour was almost compulsive. He once said to me, "I have all the feelings of everyone encased in an armour of fat." He felt that he was not attractive physically, but at the same time he recognised that he had all those same yearnings [as others had], and he was frustrated by what he perceived as a difficulty, if not an impossibility, which was to experience requited love.'

When principal photography was complete, the technical challenges would begin, consuming even longer days than filming with actors. There would be the complex process of Technicolor correction; the invention and placement of electronic sounds, for Hitchcock proscribed the use of a musical soundtrack; and the editing of a picture composed variously of live action, animation, trick shots, mechanical birds (for the scenes involving children) and thousands of live trained birds of several varieties (gulls, crows, ravens, blackbirds, finches, pigeons). Two-hour Hollywood features routinely contain between 400 and 700 separate shots; *The Birds* has over 1,500.

But before the finished film could be put together, there was a final, harrowing time for Tippi Hedren. Perhaps because he knew how dangerous the event would be, Alfred Hitchcock kept until the last week of shooting the appalling finale of the story, in which Melanie Daniels climbs alone to a room in the house, enters, and is viciously attacked by hundreds of birds. 'Hitch,' she asked him when they were in story conferences, 'why doesn't she summon Mitch [the Taylor character]? Why does she do this?' Hitchcock's reply: 'Because I tell you to do it.'

When the time came, she was at first shocked and then felt betrayed – even before the ordeal began and the cameras rolled for a week, recording a sequence that surpasses even the stylised shower murder of *Psycho*, which seems restrained by comparison.

Since work on the picture began early in the year, Hitch, his bird trainer, the production designer and the assistant director had all told Tippi that of course mechanical birds would be used for this final sequence, and that she would certainly not be subjected to the risks of a live bird attack. But when she arrived on the set early that Monday morning, it was clear that Hitchcock and company always had a different intention.

'I walked onto the set, and there was a chain-link fence all around and on top. Jim Brown [the assistant director] seemed embarrassed, he looked everywhere around the set except at me, and then he finally said, "We can't use mechanical birds after all – we have to use live birds." With that, he left, and there I was. Now what? Soon after, in came bird handlers with their long gloves and gauntlets, carrying huge boxes of squawking birds – gulls, crows, pigeons, all kinds.'

Very soon, she had her answer. 'The men stood Tippi in the corner of the room and just began throwing birds at her,' recalled Rod Taylor, 'one after another, again and again, take after take.' The agitated birds darted and swooped about, and by noon on the first day of that week, the set and the actress were (in the words of Jessica Tandy) 'just covered in bird shit.' Often the set had to be cleared for cleaning and scrubbing. Hitchcock, meanwhile, remained in his trailer-dressing room, emerging only to call 'Action!' and 'Cut!' It was as if he were both embarrassed and frightened by what he was asking his star to endure.

'All of this had been prepared well in advance,' she later learned. 'Nothing could have been done with such speed – the arrival of the birds and the handlers, the careful placing of the wire fence and everything on the set – they knew from the first day what they needed, that they had to use live birds, but they had lied to me. You can't just do this thing spontaneously – it had all taken complicated planning. And they had to leave it all to the end.' Who could predict how much of it she might be able to withstand, and what would be the physical and emotional effects of the work?

One day of filming this ordeal was insufficient for the final effect, and work continued on Tuesday. Cary Grant visited the set and told Tippi that he admired her courage. But the fact is that an experienced actress would have objected loudly to this treatment. Moviemaking often pitches actors, stuntmen and crew into uncomfortable situations, and difficult scenes, often unforeseen, often go with the professional territory. But there is no precedent for Tippi Hedren's ordeal; years later, of course, the sequence would have been easily and safely achieved by computer.

Monday and Tuesday left Tippi exhausted and unnerved, but she was told it would all be over by Wednesday morning. But the torture continued all day Wednesday and Thursday. 'It was frightening and exhausting for me, and it seemed to go on forever.'

Hollywood has a long history of imposing painful tasks on actors and stuntmen. Lillian Gish and Richard Barthelmess endured freezing temperatures and real ice floes for climactic scenes of Griffith's *Way Down East*. Harold Lloyd lost a thumb and finger for the sake of a movie and never used doubles for his most dangerous stunts. Buster Keaton took enormous risks, and Lon Chaney caused himself acute pain for the make-up and distortions that made him famous; thousands more have fallen from horses, leaped from buildings and dashed through flames while the cameras rolled. A single actor, however – especially a woman – is rarely subjected to the sort of repeated violence asked of Tippi Hedren in making *The Birds*.

Finally, on Friday, Hitchcock and his crew prepared for the last moments of the scene, when the battered character cowered in agony and shock on the floor of the room. For the first four days, birds had swept around her, pecking and nipping. Pauses were called; her costume was torn a bit more; make-up artists created facial gashes, lacerations and the impression of terrible wounds; stage blood was dripped – and then filming resumed.

There was one last technique to be applied. 'The wardrobe team applied bands around sections of my body before I put the costume on, and then thin, almost invisible elastic wires were pulled through holes in the clothes. They pulled the strings through – and then they loosely tied one leg of the birds to the strings, so that the birds would pounce all over me, unable to fly away.'

The torment continued throughout the day.

Late on Friday, after five full days, the occasion reached critical mass. 'One bird that was tied to me jumped from my shoulder onto my face and landed just near my eye, scratching my lower eyelid.'

She collapsed, sobbing hysterically and shouting that she could do no more – that the birds had to be taken off her, that this had to stop at once. Everyone withdrew, embarrassed and apologetic.

Carried to her dressing room – dazed, shaking and almost in clinical shock – she was told to rest before going home for the weekend. But when crewmen came to rouse her, she was unresponsive, and for an unnervingly long time, she did not respond. Physicians ordered her to remain at home for ten days of complete rest.

'But we can't do without her!' Hitchcock protested. 'We need her on Monday for the last few shots.'

'Are you crazy?' a doctor asked the director. 'Are you trying to kill her?'

15

The End of Art
(1963–1964)

Tippi's contract required her to travel for the promotion of her Hitchcock films, and so, on release of *The Birds* in spring 1963, she joined him (and frequently a handful of studio executives and assistants) for a publicity tour. The picture was screened at the Cannes Film Festival, and everywhere there were odd gimmicks: in some cinema foyers, for example, birds labelled 'Alfie' and 'Tippi' were suspended in cages.

That autumn, she was assigned the leading role in his next picture, *Marnie* – the story of a frigid compulsive thief trapped and black-mailed by an equally troubled man named Mark Rutland (Sean Connery).* This role she undertook as if by default, for Hitch had hoped in vain to lure Grace Kelly back to work as the star. Joseph Stefano had first worked on the treatment, and then Evan Hunter came aboard, but he was dismissed when he failed to write the honey-moon rape scene.

'I told him,' Hunter recalled,

---

* Tippi Hedren received $500 weekly as salary for *The Birds* and $600 for *Marnie*, which Hitch thought was royal compensation. She accepted these sums – much less than her modelling career had paid – in the belief that it was wiser to have a regular weekly income, guaranteed for seven years, than to depend on the uncertain income from modelling.

that audiences would lose all sympathy for the male lead if he rapes his own wife on their honeymoon. I told him that the man would be comforting, that the couple would work things out. But Hitchcock lifted his hands and sketched a rectangle in the air, framing an imaginary camera image. Then he moved his hands toward my face, as if moving in for a close shot. 'Evan,' he said, 'when he sticks it in her, I want that camera right on her *face!*'

Insisting that he would not write the scene, Hunter was fired forthwith and replaced by Jay Presson Allen, then in her maiden voyage on the seas of Hollywood scriptwriting.★With *Vertigo, Marnie* is certainly one of Alfred Hitchcock's most direct creative acts of self-revelation. 'He was always trying to put his own personal feelings up on the screen,' said Robert Boyle, 'and I think that was one of the things he was doing with *Marnie*. He was doing it through Tippi and through his filmmaking, and exploring some of his own feelings and his compulsive behaviour.'

Boyle was on the mark. In its finished form, the movie became a haunted and haunting tale of a man's desire to control completely a woman who rejects him – only blackmail forces her to comply by marrying him. 'You don't love me!' Marnie cries out to Mark. 'I'm just something you've caught. You think I'm some kind of animal you've trapped!'

'That's right – you are! And I've caught something really wild this time, haven't I? I've tracked you and caught you and by God I'm going to keep you!' As Truffaut asked, 'Can there be any doubt that Sean Connery . . . is expressing Hitchcock's own feelings as a frustrated Pygmalion?' This, of course, precisely expressed the nature of the deteriorating relationship, due to destructive demands made by the director on his star.

Jay Allen saw Hitchcock's treatment of Tippi, but she, too, was new to Hollywood and said nothing. 'He was mad for her,' Allen said,

★ In 1979, Peggy Robertson told me that Jay Allen was often in tears at the end of her daily script sessions with Hitchcock – not because of any inappropriate conduct on his part, but because Jay quickly realised she was out of her depth on a subject she couldn't write (like the honeymoon rape). Years later, Jay spoke often on the record about her apprenticeship with Hitchcock, admitting her inability to resolve some of *Marnie's* thornier script problems.

'just as he had been obsessed with a series of cold blonde actresses before. He was very Edwardian, and he put lids on himself. To work out his repressions, he created a framework – his art. It was his way of legitimising everything, of transforming his feelings.' Oddly, she came to Tippi one day: 'Can't you just love Hitch a little bit?' Tippi asked what she meant, but Jay could not elaborate, and the conversation ended. 'The problem was that Tippi wanted her own life,' Jay said years later, 'and so she couldn't help making him unhappy.'

As Tippi Hedren's predicament deepened during the filming of her second picture, she was not alone in facing unforeseen problems: Hitchcock extended his efforts to train other actresses during pre-production. Young Mariette Hartley had a smaller role, but Hitchcock took time to explain to her how he used storyboards. She recalled that the director often made jokes and kept the crew at ease. 'I was in the presence of a genius,' she said later, 'but his sense of control left little room for improvisation. Still, he taught me a tremendous amount in the short time I worked with him.' Then Hitchcock refused to speak to her, and thereafter he retained a mysterious silence to the end of production. 'I went up to him and asked if in some way I had offended him,' she recalled years later. 'His reply was, "Miss Hartley, I think you have problems with men."' This may be a classic example of projection, for it was, of course, Hitchcock who had problems with people in general.

Engaged to play the significant supporting role of Sean Connery's jealous sister-in-law, Diane Baker was offered the role without being permitted to read the script; but because this was to be an Alfred Hitchcock picture, she accepted. Diane had already appeared in more than twenty features and television films since launching her career in 1959 with *The Diary of Anne Frank*, and she had recently concluded a term contract with Twentieth Century-Fox.

'I was invited to the Hitchcocks' home,' she recalled, 'and I sat in their kitchen while Alma prepared lunch for us. She told me how much I resembled Grace Kelly, and she said that I could *become* another Grace Kelly – which astonished me. Then she brought out photos of Grace to make her point, while Hitch sat there, watching me. I felt I was in another kind of world. I didn't want to be made over into the image of another woman Hitch was still looking for, and I didn't want to sign a contract with him or any producer. My contract at

Fox had expired and I wanted to freelance.' The Hitchcocks were not pleased.

His increasingly bizarre behaviour alarmed his seasoned associates, the major Universal Studios executives and the entire company of *Marnie*. Considering the exigencies of this complex and demanding picture, Hitch was alert, creative and quick to meet its technical challenges – in other words, he had lost none of his ingenuity, nor had be become uncertain of his ability to provide artisans and actors with the precise counsel required. Diane Baker recalled that, at the outset, 'Hitch taught me so many wonderful things about camera angles and gestures and acting subtleties. He was a magnificent teacher.'

But after the first scenes were filmed at the end of November, things turned even more sour and tense. When Diane Baker arrived for work on her assigned days, she was astounded and bewildered.

> I was on the set constantly, even when I had no scenes to do, and I never saw Tippi enjoying herself with the rest of the cast and crew. She was never allowed to gather around with the rest of us, and he demanded that every conversation between her and Hitch be held in private. None of us ever saw her having a warm, friendly professional relationship with him. Throughout December, nothing could have been more horrible for me than to arrive on that movie set and to see her being treated the way she was. I had never seen that, I didn't expect it, and I didn't understand any of it.

Hitch then attempted a 'divide and conquer' strategy. 'The most uncomfortable part of it all for me,' Diane added, 'occurred when he manoeuvered me for a conversation outside Tippi's dressing-room trailer. There was a high window built into it, and he stood me there and spoke very loudly – saying negative things about her, to make her angry or jealous, or to cause some reaction. Which just showed how little he really knew her. After I'd had enough of this, I asked him one day, "What do you say about *me* behind my back?" He said oh, no, that I was just fine, and that he would never say anything bad about me.' But Hitch's tactics to create a wedge of enmity between his co-stars failed, even with Connery, who was told, 'Don't touch the girl.'

There were unfriendly, alienating strategies to secure good

performances, too, as Diane added: 'He often did strange and upsetting things. He turned his back on you just before a take – and
then he whispered to someone like [MCA agent] Edd Henry or
Lew Wasserman, who were frequent visitors to the set. He made
you feel as if he was saying something derogatory about you.'

'Nobody knew what to do about all this,' according to Tippi.
'Everyone – I mean *everyone* – knew he was obsessed with me. He
always wanted to have a glass of wine or champagne, with me alone,
at the end of the day – "to talk about the next day's work", he said.
But he was really isolating me from everyone. I wasn't flattered by
all this special attention – he was alienating me from everyone else,
and that added another level of discomfort. To make things even worse,
by this time he was drinking heavily at lunch. By late afternoon, I
just wanted to go home to my daughter, study the next day's [script]
pages and try to relax.'

That became more and more difficult – especially during the
shooting of a scene in which Marnie has been found out by Mark
and is packing her things at the riding lodge. 'Hitch came over to
me just before we shot the scene and whispered to me, "Touch me."
He made sure no one else could hear, and his tone and glance made
it clear exactly what he meant. It was disgusting, and I was furious.
I was made to feel humiliated. He had absolutely no consideration
for my feelings.' Shaken, Tippi went to see Peggy at the end of the
day. 'Peggy told him how unhappy I was, but it didn't matter to him.
He thought no one had any feelings to hurt, and the word "respect"
wasn't in his vocabulary. It was very strange, because Peggy came back
to me and reported that Hitch said only that he was so sad because
I had never invited him alone to my home for dinner! I became
almost sick thinking of being alone with him at home.

'There were so many insulting and offensive things, all during
production. This was a side of life I had never seen and knew nothing
about. At the same time, I had the huge responsibility of this difficult and demanding role.'

From that time, she was essentially not permitted to leave the studio
at the end of the day's work until Hitch gave the sign. As she recalled
years later, 'It reached the point that I just couldn't stand to see or
be with him. Every day, there was a reason for me to be unhappy,
every day he planned some private meeting with wine or champagne,
and every day I thought, "How can I get out of this one?" I remember

driving from my home to the studio every day, asking myself, "How can I get out of this job?" But of course I couldn't. They would have sued me for a great deal of money – that threat was implied more than once.'

He also began to give unwelcome signs to Diane Baker. At first, she tried to cope with the private lunches for two, but he drank wine, got red in the face, and often dropped off to sleep while working during the afternoon. 'Once at lunch he told me that actresses should never be married, which at first I thought was amusing and then very strange.' Jim Brown, the assistant director, often had to poke Hitch awake, to ask if a shot was OK to print. Diane politely refused further midday meals.

'Then came his strange topics of conversation,' she added. 'He wanted to talk to me about sex. He said he had no intimate relationship with Alma for decades – well, that's a difficult remark to respond to! And then he loved to talk about toilet matters, too. He told me, for example, about a French king who invited honoured guests to observe him defecating. I had never heard such stuff, and I didn't know what to do or say.' Since the 1930s, Hitch had scarcely altered the shock tactics employed with some vulnerable young women.

One curious interlude involved another actress who found favour in Hitchcock's eyes. Cast in a small role of one of his teleplays was Claire Griswold, wife of the actor and director Sydney Pollack. 'You and I are going to do business,' he told her – and then he signed her to a seven-year contract. A personal wardrobe was again designed ('Bring me your body, and I will dress it'), and three lavish screen tests were prepared – longest of all, a scene from *To Catch a Thief*. Claire recognised at once what was happening and decided she did not like it. 'I was very touched by his evident need to re-create Grace Kelly – or whoever it was he wanted to re-create – but I didn't really want to go along with that sort of thing.'

Invited to dine at the Hitchcock home, the Pollacks were surprised that Hitch barely addressed Claire's husband or took any interest in his career. Hitch was creating an odd kind of rivalry: on the one hand, Tippi Hedren was being openly held before Griswold as a competitor for Hitch's full attention; on the other hand, Claire was placed in the centre of a struggle between two directors.

When Hitch finally settled on Tippi for *Marnie*, Claire felt that she would be free for the next year. She discussed this at lunch with

Peggy Robertson and explained that she and her husband planned to expand their family during this time. Peggy advised Claire that there would be no appropriate time for that within the next seven years: Claire was expected always to be available, for any role, under any circumstances. Not long after, Hitchcock's office was informed that Mr and Mrs Sydney Pollack were awaiting the birth of their second child. The following year, by mutual consent, the Griswold–Hitchcock contract was terminated, and Claire settled very happily into the private life she always preferred.

Things became more tortured as the filming of *Marnie* progressed. 'One day, he came into my dressing room,' recalled Diane. 'He closed the door behind him – he didn't say anything – walked across to me, put his arms around me and planted a kiss, hard, right on my mouth. It wasn't a friendly or fatherly kiss, and I was shocked. I didn't say anything. I grabbed a tissue, wiped my lips and then wiped my make-up off his lips. I went to the door and opened it, and, still without a word, he left.

'I had never been sick during a production or because of a job,' Diane said years later, 'but before Christmas, I became so ill from the tension of making *Marnie* that a doctor was sent to my home. The whole thing was taking quite a toll on me, and of course it was even worse for Tippi.' From Hitchcock, Diane received a pink clock radio as a holiday gift, with a note: '"I want you to think of me every single night before you go to sleep." That caused me a little panic – how would I deal with this when I saw him after the holidays?'

Years later, the situation would have at once produced charges of sexual harassment. But it was virtually unknown for employees of movie studios to mention such things at the time. A platoon of powerful producers routinely acted like Hitchcock, and it was up to young actresses to find a way to cope, to submit (the better to advance their careers) or to complain in private. 'In 1963,' Diane added, 'no one thought in terms of legal recourse or sexual harassment – and we would have been completely ignored if we spoke out. In fact, we *were* completely ignored.

'I did complain to Monique James [casting agent for Universal],' Diane continued. 'I also spoke to Peggy Robertson. But nothing happened. I liked Peggy, but her loyalty was to Hitchcock, and she just wanted some information from me that she could report back to him – how upset I was, for example, and if I was going to talk to anyone about all this. I felt there was a terrible collusion going on, and I was right. Everything got back to him, and when he learned that I was unhappy and complaining, his attitude toward me changed completely. I was glad not to be under contract to him, the way Tippi was – I could finish the job and get away.'

In the new year 1964, things became more tangled still. 'Lew Wasserman and his wife Edie started in on me,' Diane added. 'Messages were left at the Universal gate for me that they wanted me to come to their home for dinner. I knew what was happening, and so did everyone else.'

Indeed, Wasserman attempted to exert damage control. He sent one of the executive team to Tippi's dressing room one day. 'We all know about your private life,' said the man nervously. When she asked just what he meant, he had to remain silent. He had no idea what he was talking about; he had hoped for some voluntary, scandalous self-revelation from her. Meantime, Hitch and Lew were still bringing the major Universal executives onto the set, to see what Hitch said was his proudest accomplishment, the creation of a major new star for whom he still planned a big future. 'You'll be making $500,000 a year,' Hitch told her expansively – a great deal of money in the 1960s. 'It was a carrot he thought I'd go for, but I remember thinking I'd give it all up for peace and freedom.'

The Hitchcock-Wasserman relationship had flourished for many years because of a long-term business arrangement. 'Lew had become a second father-figure [to Hitchcock] with all the attendant mingling of love and guilt, gratitude and resentment,' wrote John Houseman. 'Fear of displeasing him by failure to deliver his new film on time and the dread of being punished by the withdrawal of favours such as his prestigious bungalow suite at Universal Studios loomed no less "dark" [for Hitchcock] toward the end than the anxieties of sexual frustration, and had an equally destructive effect on Hitchcock's work.' In fact, the long Wasserman-Hitchcock relationship ended badly. When Hitch invited me to lunch in 1977, he was discussing his problems with the Universal executives when suddenly tears rolled down his cheeks. 'Lew never comes to see me any more,' he said, almost in a whisper.

★   ★   ★

Hitchcock really believed that Tippi would be his, that he could somehow leave Alma and have a new life: this was perhaps the extreme point of his delusion. 'He told me,' Tippi recalled, 'that he had a fantasy – that he and I were standing in his living room, and the rays of the moon were coming in and enveloping us.' The moment was certainly like a beautiful cinematic fantasy, a totem of his expectation of a new life with Tippi. But it was also astonishingly presumptuous, not least of all because she had never given him any indication that she shared his feelings. 'He was so sure that I was in love with him. That whole time was really very sad, very difficult.' That year, Tippi was making a life with her agent, Noel Marshall, whom she eventually married; Hitchcock made no secret of his displeasure at the news. 'For him,' according to Tippi, 'there was no one else in my life – *could never be anyone else* in my life except him.' One can reasonably add that *Marnie* is a triumph of one woman's performance over unimaginable circumstances.

On St Valentine's Day, 14 February 1964, Hitchcock sent Tippi a long, impassioned telegram. After recounting the legend of the two ancient Christian martyrs named Valentine, he wrote that they were probably two legends about one man – himself. He then referred to his emotional martyrdom and signed the message 'Alfredus'. About the same time, unwilling to let her out of his sight, Hitch refused permission for Tippi to make a quick journey to New York to receive the 'Star of Tomorrow' citation from *Photoplay* magazine. If an accolade did not originate with him, it had neither meaning nor relevance.

The matter reached its breaking point in March 1964, near the end of production and on the day Tippi was drenched with water for the close-ups of the scene in which Mark saves Marnie from an attempted suicide-by-drowning in a pool aboard a cruise ship. Tippi's memories were acute and indelible.

'We were ready for the scene when Hitch called me into his office on the set. He stared at me and simply said, as if it was the most normal thing in the world, that from this time on, he expected me to make myself sexually available and accessible to him – however and whenever and wherever he wanted. That was the moment, after almost three years of trying to cope, when I finally had enough – that was the limit, that was the end.'

With that, she jumped up. 'I can't go on with this,' she shouted at him. 'I can't put up with another day – I want to get out of this contract. I don't want to be around you any more.'

Hitchcock's next step was to propose what can only be called prostitution.

'He said, "Well, you can't get out, can you? What will happen to your child, and to your parents?" I replied that no one who loves me would ever want me to be in a situation in which I was so miserable.

'But he didn't stop, and then the threats began. "I'll ruin your career," he said. "You'll never work again anywhere. I'll destroy you."'

It was precisely as Connery says in *Marnie*: 'I've tracked you and caught you, and by God I'm going to keep you!' *Marnie* is, even at face value, a film about Hitchcock. 'There must be something wrong with the girl if she doesn't want me' – that is the point of Mark's exploitation of Marnie, and of Hitchcock's conduct toward his star.

After more than forty years, Hitchcock had hoped at last to make a film of James Barrie's delicate, sentimental fantasy *Mary Rose*; Jay Allen had written a first draft of the screenplay. Now, Hitchcock threatened to cancel what he called the role of a lifetime for Tippi. But she was unmoved by the threat.

This episode in the life of Alfred Hitchcock cannot be ignored, for it is a frank case of extreme sexual harassment that may not be dismissed or minimised. Nor was the successful completion of *Marnie* any justification for Hitch's conduct. The events comprise a stern cautionary tale; they also document the unfortunate decline of a great genius who lost all control over himself. *Marnie* marked the end of his art.

There has been a general feeling that one can say or write anything about Alfred Hitchcock – except the fact of his frailty, his faults, his suffering and the suffering he caused others. His status as an icon has made many people, even some surviving colleagues, blind to this appalling time. Consequently, the pain for which he was responsible, the deep unhappiness he visited on himself, has been ignored or excused; into the bargain, some people have therefore approved of sexual harassment.

Did the long, dishonourable history of some powerful Hollywood men and the so-called casting couch convince Hitchcock his actions were acceptable? To assert that this is merely the way things are sometimes done, that this is typical of this or any industry, means to dismiss it as merely a quotidian reality and therefore to assent to it: 'Well, these things happen.' Do Hitchcock's most zealous admirers minimise or shrug off this sad episode because they think such treatment of actresses is merely boyish high-jinks? Was Hitchcock so respected that his associates – and later some of his partisans – thought it of little consequence how he treated Tippi Hedren and Diane Baker?

'He was never in love with me,' Tippi insisted years later. 'He was obsessed with me, and that's very different. When you love someone, you don't frighten them, disgust them or want to hurt them. You want them to come to you, not feel repelled.' Indeed, had he behaved differently, Hitchcock might have gained the lifelong friendship of Tippi and Diane; as with others, he could have been a mentor and father figure. But he lost all discretion. 'He could not or would not control himself,' Tippi added, 'and he made no attempt to. It wasn't just selfish conduct – frankly, it was sick conduct.' She was hurt and surprised that Alma did not intervene more forcefully on her behalf: 'Alma was the Mom – she watched over him, but by this time, she couldn't control him.' The fact that Tippi never did anything to provoke Hitchcock made his sexual obsession 'his problem, really, not mine. I had no control over him, and that realisation kept me sane during those three years.'

Hitchcock followed through on his promise to ruin Tippi Hedren's career, keeping her under contract, inactive and unemployed for several years after the release of *Marnie*. An impressive list of directors contacted him, eager to borrow her. The response was invariable: 'She isn't available.' Tippi was especially disappointed to learn later from François Truffaut that he had wanted her for a film, but that Hitchcock turned him down. 'It was really a shame,' Truffaut told me. 'He was never the same Hitchcock after this time.' Eventually, Hitchcock acceded to a request from Charles Chaplin, who brought her to London for a picture; soon after, Hitch agreed to cancel her contract.

'Some people have claimed that I had some cordial meetings with Hitch in his office later, to patch things up and establish a friendship. I have no recollection of anything like that. I did agree to meet him and Alma at Claridge's once when I was working for Chaplin. I had sent Alma some roses as a welcome to London, but when I was summoned to the Hitchcock suite, the flowers were next to a steaming wall heater, so they had died very quickly. The meeting was very awkward.' British representatives for Chaplin and Hitchcock suggested that the two directors, with Alma and Tippi, be photographed together. Hitchcock refused: 'Why would I want to do that?'

Virtually every element of the truth about this time eluded him. 'Nothing ever came of her,' he said of Tippi in 1972, 'because she didn't want to do television.' That was not so: what she did not want was to be directed by him.

Diane had additional scenes in *Marnie*, but Alma convinced her husband they were unnecessary, and they were cut.

> Hitch knew that I was due in Israel for pre-production on my next picture. I had just one more shot for him – a process shot that was delayed and delayed, and finally completely postponed. I kept asking when I could do this bit of work and leave. No answer came from anyone. I missed the rehearsals in Israel and arrived late. I really believe it was a kind of punishment for me.

Diane's memories of *Marnie* were so painful that for years she said nothing. 'I wanted to forget the whole experience, and I never went to any of the tributes to Hitchcock during his lifetime or afterward.' Happily, Diane's career flourished, not only as a film and television actress worldwide, but also as a director, producer and acting teacher.

Notwithstanding her mentor's stated goal – to ruin Tippi's life and career – no such thing occurred. Certainly he made it impossible for her to accept work offers over the next two years, and by the late 1960s, as so often in Hollywood, the momentum created for her by *The Birds* and *Marnie* fell victim to changing movie fashions and the myopically lukewarm critical response to those pictures. Over the next decades, she often returned to work in film and television, but these projects were very much second place to a deeper commitment.

That dedication began in 1969, when she went to Africa to appear in a picture. 'While I was there, I became deeply concerned about the dangers to the survival of wild animals because of sport hunting, poaching and encroaching civilisation.' She and Noel Marshall, then her husband, decided to rescue some of the most endangered animals in Africa and America, and then to make the film *Roar*, which showed that wild animals are not appropriate as house pets. By the mid-1970s, she had taken in dozens of abused or abandoned lions, tigers, leopards, cheetahs, cougars, elephants on a large tract of land an hour's drive from Los Angeles.

Tippi did not establish a zoo or animal park in 1972. Instead, her non-profit Shambala Preserve (the name is from the Sanskrit, meaning a place of harmony for all living beings) is like an animal orphanage, where she has continued to rescue big cats from illegal owners, from abuse by low-life circuses, private zoos and unscrupulous men who charge fees for the sport of shooting animals. She and a dedicated staff provide veterinary care, proper nutrition and safe ground.

With great tenacity, Tippi successfully sponsored a Congressional bill making it illegal to breed exotic animals as pets in the United States. Shambala remains her life's work, a refuge for battered and rejected animals, a place where educational programmes continue to change for the better people's attitudes to wild animals. The honours and awards she had received for her tireless work on behalf of animals has been equalled by her citations for important humanitarian work – especially in relief programmes for the victims of floods, earthquakes, famine and war. In many of these efforts, she has been joined by her daughter, the actress Melanie Griffith.

For Tippi Hedren, time, distance and a purposeful life healed the memories of the three years from 1961 to 1964. But it is no exaggeration to say that Alfred Hitchcock never recovered from the misery he set in motion. A week after his death in April 1980, there was an international congress in Rome celebrating Hitchcock's extraordinary achievements – a programme of lectures and interviews sponsored by the Assessorato alla Cultura, scheduled months before he died.

The three-day event went forward. I was asked to deliver a keynote lecture and to coordinate the American contingent, and I travelled to Rome with Tippi Hedren, Farley Granger, Ernest Lehman and Peggy Robertson. It was a bitter-sweet triduum. As we sat in a coach on the morning of 6 May, awaiting transfer from the Hotel de Ville to the press events at the Parco dei Principi, Peggy turned to Tippi and said, 'You know, he never got over you.'

Afterword

The Leaden Echo and the Golden Echo
(1964–1980)

'I am convinced,' wrote François Truffaut, 'that Hitchcock was never the same after *Marnie*, and that its failure cost him a considerable amount of self-confidence. This was not so much due to the financial failure of the film (he had had others), but rather to the failure of his professional and personal relationship with Tippi Hedren.' Truffaut was on the mark. After *Marnie*, no subsequent Hitchcock picture has any emotional statement to make.

Psycho had brought him the greatest wealth of his career. But with that picture – so different from anything he had ever done – something was shifting in his personality. That movie has a pervasive sense of doom: it proclaims the triumph of the kingdom of death, of monstrous, murderous lunacy and the annihilation of personality, in a way unlike any other Hitchcock film. Even its perverse humour cannot mask the sense that the director is describing not only the world of nightmare, but also something mad and malevolent in the chilling world of everyday, recognisable situations. Therein lies its ultimate horror.

But with *Psycho*, even as he tried desperately to push back the frontiers of what was permissible in American movies, something hardened in Alfred Hitchcock – something forever closed over his fragile capacity for warmth. There would never again be films with the warmth of *Rear Window*, *To Catch a Thief* or *The Man Who Knew Too Much*, nor the mature indictment of romantic self-abnegation that characterised the genius of *Vertigo*. Poisonous politics would never be treated again with the blithe, wise humour of *North by Northwest*.

The causes for this decline cannot be reduced to a single physical or psychological ailment. On the one hand, it is unfair to expect any artist to repeat or to exceed recent successes – especially when the forms of popular entertainment shift as much as they did in the 1960s and after. Hitchcock was dependent on studio approval and public endorsement, and he was very much of his time – how could he not be? It would have been absurd for him to imitate a maverick young moviemaker.

It is tenable, however, that after 1964 he had somehow lost the resources to cope with the shifting fortunes of fame, popularity and cinematic fashion; that he could not counter his increasing terror of illness, incapacity and age; that his sense of detachment, of isolation, made him merely angry instead of pitching him into creative solitude. Always an indulgent tippler, he drank in perilous quantities after 1965, and writers working with him were often at a loss to understand how they ought to proceed. Perhaps most poignant of all was the egregious lack of friends. He might have become mentor, friend, *éminence grise* to a generation of filmmakers, actors and students, but he knew not how to offer himself, nor did he seem much to care.

After *Marnie*, indeed, something died in him. There was nothing more for him to say in art or life, and his bewilderment at finding himself an antique in a strange new Hollywood was enormous. Thenceforth, Wasserman and his colleagues at Universal made commercial demands on Hitchcock to which he was forced to yield: to cast major stars in the next picture, for example, and to dismiss the great Bernard Herrmann as composer in order to secure a more contemporary 'pop' soundtrack from others.

In addition, the Hitchcock style was dead in the 1960s. During the course of many interviews between 1964 and 1980, he was often asked to name his great pleasures in life, and making pictures was no longer among them: 'The things that make me happiest in the world are eating, drinking and sleeping. I drink like a fish – have you seen what a red face I have? And I could die eating.' He was certainly frank, but there is something humourless and pathetic in his words.

Tippi Hedren, among others, saw that Hitchcock was 'a very, very unhappy man. His only friends were his businessmen.' He increasingly isolated himself after 1964, refusing most invitations unless he was the main attraction. He made excuses for his absence, and eventually the offers dried up. 'He really had nothing else in this world except food, wine and fooling around with movies,' said Marshall Schlom, once his assistant director.

Hitchcock's fiftieth film, *Torn Curtain*, was released in 1966 but had been troubled long before production began. First, Hitchcock objected to the stars forced on him – Julie Andrews and Paul Newman. To Hitchcock's fury, their combined salaries made up a quarter of the $6 million budget. Second, he and writer Brian Moore, who later tried unsuccessfully to have his name removed from the credits, could not make the dated Cold War antics of Hitchcock's original story outline compelling or the characters anything but wooden. Filming was awkward for everyone: Newman did not get on at all with Hitch, who was in turn openly contemptuous of Andrews. 'I tried to dispense with her services on the strength that she was a singer and not a serious actress,' Hitchcock said, '[but] the studio considered her a sure box-office draw.'

To assert that Julie Andrews was not a serious actress demonstrated just how ungraciously out of touch he was: her recent performance in *The Americanization of Emily* counters this negative judgement, for Andrews was an actress of both range and stature on stage and screen. Had Hitchcock not been eager to have the singing actress Doris Day in *The Man Who Knew Too Much*? (Privately, Julie was so upset by the experience that she urged her friends not to see *Torn Curtain*.)

'Hitch just went through the motions on that movie,' Samuel Taylor said. 'He knew it was a loser, and he became very depressed and lost all interest in it.' Lila Kedrova, in a small but colourful rôle, said that Hitchcock seemed not to want to direct her or anyone else. Instead, according to uncredited writer Keith Waterhouse, Hitchcock loudly berated and even tormented minor players in a key scene of *Torn Curtain* for not jumping off a bus in the proper manner.

His almost constant anger was now both evident and alienating. Hitchcock never had the gift of friendship, but he could always attract acquaintances to be entertained. In the last decade of his life, as his old colleague Hume Cronyn sadly recalled,

> There was something tragic about Hitchcock – an element of snob in him that became really tragic in its consequences. Because

he never took people close to heart, in the latter years he became a sad and rather isolated figure. I visited him often and found him weeping. He said not only that the work was not proceeding well, but that he never went out, never saw anyone, was never invited anywhere. But all of that was Hitch's own fault. He had encouraged that kind of distance with people, and so they left him alone – which is what he'd wanted. And so he was lonely, and it was all very sad.

Nor could Samuel Taylor's nearly round-the-clock efforts salvage Hitchcock's next picture, a production Universal chose for the director after the disappointment of *Torn Curtain*. 'The trouble with *Topaz*,' Hitchcock said in 1975, 'is that there are too many foreigners – Frenchmen, Cubans, Russians and the rest – all of them speaking English. It's a letdown, really.' But there were problems far more acute than language dissociation: for one thing, Hitchcock, Taylor and Universal could not decide on an ending for the movie. Several were shot, none of them satisfactory, and for all its travelogue colour and a few inventive set pieces, *Topaz* is generally regarded (except by the most defensive Hitchcock aficionados) as cold and remote, an almost embarrassingly bad movie. Audiences, as Samuel Goldwyn said in another context, stayed away in droves.

There were other more embarrassing problems on *Topaz*. During a publicity photo session, cast members Karin Dor and John Vernon were in costume, and Hitchcock decided to pose them for the photographer. Glancing first at Vernon's cigar, Hitchcock called aloud to Karin Dor, 'Karin, put it in your mouth. Come on, Karin – you know you've had it in your mouth before.' This was not amusing to the actress, and everyone present felt awkward and embarrassed. Hitchcock angrily stopped the photo session and departed.

Frenzy, produced in London in 1971 and released the following year, restored Hitchcock's critical acclaim, but the explicitly violent story of a serial killer alienated many. Structurally, the movie is icily brilliant, but there is nowhere for the audience to apply its sympathies, no one with whom to identify or to support.

Hitchcock's final picture – *Family Plot*, released in 1976 – was a quiet coda. He was no longer the alert and spry director, but a man who had become ill, somnolent, uncaring and alcoholic. He looked terrible, moved with obvious pain and found every day a trial; his staff was alternately sympathetic, frustrated and resentful. He fired and replaced the leading man after filming had begun, and the atmosphere of the production was anxious throughout.

Still, he could surprise a young actress. Karen Black was one of two leading ladies in the picture, and when he kissed her one day before work, she was astonished that he thrust his tongue into her mouth. 'I think he was probably born an exuberant spirit,' she said coolly, 'and that's why he French-kissed me. He just felt like it.'

'Hitchcock was a neurotic,' Truffaut wrote, 'and it could not have been easy for him to impose his neurosis upon the whole world.'

The fantasies Hitchcock spun, to which his writers gave form and structure and which his actors enlivened, depended on the emergence of mysterious images from deep within him – images that were often terrifying and violent, sometimes tender. From his own secret longings and vivid imagination, there came small gems of stories. But the plots and characters would always be subordinate to the images – just as in dreams, the narrative is never quite logical or clear and is always subordinate to the images.

His tortured and lonely life – and particularly his complex, unresolved feelings about women – enabled him (indeed, forced him) to draw deeply from a common human reservoir of imagery and dream, fear and longing. Had his films been simple representations of his own fantasies and dreams, with no wider reference, he would perhaps have won a small group of like-minded admirers. But he expressed those images, desires and half-remembered dreams in terms that moved, astounded, delighted, frightened and aroused awe from millions around the world, in widely disparate cultures.

That is the secret of the unassailable genius of Alfred Hitchcock. In *The Lodger*, for example, a woman shrieks in terror when her fiancé, a detective, playfully snaps handcuffs on her as he refers to marriage bonds. In *Vertigo*, a beautiful, remote blonde, clutching a nosegay, stands dazed before an old tombstone in a cemetery garden. In *The Birds*, the failure of human relationships is marked by the sudden, inexplicable revolt of nature itself.

If there is anything that can confidently be said about dreams and longings, it is that they are intensely private. Even when they are articulated, it is hard to transmute into words the oddness of an image, the comic-grotesque distortions of inner time and space, the weird amalgams of feeling that leave us less certain of the comforting arti-fice with which we so often present ourselves to the world. In giving form to his fantasies, Hitchcock explored and exposed things not only in himself but also in others — realities more or less actual, more or less potential. He showed us not what *all* of life is like, but what *some* of life is like, all the time, everywhere, and what all of life is in constant danger of becoming.

Beginning in 1971, Alma Reville Hitchcock suffered the first of several strokes, and by the end of the decade, she was mostly confined at home. On the morning of 29 April 1980, Alfred Hitchcock died quietly in bed. Alma survived him for more than two years. Photographs of her husband bewildered and sometimes upset her, as if they were images of someone she had once known, very long ago, in a dim and half-remembered past. Finally, she set the pictures aside for ever, and then she seemed more at peace with herself, and much calmer.

Notes

*For brevity, details of interviews are supplied only at the first citation;
unless otherwise stated, subsequent quotations from the same source derive
from the identical interview with that source.*

Abbreviations: AMPAS/MHL = The Margaret Herrick Library at
the Academy of Motion Picture Arts and Sciences, Beverly Hills.
BFI = *British Film Institute, London.*

Chapter One

All my early training: to Peter Bogdanovich, in 1963.
general factotum: quoted in 'Close Your Eyes and Visualise!', *Stage*
   (July 1936) pp. 52–3.
I was quite dogmatic: ibid.
I had no intention: see, e.g., Truffaut, p. 31.
wanted to be a director: Balcon, p. 19.
I was in a cold sweat: AH, with John J. Newnham, 'My Screen
   Memories,' *Film Weekly*, 2 May 1936.
Valli was big stuff: *News Chronicle* (London), 1 March 1937.
sappy: *Variety*, 3 November 1926.
Wiener schnitzel: *Photoplay*, January 1927.
It was a very *gemütlich*: to Truffaut, p. 39.
She arrived: Bob Thomas, 'Alfred Hitchcock: The German Years',
   Action, January–February 1973 pp. 23–5; Truffaut, p. 41; and *News
   Chronicle*, 2 March 1937.
fostered the impression: Barr, *English Hitchcock*, pp. 9–10.

It hadn't taken the landlady: Lowndes, p. 46.

had sheltered him: ibid., p. 256.

Before a camera: from the British Film Institute's online notes for the career of Ivor Novello (1893–1951).

Some people: Elsie Randolph to DS, 23 January 1981.

It was just too tempting: Ackland, p. 35.

Hitch had very strong feelings: Cotten, p. 66.

spoke in a curious: June, p. 156.

Psychologically, of course: Truffaut, p. 47.

a murderous fascination: BFI 'Screen Online' notes for *The Lodger*.

Like Hitchcock himself: Philip Kemp, 'The Icy Blondes', in Mogg, pp. 126–7.

Chapter Two

The Lodger was really: to Truffaut, Bogdanovich and DS.

Hitch was ungrudgingly: Ivor Montagu, 'Working with Hitchcock,' *Sight and Sound*, summer 1980 pp. 189–90.

It is possible: *The Bioscope*, 16 September 1926.

On the genesis of *Downhill*, see Mark Duguid's comments in the BFI 'Screen Online' notes for the picture.

because she asked me to: Fallaci interview in Gottlieb, *Alfred Hitchcock Interviews*, p. 59.

I could have been: John Russell Taylor, 'The truth about Hitch and those cool blondes', *The Times* (London), 5, April 2005. AH confided this remark to playwright Rodney Ackland, who told Taylor.

Hitch and Alma: Samuel Taylor to DS, 2 December 1980.

Alma was his co-writer: Elsie Randolph to DS, 23 January 1981.

celibate: Ken Mogg's contributions to Hitchcockian scholarship include management of an important website, from which this is excerpted: www.sensesofcinema.com/contents/directors/05/hitchcock.html.

Lilian was a good: AH to DS: 21 November 1976.

His women must kill: McGilligan, p. 122.

He never stopped playing: *TV Times* (London), 29 October 1964.

It was initially set up: Barr, *English Hitchcock*, p. 81.

We made the film silent: Ronald Neame, interviewed by Matthew Sweet at the National Film Theatre (London), 19 October 2003.

Hitchcock has been so faithful: *The Times*, 1 January 1930.

Under Mr Hitchcock's guidance: *The Times*, 24 June 1929.

Hitchcock's films resemble: *The Times*, 25 May 1936.

I asked him later: Norah Baring, 'The Man Who Made *The 39 Steps*: Pen Portrait of Alfred Hitchcock', *Film Pictorial*, 23 November 1935, pp. 14–15; reprinted in Gottlieb, *Alfred Hitchcock – Interviews*, pp. 12–13.

creative artist: *The Times*, 23 September 1930.

He was a darling: Elsie Randolph to DS: 23 January 1981.

was engrossed: Ackland, p. 33.

the conversation: Kendall, p. 116.

He sent me up: Thornton, pp. 108–9.

had to be handled: AH, 'Nova Grows Up', *Film Weekly*, 5 February 1938.

Chapter Three

I had wanted: AH, 'My Screen Memories', *Film Weekly*, 23 May 1936.

You owe everything to me: From Charles Bennett's unpublished memoirs, cited in Ken Mogg's scholarly website; also Bennett to DS, November 1981.

had a monstrous ego: Mogg, p. 20.

If he decided to use you: quoted in Sullivan, p. 258.

He is blazingly ambitious: ibid.

She is both beautiful: the review excerpts are from the *New York Times*, 15 January 1934; 24 August 1930 and 26 July 1940.

There has been: AH, in 'My Screen Memories', *Film Weekly*, 30 May 1936.

Hitch, without: McGilligan, p. 4, mentions that Hitchcock much liked to use this introduction, doubtless to see people's reaction.

There they were: 'Life Among the Stars', *News Chronicle*, 5 March 1937; reprinted in Gottlieb, *Hitchcock on Hitchcock*, p. 45.

Madeleine and I shared: Barrow, pp. 75–6.

a gleeful delight: Taylor, pp. 108–9.

What interests me: *Sight and Sound* 25, no. 3 (winter 1955–6) p. 158.

There was no better: Jack Whitehead to DS, 7 November 1981.

It had long been: Montagu, p. 90.

I sometimes wonder: Frank S. Nugent, 'Mr. Hitchcock Discovers Love', *New York Times*, Sunday Magazine, 3 November 1946.

We deliberately wrote the script: Montagu, 'Working with Hitchcock', *Sight and Sound*, summer 1980, p. 193.

Bring on the Birmingham tart: ibid.

I just gave him a look: Emerson Batdorf, 'Let's Hear It for Hitchcock', *Cleveland Plain Dealer*, Sunday Magazine, 1 February 1970.

We'll do it one more time: the incident was told by Googie Withers to the Australian film historian Brian McFarlane. It is also recorded in Sweet, p. 169.

I don't exactly hate: 'Alfred Hitchcock Tells a Woman that Women Are a Nuisance', *Film Weekly*, 20 September 1935.

He was essentially: ibid., p. 192.

Nothing pleases me: ibid.

I try to make a woman human: ibid.

On AH's impotence, see McGilligan, p. 177.

Peter Lorre was: John Gielgud, in McFarlane, *An Autobiography of the British Cinema*, p. 216.

I knew that: quoted in the *New York Times*, 12 July, 1940.

Who knows if any of us: ibid.

the most glamorous woman: Heiskell, p. 45.

I knew a young Englishwoman: her speech was reprinted in the *New York Times*, 18 November 1940. Madeleine Carroll's sister Marguerite died in London on 7 October 1940.

In my French home: *New York Times*, 4 March 1945.

Don't be silly: *New York Times*, 19 December 1948.

Chapter Four

When moving pictures: AH, 'Films We Could Make', *London Evening News*, 16 November 1927.

coherent body: *un oeuvre cohérent* was the phrase Truffaut used in conversation with DS in December 1976.

what critics consider: Krohn, p. 16.

He thought movies: ibid.

I discovered: Michael Balcon, 'My Hollywood Star Captures', *Film Weekly*, 18 January 1936.

On the set: C. A. Lejeune, 'Hitchcock, The Man Korda Cannot Sign', *World Film News*, no. 2, May 1936.

she had nice understatement: Truffaut, p. 111.

really wicked wit: Nova Pilbeam to Brian McFarlane (in June 1990), *An Autobiography of the British Cinema*, p. 453.

and he finds: *New York Times*, 5 February 1938.

She imparts sincerity: *Kinematograph Weekly*, 25 November 1937; *Variety*, 8 December 1937.

her name: McFarlane, *An Autobiography of the British Cinema*, p. 453.

It's what people did: Suzie Mackenzie, 'Pat Hitchcock: The woman who
knew too much', *Guardian*, 28 August 1999; see also de Bertodano.
There was a strange: Elsie Randolph to DS, 23 November 1981.
I don't think: Helena de Bertodano, 'Even scarier than *Psycho*: his
"great production"', *The Times*, 5 April 2005.
There are the: quoted by Samuel Taylor to DS, 23 April 1981.
Poor Patty: Teresa Wright to DS, May 1983.
I suppose: Margaret Lockwood to DS, 16 January 1981.
He wasn't really: Michael Redgrave to DS, 3 September 1980.
The art of filmmaking: Truffaut, p. 124.
sloppy, stiff: Callow, p. 129.
The quotations from Maureen O'Hara and Emlyn Williams are cited
in Chandler, pp. 117 and 199; more accurate are O'Hara's extended
recollections in O'Hara and Nicoletti, p. 25.

Chapter Five

Rebecca was a very pleasant: Patricia Hitchcock O'Connell, on the DVD
of that film, released in 2001 by the Criterion Collection DVD.
analysis that was: Thomson, p. 306.
Hitchcock was not always: Whitney Bolton, 'Hitchcock Salesman for
All His Movies', *New York Morning Telegraph*, 7 July 1966.
It's not a Hitchcock: Truffaut, p. 127.
she was widely assumed: John Russell Taylor, 'The truth about Hitch
and those cool blondes', *The Times*, 5 April 2005.
She puts up: AH, 'The Woman Who Knows Too Much', *McCall's* 83
(March 1956) p. 14.
too coy and simpering: Haver, p. 319.
much in love with Joan Fontaine: Thomson, p. 305.
knew ways: ibid., p. 331.
We liked each other: Fontaine, pp. 106–7.
Joan is young, pretty, gay: Aherne, p. 286.
The British brigade: ibid., p. 108.
He seemed to want: Joan Fontaine to DS, 23 July 1974.
But he didn't give me: Chandler, p. 130.
My grandmother: Leff, p. 74, retold by Chandler, p. 125.
She was not a good: quoted in Leff, p. 74.
I am aware: Selznick, in an unsent letter to AH dated 19 September
1939: see Behlmer, p. 307.

I think Joan has been handled: Behlmer, pp. 312–313.

She was practically: quoted in Leff, p. 63.

A well-trained: ibid., p. 64.

dozens of isolated lines: Ibid., pp. 79–80.

Although Hitchcock is: Geoffrey T. Hellman, 'Alfred Hitchcock, England's Best and Biggest Director, Goes to Hollywood', *Life*, 20 November 1939.

Many of the actors: Leff, p. 52.

There were very unpleasant things: Judith Anderson to Leonard Leff, in a 1986 telephone interview included on the Criterion Collection DVD release of *Rebecca* (2001).

the dirtiest joke: Leff, p. 44.

Well, Miss Bates: ibid., p. 72.

You're supposed to be: Haver, p. 322.

His pauses: Behlmer, p. 313.

Joan Fontaine, at moments: *The Times*, 27 June, 1940.

Hitchcock had a habit: quoted in *Focus in Film*, no. 30, June 1978.

Hitch was always playing: Laraine Day, on the Warner Bros Home Video DVD release of *Foreign Correspondent* (2004).

I liked [Carole]: Chandler, p. 133.

Oh, you've looked: quoted in Leff, p. 92.

Chapter Six

He brings his wife: *Dialogue on Film*, no. 5: American Film Institute, Center for Advanced Film Studies (1972); reprinted in Gottlieb, *Alfred Hitchcock Interviews*, p. 92.

If I came on the set: quoted in Leff, p. 267.

in turmoil: Auiler, *Hitchcock's Notebooks*, p. 63: he devotes no fewer than thirty-four pages to commentaries on the various screenplays for *Suspicion*. McGilligan's account runs to thirteen pages. Ken Mogg and Bill Krohn also studied the movie's history for a lengthy website excursus (www.labyrinth.net.au/~muffin/suspicion_c.html).

Hitchcock's material: Samson Raphaelson to DS, 21 December 1980.

No, not necessarily: Truffaut, p. 44.

The whole subject of the film: ibid.

I have a raving: Harry E. Edington to J. J. Nolan, 5 February 1941; RKO production files for *Suspicion*.

Hitchcock does not appear: S. Rogell to Edington, 1 April, 1941.

The scenario: Fontaine, pp. 124–5.

stepping in: Fontaine to DS, 24 July 1974.

habit of saying: Brian McFarlane, 'Joan Fontaine', *Cinema Papers* (Australia), June 1982, p. 234; cited in Leff, p. 91.

did not feel the rapport: ibid., p. 123.

I thought the original: Nelson, p. 124.

But I'm sure I didn't: Chandler, p. 138.

far finer film: Howard Barnes, in *New York Herald Tribune*, 21 November 1941.

The ending is not up to: Bosley Crowther, in *New York Times*, 21 November 1941.

least satisfying: Nelson, p. 123.

I had heard: Houseman, *Run-Through*, pp. 479–80.

But I had to take: AH to DS, 24 November 1977; see also Truffaut, pp. 145–6.

On the Wilder–Hitchcock collaboration, see the essay by Max Alvarez, 'Wilder & Hitchcock: Writing and Re-writing *Shadow of a Doubt*, in *The Thornton Wilder Society Newsletter*, vol. 2, #2, 2007, pp. 2, 5.

This was my father's: Patricia Hitchcock O'Connell, on the Universal DVD release of *Shadow of a Doubt*.

I wouldn't say: Truffaut, p. 151.

I was seventeen: Teresa Wright spoke with DS about her early life and career very many times during our thirty-one-year friendship (1974 to her death in 2005).

uncommon charm: Brooks Atkinson, in *New York Times*, 19 November 1939.

the best actress: Harold Heffernan, 26 August 1941.

She had a genius: Stephan Talty, 'A Genius for Decency', *Film Comment*, October 1990, pp. 18–19.

Chapter Seven

We were always: Hume Cronyn to DS, 4 June 1974.

black and blue: Bankhead, p. 229.

She had no inhibitions: Brian, p. 138.

I was under contract: Ingrid Bergman spoke with DS many times from 1975 to 1982; she spoke particularly about Selznick on 8 May 1975.

Lindstrom: W. H. Dietrich to DS, 23 October 1995.

almost desperately anxious: Selznick to Margaret McDonell, 10 July 1943.

beaming: Hecht, p. 396.

I won't do: Bergman to DS, March 1979; see also Hecht, p. 481.

Selznick treated: Gregory Peck to DS, 14 April 1981.

although Hitchcock meticulously: Leff, p. 135.

I have to consider: AH, 'How I Choose My Heroines', in Reed and
  Spiers, p. xxiii; reprinted in Gottlieb, *Hitchcock on Hitchcock*, p. 75.

because I think he is entitled: Behlmer, p. 392.

Chapter Eight

Miss Bergman just can't help: Frank S. Nugent, 'That Phenomenon
  Named Bergman', *New York Times Magazine*, 16 December 1945.

You have become an industry: Bergman, p. 156.

I fell in love: Larry Adler to DS, 9 June 1996.

By the time: Bergman, p. 102.

like a cat: quoted in Harmetz, p. 146.

dominating: Leff, p. 266.

I don't get: Nugent, 'Mr Hitchcock Discovers Love' (see above).

the great privilege: AH to DS, 25 July 1975; almost identically to
  Truffaut, pp. 261–2 and to Bogdanovich, p. 26.

I almost frightened myself: Edmond J. Bartnett, 'Not Born to Evil',
  New York Times, 1 September 1946.

Chapter Nine

Whatever Miss Valli thought: Howard Taubman, 'Fact vs. Fiction in
  the Discovery of a Star', *New York Times*, 11 January 1948.

On the train: Alida Valli to DS, May 1989.

This, of course: Gregory Peck to DS, 24 April 1983.

Hitchcock [had a] lifelong: Houseman, p. 158.

he drove us crazy: cited in Leff, p. 222.

he was not a director: Alida Valli, in *Il Brivido del Genio*, a three-part
  television documentary for RAI (1985).

In the right part: *Daily Mail*, 10 March 1930.

He took the trouble: Ann Todd to DS, 19 January 1981 and in interviews thereafter through 1992. See also her book, p. 75.

a very complex man: Ann Todd, in *Il Brivido del Genio*.

We never discussed: Arthur Laurents to DS, 19 October 1981.

lived in the land: Laurents, pp. 124–30, *passim*.

not very amusing: Hume Cronyn to DS, 21 June 1974.

The really important thing: James Stewart to DS, 26 February 1982.
I realise: AH to Truffaut, pp. 180, 184.
He got such pleasure: Ingrid Bergman to DS, 8 May 1975.
I wanted to put: Selznick to Petter Lindstrom, 15 April 1944.
I am still in mourning: Chandler, p. 289; similarly, to DS, August 1978.
But he never forgave: Truffaut, p. 325.

Chapter Ten

My grandmother: Mary Stone, in the extra material 'The Hitchcocks on Hitch', on the Warner Bros DVD of *Strangers on a Train* (2004).
relied on Alma: quoted in Moral, p. 131.
with childish innocence: Brooks Atkinson, in *New York Times*, 28 January 1942 and 8 February 1942.
monotonous: Lewis Nichols, in *New York Times*, 25 October 1944.
It appears that: McGilligan, p. 428.
a bachelor: ibid., pp. 427–8.
You never knew: Brown, p. 89.
Hitch was so perverse: Lambert, p. 128.
I was stuck with her: AH to Peter Bogdanovich (1963).
I had lots: Truffaut, pp. 190–1.
When she heard: Richard Todd, p. 240.
She wouldn't do anything: Chandler, *It's Only a Movie*, p. 13.
We became inseparable: Wilding, pp. 60–76.
there is exactly none: quoted in Sullivan, p. 155.
Hitchcock was a very distant man: Richard Todd, in *Il Brivido del Genio*.
He was a strange man: Richard Todd, interviewed in McFarlane, *An Autobiography of the British Cinema*, p. 564.

Chapter Eleven

There are some actors: Arthur Knight, 'Conversation with Hitchcock', *Oui* magazine, February 1973, p. 116.
Monty was a friend: Karl Malden to DS, 10 November 2007; see also his book *When Do I Start?*, pp. 229–33; and his Oral History, pp. 17 and 163.
He gave me the impression: Anne Baxter to DS, 15 September 1980; see also her comments on the RAI production, *Il Brivido del Genio*.
Bob Burks gave Hitch: John Michael Hayes to DS, 27 February 1982.

As Nina: Brooks Atkinson, in *New York Times*, 12 May 1954.

When you compare: AH to Truffaut, p. 202.

written with inner eyes: Louise Bernikow, in *New York Times*, 19 September 1976.

I have to consider: AH in Reed and Spiers, p. xxiii; see also Gottlieb, *Hitchcock on Hitchcock*, p. 75.

When I saw the first cut: SAS The Princess Grace of Monaco to DS, 22 September 1975.

Hitchcock the voyeur: McGilligan, p. 471.

The stamp of Hitchcock's genius: John Michael Hayes to DS, 27 February 1982.

She was rather mousy: quoted in Fawell, p. 142.

Every costume: Edith Head to DS, 22 July 1975; see also Head and Ardmore, pp. 153–4.

Grace was very sweet: quoted in Chandler, *It's Only a Movie*, p. 217.

full on the mouth: the incident is recorded in McGilligan, pp. 550–1.

The former Cockney lad: Truffaut, p. 325.

Chapter Twelve

very precise: Doris Day to DS, 12 December 1981.

Hitch and Doris Day: Constance Willis to DS, 17 May 1983.

always seemed more concerned: Bernard Miles to DS, 20 January 1981.

Hitchcock never gave: Reggie Nalder to DS, 11 April 1981; see also *Kinoeye: New Perspectives on European Film*, vol. 3, no. 2, and www.kinoeye.org/03/02/delvalle02.php.

so she wouldn't: AH to Hedda Hopper, 7 March 1961.

I feel the same way: Robert Marks, 'Vera Miles – Hitchcock's New Star', *McCall's*, May 1957.

Vera Miles is the girl: *Cosmopolitan*, October 1956, p. 67; see also *Mademoiselle*, December 1959.

Hitch had an obsession: McGilligan, pp. 537–8.

Vera was a lovely girl: quoted in Rebello, p. 63.

Vera's wardrobe: AH to DS, 24 July 1975; similarly, see Fallaci, p. 256.

Over the span: quoted in Rebello, p. 64.

I lost all interest: Truffaut, p. 247.

The majority of actors: Fallaci, p. 255.

But I did see in Hitch: to DS, 17 May 1983.

She said she couldn't: Edith Head to DS, 22 July 1975.

Before shooting started: Kim Novak, interviewed by Stephen Rebello in 2003; see www.labyrinth.net.au/~muffin/kim_novak_c.html.

Miss Novak arrived: AH to Truffaut, pp. 247–8.

I'll wear anything: Head and Ardmore, p. 15.

Handle it, Edith: Head and Calistro, p. 116.

I never sat down: quoted in McGilligan, p. 555.

so much of what: Kim Novak, interviewed by Anwar Brett for *The Dark Side* magazine (UK), no. 73, June–July 1998 p. 21; see also his essay in *Film Review*, May 1997, p. 25.

I could tell: James Stewart to DS, 26 February 1982.

Anyone who saw him: Samuel Taylor to DS, interviews from 1974 through 1980.

He was never deeply friendly: John Russell Taylor, 'The truth about Hitch and those cool blondes', *The Times*, 5 April 2005.

spiritual transvestism: Edel, p. 259.

Chapter Thirteen

Hitchcock's main purpose: Ernest Lehman to DS, 12 April 1975; additional conversation with EL from 1976–2000.

My camera: Leigh with Nickens, p. 43.

Either they wear: Rebello, p. 74.

It was challenging: Janet Leigh to DS, 23 March 1982 and ff.

Some hair-raising screams: Leigh with Nickens, pp. 46–7.

Before every shot: Rebello, p. 90.

Vera was very angry: ibid., pp. 73–4.

Chapter Fourteen

I prefer a woman: AH, in *Hollywood Reporter*, vol. 172, no. 39, 20 November 1962.

a wonderful opportunity: all quotations from Tippi Hedren derive from a span of thirty-four years of my frequent interviews with her; in this book, most are drawn from our conversations of 2007.

the Svengali approach: from the Robert F. Boyle Oral History at the Academy of Motion Picture Arts and Sciences (1992); interviewed by George Turner.

It was evident: Martin Balsam to DS, 1 March 1982.

I signed her: Thomas McDonald, 'Watching "Birds"', *New York Times*, 1 April 1962.

Well, she has nothing to unlearn: 'On Style', *Cinema* 1, no. 5, August–September 1963, p. 34.

'Tippi Hedren is really remarkable' and the following citation are drawn from 'Tippi Hedren – Hitchcock's New Grace Kelly', *Look*, 4 December 1962, p. 55–8.

Hitch was becoming: Rod Taylor to DS, March–April 1982; see also, *Lifetime: Intimate Portrait of Tippi Hedren*, a Feury/Grant Production, for TV, 2001, and *Magnificent Obsession: Tippi Hedren*, Prometheus/Van Ness for TV, 2003.

just covered in bird shit: Jessica Tandy to DS, 3 June 1974.

Chapter Fifteen

I told him: Evan Hunter to DS, 3 December 1981. His remarks are virtually identical on the transcriptions of taped story conferences for *Marnie* throughout late 1962; see also Hunter, pp. 75–6.

Can there be any doubt: Truffaut, p. 346.

He was mad for her: Jay Presson Allen to DS, 12 November 1980.

I was invited: Diane Baker to DS, 3 November 2007.

You and I: Claire Griswold Pollack to DS, 1 March 1982.

Lew had become: Houseman, *Entertainers and the Entertained*, p. 159.

I discussed Tippi Hedren with François Truffaut in December 1976, when I spent several days with him during production of his film *L'Homme qui aimait les femmes*, in Montpellier, France.

Nothing ever came: Janet Maslin, 'Alfred Hitchcock', *Boston After Dark*, vol. 3, no. 24, 12–20 June 1972.

Afterword

I am convinced: Truffaut, p. 327.

The things that make: Rui Nogueira and Nicoletta Zalaffi, 'Hitch, Hitch, Hitch, Hurrah!' in *Écran*, no. 7, July–August 1972, reprinted in Gottlieb, *Alfred Hitchcock Interviews*, p. 122.

He really had nothing: Rebello, p. 97.

I tried to dispense: ibid.

There was something tragic: Hume Cronyn, in *Il Brivido del Genio*.

The incidents with Karin Dor and Karen Black are reported by McGilligan, pp. 690–1 and 726.

Hitchcock was a neurotic: Truffaut, p. 346.

Bibliography

Ackland, Rodney, with Elspeth Grant, *The Celluloid Mistress*, London: Allan Wingate, 1954.

Aherne, Brian, *A Proper Job*, Boston: Houghton Mifflin, 1969.

Auiler, Dan, *Hitchcock's Notebooks*, New York: HarperCollins, 1999.

——, *Vertigo: The Making of a Hitchcock Classic*, New York: St. Martin's Griffin, 1998.

Balcon, Michael, *Michael Balcon Presents . . . A Lifetime of Films*, London: Hutchinson, 1969.

Bankhead, Tallulah, *Tallulah: My Autobiography*, London: Victor Gollancz, 1952.

Barr, Charles, *English Hitchcock*, Moffat (Scotland): Cameron & Hollis, 1999.

——, *Vertigo*, London: British Film Institute, 2002.

Barrow, Kenneth, *Mr Chips: The Life of Robert Donat*, London: Methuen, 1985.

Behlmer, Rudy (ed.), *Memo from David O. Selznick* (rev. ed.), New York: The Modern Library, 2000.

Belton, John (ed.), *Alfred Hitchcock's* Rear Window, Cambridge: University Press, 2000.

Bergman, Ingrid, and Alan Burgess, *Ingrid Bergman: My Story*, New York: Delacorte Press, 1980.

Bogdanovich, Peter, *The Cinema of Alfred Hitchcock*, Garden City: Doubleday, 1963.

Brian, Denis, *Tallulah, Darling*, London: Sidgwick & Jackson, 1972.

Brown, Geoff, *Launder and Gilliat*, London: British Film Institute, 1977.

Brown, Peter Harry, *Kim Novak, Reluctant Goddess*, New York: St. Martin's, 1986.

Callow, Simon, *Charles Laughton: A Difficult Actor*, London: Methuen, 1987.

Chandler, Charlotte, *Ingrid: A Personal Biography*, London: Simon & Schuster, 2007.

———, *It's Only a Movie – Alfred Hitchcock: A Personal Biography*, New York: Applause Theatre & Cinema Books, 2005.

Cotten, Joseph, *Vanity Will Get You Somewhere*, San Francisco: Mercury House, 1987.

Edel, Leon, *Henry James, 1895–1901: The Treacherous Years*, Philadelphia: J. B. Lippincott, 1969.

Falk, Quentin, *Mr Hitchcock*, London: Haus Publishing, 2007.

Fallaci, Oriana (trans. Pamela Swinglehurst), *The Egotists: Sixteen Surprising Interviews*, Chicago: Henry Regnery, 1963.

Fawell, John, *Hitchcock's* Rear Window *– The Well-Made Film*, Carbondale and Edwardsville: Southern Illinois University Press, 2001.

Fontaine, Joan, *No Bed of Roses: An Autobiography*, New York: William Morrow, 1978.

Forster, Margaret, *Daphne du Maurier*, London: Arrow, 2007.

Gielgud, John, *An Actor and His Time*, New York: Clarkson N. Potter, 1980.

Glancy, Mark, *The 39 Steps: A British Film Guide*, London: I. B. Tauris, 2003.

Gottlieb, Sidney (ed.), *Alfred Hitchcock Interviews*, Jackson: University Press of Mississippi, 2003.

———, *Hitchcock on Hitchcock*, Berkeley: University of California Press, 1995.

Harmetz, Aljean, *The Making of* The Wizard of Oz, New York: Knopf, 1977.

Haver, Ronald, *David O. Selznick's Hollywood*, New York: Knopf, 1980.

Head, Edith and Jane Kesner Ardmore, *The Dress Doctor*, Boston: Little, Brown, 1959.

Head, Edith and Paddy Calistro, *Edith Head's Hollywood*, New York: Dutton, 1983.

Hecht, Ben, *A Child of the Century*, New York: Simon & Schuster, 1954.

Heiskell, Andrew, with Ralph Graves, *Outsider, Insider: An Unlikely Success Story – The Memoirs of Andrew Heiskell*, New York: Marian-Darien Press, 1998.

Hotchner, A. E., *Doris Day: Her Own Story*, New York: Morrow, 1976.

Houseman, John, *Entertainers and the Entertained*, New York: Simon & Schuster, 1986.

——, *Run-Through*, New York: Simon & Schuster, 1972.

Hunter, Evan, *Me and Hitch*, London: Faber and Faber, 1997.

June, *The Glass Ceiling*, London: Heinemann, 1960.

Kendall, Henry, *I Remember Romano's*, London: Macdonald, 1960.

Krohn, Bill, *Hitchcock at Work*, London: Phaidon, 2003.

Lambert, Gavin, *On Cukor*, New York: Putnam's, 1972.

Laurents, Arthur, *Original Story By: A Memoir of Broadway and Hollywood*, New York: Knopf, 2000.

Lawrence, Gertrude, *A Star Danced*, Garden City, NY: Doubleday Doran, 1945.

Leff, Leonard, *Hitchcock and Selznick*, Berkeley: University of California Press, 1987.

Leigh, Janet, with Christopher Nickens, *Psycho: Behind the Scenes of the Classic Thriller*, London: Pavilion, 1995.

Leitch, Thomas, *The Encyclopedia of Alfred Hitchcock*, New York: Checkmark/Facts on File, 2002.

Lowndes, Marie Adelaide Belloc, *The Lodger*, Doylestown, PA: Wildside Press, n.d. (reprint of the 1913 British and the 1914 American publications).

Malden, Karl, *An Oral History with Karl Malden* (Douglas Bell, interviewer), Academy of Motion Picture Arts and Sciences Oral History Program/Margaret Herrick Library, Beverly Hills: Academy Foundation, 2007.

Malden, Karl, with Carla Malden, *When Do I Start? – A Memoir*, New York: Simon & Schuster, 1997.

McFarlane, Brian, *An Autobiography of the British Cinema*, London: Methuen, 1997.

McFarlane, Brian, (ed.) *The Encyclopaedia of British Film*, London: Methuen, 2005.

McGilligan, Patrick, *Alfred Hitchcock: A Life in Darkness and Light*, New York: ReganBooks, 2003.

Massey, Anna, *Telling Some Tales*, London: Arrow, 2007.

Mogg, Ken, *The Alfred Hitchcock Story*, London: Titan, 1999.

Montagu, Ivor, *With Eisenstein in Hollywood*, Berlin: Seven Seas, 1968.

Moral, Tony Lee, *Hitchcock and the Making of Marnie*, Lanham, MD: Scarecrow Press, 2002.

Nelson, Nancy, *Evenings with Cary Grant*, New York: Citadel/ Kensington, 2002.

O'Connell, Pat Hitchcock and Laurent Bouzereau, *Alma Hitchcock: The Woman Behind the Man*, New York: Berkley Books, 2003.

O'Hara, Maureen, with John Nicoletti, *'Tis Herself: A Memoir*, New York: Simon & Schuster, 2004.

Powell, Michael, *A Life in Movies*, New York: Faber and Faber, 2001.

Rebello, Stephen, *Alfred Hitchcock and the Making of Psycho*, New York: HarperPerennial, 1990.

Reed, Langford and Hetty Spiers, *Who's Who in Filmland*, London: Chapman and Hall, 1931.

Ryall, Tom, *Alfred Hitchcock and the British Cinema*, London: Athlone, 1996.

Spoto, Donald, *The Art of Alfred Hitchcock*, New York: Hopkinson and Blake, 1976; New York: Doubleday Dolphin, 1999 (centennial edition).

——, *Blue Angel: The Life of Marlene Dietrich*, New York: Doubleday, 1992.

——, *The Dark Side of Genius: The Life of Alfred Hitchcock*, Boston: Little Brown, 1983; New York: Da Capo, 1999 (centennial edition).

——, *Laurence Olivier: A Biography*, New York: HarperCollins, 1991.

——, *Notorious: The Life of Ingrid Bergman*, New York: HarperCollins, 1997.

Sullivan, Jack, *Hitchcock's Music*, New Haven and London: Yale University Press, 2006.

Sweet, Matthew, *Shepperton Babylon*, London: Faber and Faber, 2005.

Tavistock Marchioness of, and Angela Levin, *A Chance to Live*, London: Headline, 1991.

Taylor, John Russell, *Hitch: The Life and Times of Alfred Hitchcock*, New York: Pantheon, 1978.

Thomson, David, *Showman: The Life of David O. Selznick*, New York: Knopf, 1992.

Thornton, Michael, *Jessie Matthews: A Biography*, London: Hart Davis, 1974.

Todd, Ann, *The Eighth Veil*, London: William Kimber, 1980.

Todd, Richard, *Caught in the Act*, London: Hutchinson, 1986.

Bibliography

Truffaut, François, *Hitchcock* (rev. ed.), New York: Simon & Schuster, 1983.

Walker, Michael, *Hitchcock's Motifs*, Amsterdam: Amsterdam University Press, 2005.

Wilding, Michael, *The Wilding Way*, New York: St Martin's Press, 1982.

Wood, Robin, *Hitchcock's Films Revisited* (rev. ed.), New York: Columbia University Press, 2002.

Index